LIVING ON FIRE

LIVING ON FIRE

The Life of L. Brent Bozell Jr.

Daniel Kelly

WILMINGTON, DELAWARE

Copyright © 2014 by Daniel Kelly

All rights reserved. No part of this publication may be reproduced or transmitted in any form or by any means, electronic or mechanical, including photocopy, or any information storage and retrieval system now known or to be invented, without permission in writing from the publisher, except by a reviewer who wishes to quote brief passages in connection with a review written for inclusion in a magazine, newspaper, or broadcast.

Library of Congress Cataloging-in-Publication Data

Kelly, Daniel, 1938–2012.
  Living on fire : the life of L. Brent Bozell Jr. / Daniel Kelly.
    pages cm
  ISBN 978-1-61017-086-4 (hardback)
        1. Bozell, L. Brent, 1925–1997. 2. Journalists—United States—Biography. 3. Triumph (Washington, D.C.) 4. Catholics—United States—Biography. 5. Conservatism—United States—History—20th century. 6. Radicals—United States—History—20th century. 7. Ghostwriters—United States—Biography. 8. Manic-depressive illness—Patients—United States—Biography. 9. Alcoholics—United States—Biography. I. Title.

CT275.B586133K45 2014
973.917092—dc23
  [B]
                       2013040688

Published in the United States by

ISI Books
Intercollegiate Studies Institute
3901 Centerville Road
Wilmington, Delaware 19807-1938
www.isibooks.org

Manufactured in the United States of America

CONTENTS

Foreword *by Neal B. Freeman*		vii
Preface		xiii
One	The Bozells of Omaha	1
Two	Bulldog	9
Three	McCarthy and His Friends	23
Four	Standing athwart History	35
Five	Ghostwriter	47
Six	Magic Kingdom	61
Seven	Pulling Up Stakes	77
Eight	Defender of the Constitution	93
Nine	Defender of the Faith	103
Ten	The Cutting Edge	117
Eleven	Autumn in America	137
Twelve	Phantom Empire	155
Thirteen	Time to Die	173
Fourteen	Manacled to a Roller Coaster	189
Fifteen	Mercy	203
Epilogue		219
Notes		221
Acknowledgments		241
Index		243

FOREWORD

by Neal B. Freeman

Daniel Kelly, the author of the book you hold in your hands, was a rare blessing to me—a good friend made late in life. When I met him seven years ago, he was toying with the idea of writing this book. I urged him to do it and, over the subsequent years, I pestered him to finish it. He seemed for several reasons to be the right man for a very challenging assignment.

Most important, Dan had seen the young Brent Bozell on a public platform. When Dan was a graduate student at the University of Wisconsin, Brent had come through Madison on a speaking tour. I asked what he thought of Brent's performance and Dan's one-word, decidedly unprofessorial review was: "Wow." That settled the threshold question. Nobody would have to persuade Dan Kelly that Brent had been an electric speaker, a special forensic talent combining folksy, midwestern affability with a razor-sharp, legally trained mind. (As just one point of reference, Brent's debate partner—some would say, junior partner—when Yale beat a previously undefeated Oxford team was a fellow named William F. Buckley Jr.)

Second, Dan had previously published a full-length biography of James Burnham, the longtime senior editor of *National Review* magazine. Jim Burnham was a man of the file, the comprehensive file, a habit born of his early experience as a CIA analyst. If Dan had spent a few years immersed in Burnham's papers, one could be confident that he knew the story of the conservative movement from the ground up. So that box was checked, too.

Finally, Dan was a Catholic mensch. That a man named Daniel Kelly should have sprung from Catholic roots was not much of a surprise, but beyond any theological affinity with Brent, who was a convert to Catholicism, Dan was acutely aware of the vicissitudes of this earthly life. When I met him, Dan was still recovering from liver-transplant surgery. He soon developed a virulent cancer and, perhaps worst of all for a historian, a creeping diabetes that was stealing his eyesight. To borrow a phrase from this book, Dan was suffering from "a Homeric catalogue of infirmities." He succumbed to those infirmities in late 2012, but not before finishing the manuscript that would become this fine biography. (That Dan completed the book at all was an act of gallantry: in the dimming light of his own life, Dan told me that he couldn't bear to default on his promise to Brent's widow, the luminous Patricia Buckley Bozell, who had entrusted Dan with the unvarnished tale of her time with Brent.)

The subject of this book, L. Brent Bozell Jr., had been my predecessor as Washington correspondent for *National Review*. That gig was my dream job. But in 1964, after only a few months in grade, I resigned to join the Bozell-for-Congress campaign in Maryland. That was a rash career move, obviously, but it was not quite as crazy as it may have appeared. Those of us who worked on Brent's campaign felt privileged to be boarding the bullet train of contemporary politics. There was much chitchat about John F. Kennedy's race for a Boston congressional seat back in the 1940s. We Bozellites liked to think that we were on something of that same JFK trajectory. A couple of terms in the House, a U.S. Senate race, and soon after that, we fantasized, it would be off to the *Casa Blanca* for us. That was the raw expectation, anyway. I don't mean to suggest that we saw it as a slam dunk, Joe and Jack Kennedy–style, but neither did it appear to be a desperation three-ball. Brent was that good.

In Dan Kelly's sober judgment, that campaign became not the

first rung on a ladder reaching to the sky but, in the clear rendering of hindsight, the apogee of Brent's political career.

In this absorbing and moving account, Dan tells the full story of Brent Bozell, both the early triumphs and the heartbreaking stumbles.

By the time he had reached his late thirties, Brent was a man not just of youthful promise but of precocious achievement as well. Among his signal contributions, to my eye at least, were these: He launched the Goldwater movement, which triggered a seismic shift in American politics; he was one of a handful of men who salvaged the anticommunist cause from the missteps of its boisterous champion, Senator Joseph McCarthy; and he was the lawyer-cum-policy wonk who framed the telling arguments against judicial activism—at the time, fresh and potent arguments—that reverberate to this very day in our national dialogue. (You will hear those arguments yet again when a candidate is nominated for the next vacancy on the Supreme Court.) Based on these early accomplishments, Brent Bozell must be reckoned, along with Buckley, Burnham, Frank Meyer, and Russell Kirk, as one of the founding fathers of the modern conservative movement.

The second half of Brent's life was not always pretty. After his early success, he turned from defending the country to defending his faith. From there, in stages, he became consumed by fervor, fanaticism, and, off at the end, delusion. His life became a protracted struggle in which a brilliant intellect fought valiantly against insidious maladies of the mind. Brent's downward drift became an agony not only for him but also for those who loved him—his wife and ten children, his devoted friends, and his many distant admirers who had been exhilarated by his brief turn on the public stage. Dan Kelly tells this part of the tale with candor and compassion—a story that, in the last chapter of Brent's life, was entirely new to me, as I suspect it will be to most of Brent's other friends. I won't ruin it for you here, but I can tell you this much—how Brent spent his last days was both astonishing and, ultimately, redeeming.

The story of Brent Bozell is an American story, a *big* American story, and one that should be more widely known. Thanks to Dan Kelly, it will be.

Neal B. Freeman *is chairman and founder of the Blackwell Corporation. Previously he served as an executive with the Hearst Corporation, as director of the Corporation for Public Broadcasting (appointed by President Ronald Reagan), and as an award-winning television producer. A graduate of Yale, Freeman has written for the* New York Times, USA Today, *the* Washington Post, *the* Weekly Standard, *the* American Spectator, *and* National Review, *among other publications.*

LIVING
ON FIRE

The fiery orator

PREFACE

I never met Brent Bozell, but I once saw him give a speech. The time was 1960; the place, the University of Wisconsin, where I was enrolled as a graduate student; the topic, the need to outlaw the Communist Party.

Bozell, then *National Review*'s Washington columnist, cut an impressive figure on stage. In his midthirties, he was tall, slim but solid looking, with a strong, clear voice and a self-assured manner. But what seized and held my attention was his hair. Assertively red, it stood out brightly in the gray atmosphere of the lecture hall, and sometimes more than brightly thanks to an optical illusion produced by the hall's ceiling lights. When he moved forward a few inches, his hair would appear to catch fire, as if to stress the importance of the point he was making. When he moved back, the fire would dim, but a new step forward would rekindle it. Illusory though it was, as a rhetorical device self-igniting on stage was sensational.

After the speech I wanted to meet the speaker, but too many others in the audience had the same idea. The odds that I would reach the podium looked long, so after a few minutes of waiting I gave up. I never saw Bozell in person again.

But now and then I had news of his latest doings (news, it turned out, that in some cases wasn't reliable but a badly garbled version of the truth). Word had it that he had ghostwritten Senator Barry Goldwater's bestseller *The Conscience of a Conservative*; that he had moved his family to Spain to escape what he saw as America's decadent culture; that he was seeking the Republican nomination for a Maryland congressional seat; that he had abandoned politics and fled to the solitude of the Blue Ridge Mountains; that he was finally publishing a book on the Warren Court that he had been working on for many years; that he had launched a conservative Catholic magazine, which was now turning radical; that he had given up *National Review*–style conservatism in favor of a neomedieval traditionalist brand; that he had repudiated the U.S. Constitution on the ground that it made man's will, not God's, the highest law; that he had rounded fiercely on the post–Vatican II American Catholic episcopate; that he had joined a movement of dissident Spanish royalists and now went around dressed in its militia's uniform; that he was leading a paramilitary group called the Sons of Thunder in assaults on abortion clinics; that he had fallen prey to manic depression; that he had ruined his health with alcohol and prescription drugs; that he had turned theologian and was writing on the subject of mercy; that he had given up writing to work for Mother Teresa; that he had joined an exotic order of barefoot monks.

And then came the news—this time, all too accurate—that he had died. Thirty-seven high-voltage years had passed since his Wisconsin speech.

I still envisaged Bozell as a man on fire. But the blaze I had once thought of as merely an optical illusion now struck me as something more: a symbol of major defining features of his life. The political ardor, the impassioned religious commitments, the restlessness that drove him fiercely from "mission" to "mission," the searing attacks of mania—all found symbolic expression in his flaming hair.

Surveying Bozell's life (*lives* might be better, given the successive mutations), I came to see it as one well worth chronicling. For one thing, Bozell played a key role in one of recent American history's central developments: the rise of the conservative movement, whose brightest moment was Ronald Reagan's election to the presidency. For another, he had founded present-day America's first activist

"Christian Right," a movement bent on making the country officially Catholic. But my interest in Bozell went beyond his public activity. I became equally interested in the private man who sometimes suggested a Dostoyevsky character more than a modern American from Omaha, Nebraska. It was the story of the private man as much as of the public man that led me to write this book.

ONE

The Bozells of Omaha

The year 1921 was a good one for Leo Bozell, the thirty-five-year-old city editor of the *Omaha Daily News*. That year, a *News* reporter named Morris Jacobs, who had been doing public relations work on the side, proposed to him that they team up to start an advertising and public relations agency. Leo bought the idea and was soon glad he had. Propelled by its founders' imagination, hard work, and reputation for honest dealing, the firm of Bozell & Jacobs quickly prospered.

As the agency grew, it moved beyond the normal scope of such businesses to work out rescue plans for local institutions in financial trouble. One such operation involved Omaha's Jesuit-run Creighton University, which the Depression was pushing toward bankruptcy. Heeding an appeal from the city's Catholic bishop, and waiving a fee for their services ("We have to pay rent for the space we occupy on this earth," Morris used to say), the Episcopalian Leo and the Jewish Morris devised a plan that kept the university solvent.

A similar cry for help came from a Catholic priest, Edward J. Flanagan, who was struggling to save a shelter for homeless boys. Leo and Morris came up with a plan for the shelter, but didn't stop there. Thinking the shelter would profit from a catchy name, the two ad men suggested "Boys' Town." They then negotiated a deal with Hollywood mogul Louis B. Mayer for a movie about the shelter. The result reached the screen in 1938 as *Boys' Town* and won Spencer Tracy, who played Father Flanagan, an Oscar. Such efforts brought Leo and Morris wide acclaim. In the eyes of the Omaha business community, they came to embody the city's civic spirit. In 1943 Leo was chosen to head its Chamber of Commerce.[1]

But Leo launched more than a business in 1921. A childless widower, he married again that year and in the decade that followed fathered two sons and a daughter. The second son, born on January 19, 1926, was named Leo Brent Bozell Jr. Growing into a lanky boy with strong features and striking red hair, Brent, as he was called, brings to mind a Norman Rockwell illustration. He had loving parents to whom he was strongly attached; an older brother, John, who good-naturedly put up with his teasing; and an adoring younger sister, Patricia, whom he walked home from school each day and allowed to tag along when he went off to play with his friends. He shot baskets at a hoop behind the house, romped with the family dog, and directed traffic with a stop-go sign at his school crossing.[2]

Unlike Rockwell's children, he also spent time in reflection, sometimes on matters unusual for a boy his age. One day his mother, Lois, found him deep in thought. What was he thinking about, she asked her nine-year-old son. How the Great Powers should divide Europe, he answered.[3]

Still, if Brent's childhood was a happy one, it wasn't a Rockwellian idyll from start to finish. As a boy, he was highly susceptible to respiratory diseases, especially bronchitis, asthma, and pneumonia (which, before antibiotics, was more dangerous than it is today). At age ten he came down with an especially bad case of pneumonia. Warned by the family doctor that a full recovery would require winter weather milder than Omaha's, the Bozells left their home for a bungalow in San Antonio, Texas, where a feverish Brent waited out the cold.

A religious man, Leo was raised in a rigorously Protestant faith but as an adult became a high-church Episcopalian. Lois, who had grown up a Congregationalist, adopted Leo's religion when they married but never took to its quasi-Catholic trappings. Even less, then, did she feel drawn to full-blown Catholicism, and when Leo revealed that he had conceived an interest in the latter, she made it clear that if he converted she wouldn't join him.[4] This was enough to brake his turn to Rome, but his attraction to Catholicism persisted, and eventually he found a way to give it vent.

Linked with Creighton University was a Jesuit high school, Creighton Prep, which enjoyed a good reputation and let non-Catholics enroll. The high school, Leo decided, would be perfect for Brent. Lois's reaction to this idea hasn't been recorded, but if she resisted, she must finally have given in, for in 1940 the Episcopalian Brent was enrolled at Creighton Prep.

During high school, Brent (or "Boz," as his classmates called him) applied himself to his studies and also found time for the football and basketball teams. But his passions were public speaking and debate. In 1943 he entered the American Legion's nationwide competition for the title of America's best high school orator and took top spot in the contest's Nebraska division. A year later he competed again, and this time, out of a national field of 127,000 contestants, he came in first.

Ordinarily, speeches composed for high school oratory contests are unlikely to hold any interest decades later. But given the adult Brent's work as a ghostwriter for two U.S. senators, a political columnist, and a constitutional scholar, these speeches, offering a glimpse of his early political views, are worth a glance.[5]

His "prepared" speech (the first of the two speeches the competition called for), "Our Constitution: The American Philosophy of Government," reported mounting worry among Americans that their government was no longer "sound," that it had fallen into the hands of people who either held a totalitarian philosophy of government or thought the purpose of government was to cater to special interests. How were things to be put right? In the armed forces, the speech went on, there was talk of servicemen carrying out a cleansing revolution once the war was over. But the right way to recovery lay in returning to the Constitution, which expressed the "true" American philosophy of government: defense of the people's "inherent rights" and use of the government "to secure the common good."

Brent's second, "extemporized," speech delivered a related message. Its subject, which he drew by lot, was the Constitution's Tenth Amendment, which reserves to the states or the people all powers the Constitution doesn't specifically assign to the federal government. This amendment, Brent argued, was the Constitution's most important provision, for it summed up the basic American ideal of government: that the ultimate sources of authority are the states and the people.

Brent's parents were Democrats, and so, by inheritance, was he. Yet he clearly viewed the New Deal with some ambivalence. Thanks to New Deal policies, he said in his prepared speech, "tremendous economic and social gains were made," yet this same New Deal was responsible for Washington's "totalitarianism." Although it had been conceived as an "emergency policy" to fight the Depression, the New Deal had developed into a "philosophy of governmental preeminence," and many of its supporters doubted the people's aptitude for self-government.

On the basis of these speeches, the teenage Brent might best be described as an old-fashioned liberal, one whose hostility to large-scale, centralized, bureaucratic government placed him closer to Jefferson than to Roosevelt. This outlook brings to mind a certain kind of conservatism (which in the 1940s rarely went by that name) whose partisans saw themselves as "true" liberals and distinguished themselves from New Deal liberals by dismissing the latter as "pseudo-liberals" or by enclosing the word *liberal*, when applied to New Dealers, within irony-laden quotation marks.

Photographs of Brent taken at the competition again bring to mind Rockwell's *Saturday Evening Post* covers. In some of these photographs he looks like a study in lengths. He is tall (an inch or two over six feet) and thin, and has a long, serious face, a long, straight nose, long, prominent ears, long front teeth, and a long, lean jaw ending in a long, assertive chin. His dress is sober, even solemn. In one of the photos, he wears a dark suit, a white shirt, and a quiet necktie (whose thinness and verticality reprise the lengths theme). All in all, he embodies a cherished American stereotype: an unpolished youth whose face radiates decency and earnestness.

Brent's success won him the prize of a $4,000 college scholarship contributed by the National Association of Manufacturers (worth more than $53,000 in 2013 dollars). Local newspapers reported that he planned to use it at Yale and then go into the diplomatic corps, but first he would serve in the Navy, which he would enter right after graduating from high school.

But in fact he had already set out on a different course. In a letter dated May 1, 1944 (about two weeks after Brent's oratorical triumph), Leo wrote to a relative, "Brent is now in San Mateo in the [cadet school of the] Merchant Marine."[6] And in his Yale class book entry, Brent recorded his Merchant Marine service as having begun in March 1944, several weeks before the oratory contest's final round.

Ardently patriotic, Brent had been eager to go to war since Pearl Harbor, but because of his age, he knew he would have to wait. In January 1944 he turned eighteen. His final term at Creighton Prep still lay ahead, but because he had already earned enough credits to graduate, the school let him leave early to enlist. (His sister, Patty, attended graduation and picked up his diploma.)[7]

After little more than a year in the Merchant Marine and several months at sea in the Pacific, he transferred to the Navy. Following basic training, he again shipped out to the Pacific, where he was assigned to an assault vessel. He preferred the Navy to the other services, he told Patty, because it was the military's "most democratic" branch. He dismissed out of hand the idea of officer training. He didn't want to be an officer, he said, just a "common sailor." In his telling, "there wasn't much to do" in either the Navy or the Merchant Marine: he had spent his time mostly chipping paint. When discharged, he had reached the rank of quartermaster third class.

Meanwhile, another of his high school interests was growing. Before his years at Creighton, Brent had paid no particular attention to religion. But as a student at a school where a Catholic ambience reigned, he began to feel himself drawn to the Catholic Church. His awareness of his father's feelings probably influenced him. So may have his Jesuit teachers' skill at debate, an ability he prized and was especially well prepared to appreciate. His absorption in Catholicism took place gradually, not all in a rush, but it steadily deepened. As time passed, his principal mentor at Creighton, the Reverend Lucius Cervantes, SJ, noticed that he often went to the school chapel to pray. (Some years later Brent told Patty that belief in the Church required more than "reason and logic." The most important thing was "an implicit faith from God," a gift that had to be prayed for "fervently and constantly.") Decades later he wrote that his conversion had had a single cause: "my disbelief in the validity of Anglican orders."[8]

In March 1946 Leo went to San Francisco to visit Brent, who, not yet discharged, was there on leave. He had definitely decided to convert to Catholicism, Leo told his son. To his delight, Brent replied that he had made the same decision. Eager for the Bozells to enter the Church as a family, Leo proposed that he and Brent delay converting for the moment. Given time, he believed, Lois might join them. Bowing to this wish, Brent agreed to wait.

But the day that Leo hoped for never came. Back in Omaha, he felt unwell. He attributed the feeling to fatigue from his recent trip and to the strain of the harsh Nebraska winter, but the real cause proved to be a failing heart. A few days after his return home, he suffered a massive heart attack and died.

Brent was discharged from the Navy in July 1946. In one respect his postwar future seemed settled, for in September he would matriculate at Yale. But in another, it was hardly settled at all, since his father's death had ruined his plans for conversion. How, he worried, would his mother react to the step. Already deeply upset by her husband's sudden death, she might suffer a breakdown if her son abruptly turned Catholic.[9]

His worry may have been unwarranted. Long aware of her husband's attraction to Catholicism, Lois probably knew that Brent was attracted too and might not have cared at all if he converted. In early 1946 he had asked her to send him a book called *Catholic Principle*, and she had promptly done so, without any hostile comment. All the same, Brent remained uneasy. When he converted was now up to him, and without his father he wasn't sure how to proceed.

TWO

Bulldog

Brent arrived at Yale a Democrat and an Episcopalian. He left a Republican and a Catholic. His political conversion shaped his life for the next two decades. His religious conversion did so—and with growing intensity—until his death. In other ways, too, Brent's future grew out of his college years. It was at Yale that this son of the Great Plains began his transplantation to the East Coast, the region in which he would spend the bulk of his life. It was at Yale, too, that he formed his closest friendship and met the woman who would become his wife and the mother of his ten redheaded children.

Like his Omaha childhood, Brent's Yale years look idyllic. He joined the Elizabethan Society (for students with literary interests); played football and basketball for Trumbull, his residential college (Yale dormitories for upperclassmen); and pledged the Fence Club, the most fashionable fraternity of the day.

He also gave attention to his courses, doing well enough to be admitted to an academic honors society. In one feat of cramming, he plowed through *The Brothers Karamazov* (930 pages in the edition he read) in thirty-six hours, stopping only for quick meals and a two-hour nap. Upon finishing the book, he pronounced it "very enjoyable."[1]

He spent further time counseling his sister, Patty, now a student at Carleton College, who turned to him for advice on college life. "I think you should make a habit of drinking a beer every once in a while," he told her, since "you have to get used to it sometime. Better getting used to that amount of alcohol gradually than passing out with a couple of cocktails in a couple of years from now." But "be sure," he added, "to keep off the hard stuff." On what Patty called "smooching," he advised, "Never kiss a boy unless you want to . . . in the sense of being in the mood for a kiss." And she ought to keep in mind that "the mere kissing itself is not nearly as important as the *intensity* of the kiss." As for marriage, he said, "Don't be in a hurry! You are still a *little* girl yet. Ha!"[2]

But his deepest interest at Yale lay in politics. He chose his courses accordingly, pursuing a major combining political science and economics. Well into his sophomore year he identified himself as a liberal, supporting New Deal–style economic and social legislation and calling for a United Nations–based system of world government. As a sophomore, he became chairman of the United World Federalists' Yale chapter, in the postwar years an important group on campus.

To his efforts for global union he brought his talent for oratory as well as a flair for advertising recalling his father's. One morning, freshmen opened their mailboxes to find amid their regular mail live turtles whose shells bore the slogan "Hurry World Government." Very quickly, however, Brent's promotion ran aground. Alerted by outraged animal lovers, the New Haven ASPCA stepped in, and the World Federalist marketing campaign abruptly ended.[3]

Yet Brent broke with liberalism on the issue of national security. A hard-liner on the question, he thought liberals underestimated the danger of communism—whether as Soviet expansion abroad or infiltration and espionage at home—and that therefore liberals themselves could pose a threat.

Brent's passion for politics drew him to Yale's Political Union, a student debating forum modeled on the Oxford Union. No place for the tongue-tied and the bashful, the Union offered the perfect showcase for his talents, and in this arena for gladiators whose sword was the spoken word, the tall, redheaded Nebraskan soon made his mark.

Brent also won a place on Yale's debating team, one of the top squads on the college debating circuit. It was at a tryout for the team that he first met William F. Buckley Jr., who would play a decisive role in his life. Buckley was the sixth of the ten children of a Texas oilman and his Louisiana-born wife, who, after much wandering, had settled in Sharon, Connecticut. Twenty-one when he met Brent, Buckley too was a veteran, having recently finished a two-year hitch in the Army. From his parents he had learned a devoutly observant Catholicism; from his father, the views that defined conservatism at the time: a libertarian dislike of the New Deal's big-government philosophy and a hard-line brand of anticommunism in which concern for internal security played a major part. Buckley's political tilt at first often clashed with Brent's. (For Buckley, World Federalist schemes meant nothing but trouble.) But hard anticommunism forged a powerful bond between them, and despite their differences the two became the closest of friends.[4]

Both were talented debaters, though different in style—Brent a Roman orator, a man of gravitas; Buckley a stage aristocrat with high-bridged nose and chiseled chin, a blender of wit and hauteur. When both made the team, they became partners, to devastating effect. They won their biggest victory against a team from Oxford that had bested every American team it had faced. Opposing a resolution that American industry should be nationalized, the Yale debaters ran rings around the visitors. Brent unleashed a relentless attack against socialism, while Buckley deftly wielded his verbal rapier and then, as if finding his opponents too boring to bother with, turned to flipping his handkerchief back and forth. The judges awarded the laurels to the home team, and the Oxonians stalked off without shaking hands.[5]

Brent's peak moment as a solo debater came as the climax of a running feud with Yale fellow travelers. In October 1947 he had gone to a New Haven rally of the communist-led Progressive Citizens of America (PCA), which intended to run former vice president Henry A. Wallace for president. Wallace had been scheduled to speak that night, and Brent planned to protest. But the rally's organizers thwarted the plan, dousing the lights before the protest could begin.

The following January, Brent and the PCA clashed again, this time at a rally put on by Students for Wallace, the PCA campus group at Yale. During the question period following the speeches, the Wallacites' leader, a graduate student named P. J. Vecchione, called on many in the audience but pointedly refused to take a question from Brent. But Brent persisted, stubbornly keeping his hand raised till the meeting ended. He then observed to the departing audience that Vecchione's refusal to take his question was typical of communists, the people the PCA had been formed to serve.

A few days later Vecchione counterattacked, calling Brent a "liar" and a "smearer" for applying the communist tag to the PCA. In response Brent again labeled the PCA a communist front and challenged Vecchione to debate him on the charge. Yale's student newspaper, the *Yale Daily News*, stepped in, offering to arrange a public meeting at which the two adversaries could "discuss" Brent's accusation.

Vecchione refused, offering to discuss instead whether other (that is, communist) affiliations of PCA members had any bearing on the merits of the PCA platform. Brent was willing, so the *News* scheduled a "full discussion" for a date in February.

On the appointed evening, an overflow crowd filled the law school auditorium, eager as fight fans coming to a championship bout. Brent climbed into the ring in top form. He had just won another prize for oratory, a Yale-sponsored award to the sophomore who gave the best short speech on patriotism. He was also lusting for battle. A few days earlier, in response to Vecchione's demand that he furnish evidence for his charge, he had published a statement in the *Yale Daily News* listing federal criteria for identifying communist fronts and pointed out how well they fit the PCA.

The bout began with a flurry of jabs by Vecchione, who repeated his charge that Brent was a "liar" and a "smearer." All that mattered, he insisted, was the "validity" of the PCA platform, not the other affiliations of some of its members.

Brent came out of his corner throwing haymakers. Declaring himself a "liberal," he poured scorn on the PCA's use of that term. As a third party that would take votes mainly from Democrats, he noted, the PCA was "knowingly" helping the GOP, a course genuine liberals would never pursue. And the PCA unfailingly backed Soviet interests. Had it ever opposed a position favored by Stalin? What could be clearer than its role as a communist front? Buckley, a spectator at ringside, called the bout "the highest political moment" of his years at Yale. But since the event was billed as a "discussion," not a debate, no judge was present to decide which contender had won.[6]

By his junior year Brent was clearly moving right. The main force propelling the move was his anticommunism, but his Jeffersonian liberalism, his long-standing dislike of what he saw as overgrown government, helped smooth the way.

Buckley played the key part in Brent's conversion, but he had help. This came from a political scientist named Willmoore Kendall, who joined the Yale faculty in 1948. An Oklahoman with steel-gray hair and rough-hewn features, Kendall had briefly been a communist in the 1930s but then had rounded sharply on the Left. In addition to pursuing an academic career, he had worked for American intelligence as an expert in U.S.–Latin American relations (in which role he would furnish the model for the title character in Saul Bellow's story *Mosby's Memoirs*). Endowed with a penetrating mind and a taste for polemics, Kendall also harbored a streak of irascibility. The critic Dwight Macdonald once described him as "a wild Yale don . . . who can get a discussion into the shouting stage faster than anyone I have ever known."[7]

Kendall's political thought antagonized his liberal colleagues. In Kendall's view, the liberal ideal of the "open society," in which all opinions enjoyed equal rights in "the market place of ideas," posed a threat to social cohesion and even survival. Every society, he argued, was—and should be—"closed"; that is to say, it would—and should—rest on an orthodoxy and would—and should—meet heresy with sanctions. This blunt endorsement of sanctions-backed social conformity provoked liberal outrage, and not simply because it was heresy. Put forward in the political climate of the late 1940s, Kendall's views seemed crafted to justify congressional "witch hunts."

As Kendall's liberal colleagues sent him to Coventry (thereby demonstrating his thesis), Brent and Bill became his students and then his friends. Despite the friction that later arose between them, Brent always paid homage to Kendall as a mentor.[8]

Identifying himself as a conservative in the fall of 1948, Brent joined the Political Union's Conservative Party. He also started a four-page newspaper, the *Conservative View*, "to propagate conservative thought." At first he hoped to publish every two weeks, but from the outset that schedule proved too ambitious. As things turned out, the *Conservative View* appeared only twice, once in 1948 and once in 1949.[9]

Brent's opinions were not widely shared at the Political Union. Nonetheless, midway through his junior year, he was elected the Union's president as the candidate of a coalition formed to deny the Liberal Party candidate that post. He owed his victory largely to his personal appeal and to the respect his skill as an orator had brought him.

For all his newfound attachment to conservatism, Brent retained his loyalty to World Federalism well into his junior year. In the summer of 1948 he attended a World Federalist Congress in Luxembourg. It was his first trip to Europe, and he seized the chance to do some traveling. Besides France and Belgium, he visited Spain, a country that would one day loom large in his life. This time, however, it seems to have made little impression on him. In Madrid he went to a bullfight and found it unappetizing. It contained "too much cruelty," he said, and "too little sport." As late as November 1948, he expressed disappointment at having had to miss a World Federalist gathering recently held in Minneapolis.[10] But his days with the cause were numbered. Buckley had been working hard to win him away from it, arguing that in practice it would aid communism. By his senior year Brent had put World Federalism behind him.

Buckley matched Brent's status as a campus notable, becoming chairman (editor in chief) of the *Yale Daily News*. Conservative lore has it that as graduation drew near, the two agreed to seek positions of national prominence corresponding to the eminent posts they held at Yale. Buckley, the journalist, would wield influence through the written word, while Brent, the orator, would orate his way into the White House, and working together they'd end up running the country.

Brent's religious conversion took a more private path. He had already turned Catholic "inwardly" before coming to Yale but hadn't yet officially entered the Church. Nonetheless, his religious commitment showed no sign of wavering. He viewed materialist philosophy with a jaundiced eye and delighted in citing the arguments of its critics. He wrote enthusiastically to Patty about *Human Destiny*, a book by the French scientist Pierre Lecomte du Noüy that he thought decisively debunked "the materialist theory of a mechanistic, purposeless universe." The book was a "must," he told his sister.[11]

Although he formally entered the Church while an undergraduate, just when he took the step is hard to say. In 1964 he wrote that he had converted in 1947; in 1986 that he had done so at the age of twenty, which would have been in 1946.[12] He seems never to have spoken of religious instruction before his admission to the fold or of the church where the admission took place or of a baptismal ceremony (which may not have been necessary, given his Episcopal background).

In his 1971 book *Cruising Speed*, Buckley, who at some point became Brent's sponsor (godfather to an adult convert), wrote that Brent had converted as a sophomore, which would have meant fall

1947 or spring 1948. Later, however, Buckley changed his mind, deciding his friend had probably done so as a freshman. "I'm pretty sure that Brent did it on the sly," he said late in his life. "I mean avoiding any ceremony to which people might be invited . . . Just one day . . . I knew he had become [Roman Catholic] but none of the intervening thoughts or events."[13]

Brent's wife, who may not have known him before his conversion, thought he had entered the Church as a freshman, but she couldn't be sure. She dismissed the idea that he may never have "officially" converted, saying that if this were so, he would never have received the sacraments.[14]

It looks, then, as if Brent, who disliked and avoided "occasions," slipped quietly into the Church one day in his freshman year without saying a word even to his closest friends. Buckley, who had much to do with Brent's conversion to conservatism, played no active part in his conversion to Catholicism. Nor, after Brent's entry into the Church, did the two talk much about religion or Church affairs. Still, Buckley later wrote, "our common faith strengthened a bond."[15]

How Brent's mother reacted when she heard the news seems to have gone unrecorded.

Buckley's redheaded sister, Patricia, was her parents' seventh child, the one who came next after him. Because of their closeness in age, Trish and Bill were often teamed together under their parents' scheme for organizing a numerous brood, and they became each other's favorite sibling. Trish led a nomadic early life. In 1929 her father moved the family temporarily to France, and in 1931 from France to England. Not until 1933, when the Buckleys returned permanently to Connecticut, did the six-year-old Trish's (mostly) American life begin.

Trish's childhood in Sharon, like Brent's in Omaha, suggests an idyll, but unlike his, not one Norman Rockwell would have painted.

She received her primary education at home from tutors, studied piano under a resident music teacher, swam in the family pool, took up riding, and when old enough competed in horse shows and rode in hunts. At her father's urging, she began to express her opinions, and in dinner table talk she challenged her siblings fiercely.

But in 1938 a kind of death entered her Arcadia: her father announced that she, Bill, their sister Jane, and their brother Reid were going to continue their education in England. The children vehemently protested, but to no avail. In September 1938 she, Jane, and Bill (Reid followed later) boarded an ocean liner and crossed the Atlantic. As it happened, they arrived in Southampton at the height of the Sudeten crisis, and on docking they were handed gas masks, a precaution against a possible German air raid.

At St. Mary's Convent, a Catholic girls' school at Ascot, the sisters were miserable. "Jane and I simply hate, loathe, can't stand, detest, #*&! [St. Mary's]," Trish wrote to her parents. "Jane and I cry almost every night. I don't see how I can stand it. I don't know what I would do if I came back after Christmas."[16] But her father was adamant. Not until the summer of 1939, when Europe was clearly on the brink of war, did he relent and bring the children home.

Trish's parents next sent her to the Ethel Walker School, a boarding school near Hartford that it was customary for Buckley girls to attend. But she hated Ethel Walker also and eventually transferred to New York City's Nightingale-Bamford School, from which she graduated.

If Trish dissented from her father's preferences in schools, her loyalty to him nonetheless ran deep, and she fully embraced his conservative political views. She once flaunted this allegiance at a fair in Dutchess County, New York, where she had gone with her father to compete in a horse show. Also there was the county's leading citizen, President Franklin D. Roosevelt, whose policies the senior Buckley strongly opposed. Trish won a blue ribbon in the competition, and as she took the traditional ride around the ring, she was warmly applauded by the president. But as she rode past him, instead of nodding, as custom instructed, she ostentatiously turned her head the other way. When her father asked why she had snubbed FDR, she replied, "I thought you didn't like him."[17]

Trish also shared her parents' firm Catholicism, though she didn't mind joining piety with pranks. Hearing one day that two houseguests had never been baptized, she and Bill decided to make good the fatal lapse. After dipping their fingers in water, they went to the houseguests' room and explained that they were looking for Bill's dog. Pretending to lose their balance during the "search," they "accidentally" brushed their wet fingers across the guests' foreheads while silently reciting the Church's baptismal formula. Thus the visitors left Sharon unwitting, but baptized, Christians.[18]

Trish completed her education at Vassar, where she majored in music. She also found time for politics, helping to edit a conservative student paper, *The Chronicle*, for which she wrote music criticism. Now a slim bundle of energy with (as the *New York Post* would one day write) "huge light blue eyes, orange-red hair, and a fighting temper," she was able to make a considerable impression on others. Rollin G. Osterweis, a historian at Yale and coach of the debating team, described her as "beautiful and headstrong, a young woman of decided views." This comment may read like an ad for a Katharine Hepburn movie, but it wasn't unwarranted. Trish's sister Carol seconded Osterweis. "My sister Patricia has shining red hair and a temper to match, and likes to break rules," she wrote.[19]

One rule Trish broke often was Vassar's regulation forbidding students to spend more than one weekend a month off campus. Many weekends she slipped off to New Haven to visit Bill, and on one of these jaunts he introduced her to his friend Brent. At first she took no notice of the tall Nebraskan, thinking of him simply as "someone who was around."[20] But in 1948 her feelings abruptly changed. The catalyst was political: the communist coup in Prague.

The communist seizure of power in Czechoslovakia, a country that had looked as if it might escape postwar Soviet rule, caused shock and indignation in the West. But Vassar's left-wing student papers, far from mourning, reacted to the takeover complacently. Up in arms over these Soviet fellow travelers, an outraged Trish yearned to rout them in debate but held back out of fear that she had no talent for debating. Hoping to relieve her frustration, Bill offered to come to Vassar with Brent and take on the job. When the editors of one left-wing paper agreed to debate them, a date was set. The clash, Trish recalled decades later, turned out splendidly. The visitors wiped the floor with the locals.

Thrilled by the triumph, Trish suddenly saw Bill's friend in a whole new light. "I think I'm falling in love with Brent," she told her brother. Bill said nothing, just squeezed her hand. But he seems to have passed her confidence on to Brent.[21] Brent, it turned out, reciprocated Trish's feelings, and by the time she graduated from Vassar later that spring, it looked as if she and Brent might be headed for marriage.

The following year, possibility turned into reality. In mid-January 1949 Patty Bozell received a one-sentence telegram from Brent: "Tish [as he called Trish] and I are engaged." Many years later Trish told a visitor what had happened. On a winter's day soon after the start of the new year, she had taken a train from New York, where she was working, to New Haven to meet Brent. They had plans to attend a speech at Yale by Eleanor Roosevelt. Tired after a hard day's labor followed by a long train ride, and in any case no great fan of the former first lady, Trish found the evening politically and physically painful. After the speech, they went to Mory's, the famous dining club near Yale, and there things took an unexpected turn. As they sat with their drinks, Brent suddenly proposed. Trish said yes, and they finished the drinks engaged.

Brent gave his version to Patty soon after the event. "Tish happened to be in New Haven," he said, "and I happened to get that 'God helping me I can do no other' feeling whilst in a beer joint," so they got engaged. He had yet to give his fiancée a ring, he went on, an excited twenty-three-year-old trying to sound blasé: "[I] haven't gotten around to it. Please remind me the next time you write to get the ring. I really should do it soon because I have an idea that Tish is as silly as most women about something like that."[22]

He added that in gaining a wife he was also gaining a secretary. While still a child, Trish had become a speedy typist, a fact of which her fiancé was well aware. So along with her job and the wedding preparations she now faced, she found herself saddled with much of his correspondence. He would delay Political Union business till the weekend, when he would dictate letters to her and she would type them. "It goes a lot faster that way," he explained to Patty.[23]

By autumn, plans were completed for a holiday wedding. Brent and Trish were married four days after Christmas (the senior Buckleys' wedding anniversary) in Camden, South Carolina, where the Buckleys kept a winter home. The Bozells arrived from Omaha by train, and Patty took part as one of Trish's bridesmaids. Brent's Creighton mentor, Father Cervantes, said the nuptial Mass.

After a brief honeymoon on Cuba's Isle of Pines (paid for with a gift check from the Buckleys), the newlyweds returned to New Haven. Brent still had his senior year to finish and was slated to enter Yale Law School in the fall, so they rented a house in nearby Hamden, a place to live while Brent went on with his studies.

Three months later, during Yale's spring break, they went on a longer honeymoon. Traveling by car, they drove to New Orleans, Austin, and Dallas, where they called on a number of Buckley relatives, and then to San Antonio, where they visited the bungalow in which Brent had weathered pneumonia. Back on the road, they headed for Mexico City, where they rented rooms with meals, laundry service, and a piano for $1.33 a day (unaware that Trish's father was footing the bill). Trish, an avid pianist, practiced her keyboard technique, while Brent made plans to write what he described as "a small book on the morality of war, killing, etc." He hoped to "convince the country that we should go to war [with the USSR]" but doubted he would succeed in doing so. "Alas," he lamented, "I wish I knew how to write."[24]

In the spring of 1950 Brent's long-term prospects looked bright. Nature had showered an abundance of gifts on him. He would soon graduate from one of the country's leading colleges and then go on to one of its leading law schools. He seemed destined not for conventional success in life but instead for some unpredictable kind of stardom.

THREE

McCarthy and His Friends

Brent graduated from Yale in early June 1950, shortly before the outbreak of war in Korea. At commencement he was named the winner of the Ten Eyck Award, the most glittering prize Yale bestowed for public speaking. But oddly, his 1950 class book listing (a brief summary of a graduating senior's background, college achievements, and plans for the future) lacked the photograph such entries usually include. Trish later attributed this absence to his impatience with time-consuming "fuss." He wouldn't have wanted to bother having his picture taken, she said. In fact, he even stayed home from graduation.[1]

Meanwhile, Brent's bond with Buckley was growing stronger. They were now not only close friends but also brothers-in-law joined together through Buckley's favorite sister. Just after graduation, Buckley, too, got married, and he and his bride (whom Trish had known at Vassar) also settled in Hamden. When Trish gave birth to her first child, Christopher, in November 1950, the Bozells asked the Buckleys to be his godparents. Two years later, when the Buckleys' son was born, he too was named Christopher, and the Bozells became his godparents.

Brent's main business in Hamden was studying law. Trish's was motherhood and running the Bozell household. Buckley's was a book he was working on while waiting to report for duty with the Office of Policy Coordination (OPC), the CIA's covert action arm, to which he had gained admission with the help of Kendall. The book, entitled *God and Man at Yale*, criticized Yale for a faculty Buckley thought biased toward the Left and for making no effort to achieve philosophical balance. The alumni, the book advised, should have more say in university policy and should use their financial leverage to ensure balance. Brought out in 1951 by the conservative publisher Henry Regnery, *God and Man at Yale* sold briskly, raised an ear-splitting ruckus over academic freedom, and launched its author (who resigned from the OPC in 1952) on his more than fifty-year career as a conservative author, editor, columnist, critic, and celebrity. Conservative readers generally praised the book, but Brent demurred, doubting Yale alumni were qualified to make academic policy.[2] This wouldn't be the only time he'd resist a conservative consensus.

In the early 1950s the most controversial figure in American politics was undoubtedly Wisconsin's Republican junior senator, Joseph R. McCarthy. Elected in 1946, McCarthy drew little attention until February 1950, when, in a speech delivered to a women's group in Wheeling, West Virginia, he claimed to have in his possession a list of State Department employees who were communists. So began five years of nonstop uproar, as the Wisconsin senator, hurling accusations far and wide—in one of his more outré moments, he charged former Army chief and secretary of state George C. Marshall with being a traitor—held fast to the spotlight as America's most determined foe of communists.

McCarthy's activities called forth a variety of responses. Millions hailed him as an indispensable man, the tireless guardian of the nation's internal security. Some of these fans were well aware of his shortcomings, but seeing in him a national symbol of anticommunist resolve, they thought it necessary to support him. Others, while equally hostile to communism, nevertheless condemned the methods they accused him of favoring: "smear tactics," "mudslinging," "shooting from the hip," and assuming "guilt by association" and disloyalty in what were probably instances of poor judgment—all summed up by a new political term, *McCarthyism*. Still others condemned both McCarthy's methods and his aims, which they alleged put the Bill of Rights in jeopardy. Most of the country's intellectuals detested McCarthy, so most serious writing about him took a negative view.

Brent and Buckley held a favorable opinion of the senator. They considered him to be an honest anticommunist who, careless and irresponsible though he might sometimes be, was doing a job that badly needed to be done. This judgment led them to take action in his defense. In 1952 Buckley read an article in *The Freeman* (one of the few conservative journals of the day) in which he sensed a latent hostility to McCarthy. Unwilling to let the *Freeman* piece go unchallenged, he decided to write a counterarticle for the magazine and invited Brent to join him in the project. That summer the two discussed their plans with McCarthy himself and received his blessing.[3] Back home, they embarked on a lengthy research effort, and by year's end they had amassed so much material that at the urging of Buckley's publisher, Henry Regnery, they replaced their article project with one for a book.

In 1953 they began to write. Also involved in the project by this time was Kendall, whose ideas on social consensus and its enforcement furnished the book's underlying interpretive framework. Kendall eventually took part in the writing. A typescript unearthed decades later in the Buckley house in Sharon shows revisions in his signature green ink interwoven with some in Buckley's red and Brent's blue ink.

With Kendall cracking the whip, the book was completed toward the end of 1953. Published by Regnery in March 1954, *McCarthy and His Enemies: The Record and Its Meaning* examined McCarthy's first three years of notoriety (1950 through 1952), giving most of its attention to his 1950 allegations concerning the State Department and to a Senate inquiry into his conduct in that affair. It acknowledged that he was no blameless victim of his accusers. For one thing, it noted, he had lied in his testimony at the Senate inquiry, and for that, the authors asserted, he "deserve[d] to be censured." For another, he had engaged at various times in exaggerations that might have "unjustly damaged" persons who had come under his scrutiny.[4]

Nevertheless, the book concluded—and here lay the nub of its argument—"*McCarthy's record is . . . not only much better than his critics allege but, given his métier, extremely good.*" As for the charge of smearing, "the case-by-case breakdown clearly renders a verdict extremely favorable to McCarthy." When people decried his methods, what they were really complaining about were his refusal to "understate" his cases and his preference for "the hypothesis that favors our national security" (though most federal employees who seemed soft on communism were neither spies nor traitors, the authors conceded, but loyal Americans). All told then, if McCarthy had sometimes gone too far, his campaign against communist infiltrators in the federal bureaucracy remained one "around which men of good will and stern morality [could] close ranks." Only when communist spying had been fully suppressed would the country be able to do without McCarthy.[5]

Joining a debate in which shouting and name-calling were frequent, the authors took pains to present their case with restraint. The book laid out its arguments in even-tempered prose that deepened the tone of reason and authority the authors sought. Closely examining accusations against McCarthy, the book either accepted a charge as valid or, more often, denied it with a quietly delivered rebuttal. It departed from its analytical approach only to drop an occasional dry remark, but one that always stopped short of sarcasm. It presented a McCarthy who was less a grandstander than a conscientious public servant whose zeal for his cause sometimes led him to bend rules.

Before publishing, Regnery sent galley sheets to McCarthy for review. The senator didn't read the entire text. "I don't understand the book," he later confessed. "It's too intellectual for me." But he complained to Regnery that it handled him too roughly. His wife, Jean, went well beyond this in her displeasure. Her husband's fiercest partisan, she denounced all the book's criticisms as unfounded and treated its authors as a pair of character assassins. Brent and Buckley agreed to tone down some criticisms, a concession that mollified McCarthy. Invited to the publication party, he happily attended, describing the book to reporters as the first one about him "not written by an enemy." Nonetheless, Jean McCarthy stood fast in her contrary view.[6]

Conservative reviewers applauded *McCarthy and His Enemies*. While some liberal reviewers treated the book seriously (if offering a negative view), others assumed a condescending tone, never failing to point out the youth of the authors and finding their work intellectually and morally shallow. A few wrote with venom. The historian Arthur Schlesinger Jr., for example, called the book "sick" and likened its authors to the bright young Stalin-worshipping intellectuals of the 1930s, who had also cleverly defended an evil cause.[7] Neither *The Nation* nor the *New Republic* ran a review.

Sensing a strong market for the book, Regnery thought about basing a television documentary on it in hopes of reaching a larger potential readership. "The more publicity the book gets, the better," he told Brent. The television idea never got off the ground, but to try to increase sales, the publisher rushed the book into print from what he admitted was "a pretty illegible manuscript." The result dismayed Brent. Eager for success and concerned about the book's appearance, he found appalling the number of errors it contained.

Brent also kept a sharp eye on Regnery's marketing decisions. For example, noticing that Regnery was advertising in the *San Francisco Chronicle*, the paper that enjoyed the largest circulation in San Francisco, he suggested using the *San Francisco Examiner* instead. Not only did the *Examiner* have a bigger circulation in the Bay Area as a whole, the son of Leo Bozell reminded Regnery; as part of the Hearst chain and friendly to McCarthy, it also reached people who were "much more our way" of thinking and hence more likely to go out and buy the book.[8]

Brent's attention to marketing stemmed from his ambition for success and his wish to help McCarthy, but also from a need for money. Frugality had never been his strongpoint. At Yale he had overdrawn on his checking account so heavily that his Omaha bank had closed it. (In response, while home on vacation, he had gone to the bank's president—not to apologize but to complain. "You've known me all my life," he protested. "You know I'm good for the money.")[9] Although he had inherited some money from his father and Trish had family money, the Bozells weren't able to disregard expenses. Brent had spent much of his inheritance paying college and law school bills, and the Bozell family overhead was rising.

Brent had graduated from law school by the time *McCarthy and His Enemies* came out, and he found a position at a leading San Francisco law firm, which meant transferring his household to the opposite side of the country. The Bozells bought and began furnishing a house in Atherton, an upper-middle-class suburb south of San Francisco. On top of the outlays these major purchases required, part of their transcontinental moving bill remained to be paid. Meanwhile, two more children, Kathy and Michael, had arrived, and a fourth, who would be christened Maureen, was on the way, so domestic help was necessary.

In June 1954 Brent asked Regnery for a $1,000 advance on royalties. There was evidence, he joked, "that writing from a cell-block is the best way to guarantee a best-seller, so maybe you ought to consider entering me in that field." The publisher came through with a check for $2,500 and the promise of another $5,250 in the near future.[10]

Regnery could afford to be generous, for the book was selling well. It did best in the East, where its New York sales led the way. California sales varied sharply from region to region. Los Angeles proved to be a receptive market, but San Francisco showed hostility. Several San Francisco bookstores refused to stock a book they considered pro-McCarthy, and a Regnery salesman at work in Berkeley reported that booksellers there had reacted to his sales pitch so belligerently that he felt lucky to have escaped the town alive. But elsewhere a more hospitable attitude prevailed. The Yale Co-op, for example—perhaps recalling its success with *God and Man at Yale*—arranged its stock of the book in a special display. Six months after publication, thirty thousand copies had been sold nationwide, a number Regnery called "all things considered, . . . very good"—good enough, in fact, to warrant a paperback edition. Paperback sales were also satisfactory, bringing Brent an income that continued into the 1960s.[11]

Convinced that McCarthy had further sales potential, Regnery proposed that Brent write a second book about the senator—maybe something on McCarthy's recent Army hearings, he suggested. Brent, however, had another project in mind. How about a book on the possible benefits of a U.S. attack on the USSR, he countered, still taken with the project he had written of in Mexico four years earlier. Half the book would concern the "moral ramifications" of a preventive war, and the other half the "political desirability" of such an action. Regnery pronounced himself "not too enthusiastic" about this idea, but eager to get a new McCarthy book out of Brent, he next proposed one on the liberal campaign to destroy the senator.[12] Again, however, Brent turned the publisher down, for he now had a matter of urgency to deal with.

After only a year of practicing law, Brent obtained a leave of absence from his firm. The reason was that McCarthy now faced serious trouble in the Senate and turned to Brent for help.

A few weeks after the appearance of *McCarthy and His Enemies*, McCarthy opened hearings on communist influence in the Army. Nationally televised in their entirety, the hearings gave a mass audience its first long look at the senator in action. Many viewers found their tribune distinctly unappetizing, and in the aftermath his political future began to dim.

At this point, some Republican senators turned on their Wisconsin colleague. In their eyes, his political value had rested solely on his talent for tying the communist problem to the Democrats, a talent that after two decades of Democratic rule could help return Washington to Republican hands. Their prayers were answered in 1952, when Republican Dwight D. Eisenhower was elected president and the GOP won control of both houses of Congress. As a result McCarthy lost much of his usefulness. In fact, he threatened to become a liability, because his probing of federal agencies, which Republicans now headed—the CIA, for example, figured on his hit list—could cause the administration no end of trouble. The time had come to shut McCarthy down. But as long as McCarthy enjoyed broad support among Republican voters, he remained untouchable.

The Army hearings drained away much of that support. The moment McCarthy's Republican enemies were waiting for had finally arrived. In August 1954 the Senate set up a committee, chaired by Republican Arthur V. Watkins of Utah, to look into McCarthy's behavior as an investigator. Its aim was to send the Senate a censure resolution that would deliver the coup de grâce to the now irksome senator.

Soon after the Watkins committee formed, McCarthy's lawyer phoned Brent to ask for his help in staving off censure. Brent was a lawyer, an able man with words, and, by the evidence of *McCarthy and His Enemies*, an expert at defending the senator. He agreed to help, even though he and Buckley had written that McCarthy deserved censure for lying to the Senate committee investigating his Wheeling speech claims. Brent obtained his leave of absence and, with Trish at his side, set out for Washington.

The situation he found awaiting him looked grim. McCarthy, who had been drinking heavily and looked exhausted, bristled with anger and defiance. Compromise, he insisted, was out of the question: to admit that perhaps occasionally he had behaved badly, to apologize for "excesses" in hopes of winning over undecided Republic senators, would benefit only his enemies. His best option, in his view, was to stand his ground and fight.

In November the Watkins committee passed a censure resolution, which went on to the Senate for debate and a vote. McCarthy planned to speak against the resolution and assigned the task of writing his speech to Brent. Following his boss's wishes, Brent drafted a combative and provocative text that did full justice to McCarthy's will to fight, not only refusing to admit any wrongdoing on the senator's part but also giving him a turn at playing prosecutor. The communist conspiracy now reached right into the Senate, the speech announced, and the Watkins committee was serving as "its unwitting handmaiden." Moreover, it added in a mordant dig, in doing the communists' dirty work for them, the committee was using such typical communist methods as misrepresentation, omission, and distortion—the very tactics that now went under the name McCarthyism.[13]

When the votes were counted, the censure resolution passed handily. Those in favor included twenty-two Republican senators, which suggests that McCarthy's pugnacity may have cost him votes. Brent had done his job well; the speech vividly conveyed McCarthy's battle lust. But its words were also the nails that sealed the senator's coffin.

After the censure, the Bozells returned to Atherton, but not for long. In the spring of 1955, making the phone call himself, McCarthy asked Brent to join his staff and write speeches for him. Sinking into has-been status, no longer wielding power that could make others quake, he craved the presence of people he liked and trusted. Meanwhile, Jean McCarthy had shed her hostility toward Brent, whom she now saw not as her beloved husband's libeler but as the man who had dropped everything to ride to her husband's rescue.

Brent quickly decided to accept the invitation. He was doing well at his law firm despite his open and unfashionable support of McCarthy. But restless by nature, he had begun to balk at what he thought the tedium of the legal profession, especially after the excitement of his weeks in Washington. "He hated practicing law," Trish later told an inquirer, and growing "itchy [was] part of his makeup." (Nor did Trish think much of life in a San Francisco suburb. "Atherton was a lovely place," she said, "and I recall being bored silly.")[14] Thus did Brent's life as a lawyer come to an end and his life in Washington politics begin.

Brent's decision to join McCarthy also stemmed from the liking he had conceived for the senator, who had treated him and Trish, little-known people in their twenties, as equals and friends. This wasn't an unusual response to McCarthy. The offstage McCarthy struck many people as charming. Unlike the thug of Herblock's cartoons or the grim inquisitor glowering from television screens, McCarthy in person could radiate affability.

But above all, to Brent, the student of Willmoore Kendall, McCarthy personified the nation's revulsion against communism and insistence that communists be put beyond the pale. An enemy threatened the community, and McCarthy was the sanction such threats were bound to call forth. What was more, given McCarthy's national prominence as an anticommunist, no substitute figure could possibly fill his shoes. Hence, internal security required less stress on his sins (though they couldn't be condoned), and if his career in government could be salvaged, then it should be.

This time, Brent and Trish arrived in Washington with four children in tow (and a fifth, Brent, due that summer). While they looked for a house, Brent and Trish stayed with the McCarthys and the children moved temporarily to the Buckley place in Camden.

The entry of another Bozell household member into the senator's home furnished conclusive proof of his eagerness to enlist Brent as an aide. McCarthy feared cats, yet he opened his door to Trish's Siamese, Kiki. And in a moment of crisis involving the cat, he topped even that gesture. One night the Siamese vanished. Hours later, in predawn darkness, some policemen (the Washington police were among McCarthy's biggest fans and informally kept a protective eye on his property) spotted suspicious movements in a clump of bushes behind the house. Advancing on the swaying shrubbery with guns drawn, they found no infiltrators but only McCarthy himself, clad in his underwear and armed with a flashlight, creeping through the underbrush in search of the missing cat.[15]

Brent worked for McCarthy as a speechwriter and an adviser. He also supplied the senator with at least one ghostwritten book review, which knocked former secretary of state Dean Acheson's *A Democrat Looks at His Party* and called Acheson "the worst Secretary of State in American history." McCarthy in turn gave political advice to Brent, who had developed a serious interest in running for office. Discussing the possibility of Brent's seeking a Senate seat someday, they talked about whether he should try his luck in New Mexico, a state he had visited as a child and very much liked.[16]

At first Brent's association with McCarthy worked out well, but after a year or so it ran into trouble. Now a ruin physically and psychologically as well as politically, the senator was sinking into acute alcoholism, and his erratic behavior was making him harder to work for. But the end was near. In the spring of 1957, with his liver undermined by hepatitis, McCarthy checked into Bethesda Naval Hospital, and a few weeks later he died there. After five years, Brent's McCarthy adventure was over.

Disapprove though he did of actions he called "Joe's extravagances," Brent found himself deeply moved by the senator's death.[17] In an elegy titled "This Was a Man," he reflected on McCarthy's final years, never referring to the senator by name but always by pronoun. After the Senate censure, Brent wrote, "he" had "the mind, the will, the spirit" to resume the fight, "but nothing would move." His strength had run out, leaving him like a boxer flattened by a roundhouse punch who wants to get up and return to battle but can't. "The Senate had turned on him, and that ruined him," the piece ended. "God was merciful to stop his heart."[18]

As McCarthy's career moved inexorably into its twilight, Brent's took a turn in a new direction. He agreed to contribute to an enterprise envisaged by Buckley, a weekly conservative "journal of opinion." The first issue of *National Review* (as the new magazine was called) appeared in November 1955 and contained a piece on Republican politics by Brent.[19] With this article, the lawyer turned political aide took up another new career, journalism, a profession he would pursue with passion for years to come.

FOUR

Standing athwart History

Bill Buckley saw *National Review* as a conservative counterpart of the two leading liberal weeklies, *The Nation* and the *New Republic*. *NR*, too, would appear each week (though in 1958 it became a biweekly) and publish editorial comment on the news, analytical articles, policy criticism, book and sometimes music reviews, and columns. The magazine's grand purpose, announced a "Publisher's Statement" in the first issue, was to "stand athwart [left-trending] history, yelling Stop."

Wanting to advance only "responsible" forms of the Right, and to unite these forms in a broad coalition against the Left, Buckley made the magazine simultaneously exclusive and inclusive. On one hand, *NR* would have no truck with racism, anti-Semitism, conspiracy theory, or any other strain of the crackpot Right. On the other, it would open its pages with a latitudinarian welcome to all of the many varieties of the respectable Right, including, among others, antistatists, traditionalists, free-market enthusiasts, southern agrarians, constitutional monarchists (who could be found here and there along conservative highways and byways), and strict anticommunists. Such people might differ on any number of points, but all shared an antipathy toward modern-day liberalism, in their eyes a mixture of intrusive government, collectivism, and softness on communism. Antiliberalism, then, was the glue that held them together.

Reflecting *NR*'s hospitality toward the Right in its several guises, the magazine's masthead listed, among others, such editors and columnists as the hard-line policy analyst and strategist James Burnham, whose regular column, "The Third World War," dealt mainly with American policy and the Cold War; the traditionalist conservative Russell Kirk, who contributed "From the Academy," a column focused on trends in American education; the libertarian conservative Frank Meyer, whose column, "Principles and Heresies," alerted readers to threats (especially on the plane of ideas) to the freedoms of the West; and Willmoore Kendall, who in his column, "The Liberal Line," regularly flayed his favorite whipping boy, "the liberal establishment." Buckley, for his part, avoided specialization, commenting in his column, "The Ivory Tower" (later renamed "On the Right"), on a broad range of issues and topics of general interest.

The overall viewpoint propounded by this motley crew favored libertarianism in government and the economy (limited, as opposed to expansive, New Deal–style, government; free, competitive markets), traditionalism in the social and cultural realms (individual responsibility as opposed to welfare culture dependency; conventional as opposed to "progressive" education; parental authority over "permissive" child rearing; Mark Twain over Jack Kerouac; whiskey over vodka), a hawkish stance in matters of internal security (*NR* took a generally benign view of McCarthy), and a policy of "liberation" or "rollback" rather than "containment" regarding the Soviet empire.

Brent's ties with *National Review* began early in its history: several months before *NR* started publishing, Buckley, hoping to drum up money for the venture, gave him a fund-raising letter to deliver to McCarthy, over whose signature the letter was to be mailed.[1] *NR*'s maiden issue introduced Brent's column, called "National Trends." In the column, Brent made national politics his usual beat but sometimes shifted his focus to foreign affairs, mostly to topics connected with the Cold War. Besides his column, he provided *NR* with articles, book reviews, and unsigned editorials and paragraphs, in the process becoming one of the magazine's more prolific contributors. Like other *NR* writers, he also delivered his message through the spoken word, appearing at colleges and other venues where audiences interested in politics could be found. At first, *NR*'s masthead identified him as a "contributor," but he soon ascended to the rank of "senior editor," joining such notables as Burnham and Kendall.

Brent proved to have a flair for his new profession. A painstaking researcher, as *McCarthy and His Enemies* had demonstrated, he could also turn out fluent and vigorous prose. His work habits, on the other hand, were a good deal less than exemplary, nearly causing the managing editor's secretary a nervous breakdown. Slow to get down to business, he would write his column at the very last moment, then phone it in with just minutes to spare before it was sent to the printer. Although he never missed a deadline, it was rumored that the day an issue closed, the secretary began downing tranquilizers at noon.[2]

But his dilatory ways don't seem to have earned him ill will. When editorial conferences brought him to *NR*'s New York office, the editorial staff always gave him a friendly welcome. His unassuming manner, wry humor, broad smile, and classic red-hair-and-freckles American-boy look, still vivid as he entered his thirties, instantly disposed people in his favor. In their correspondence, Buckley addressed him as "Butch," a nickname that perfectly captured Brent's Rockwellian side.

Brent's picture of American political life in the late 1950s stressed a deep-seated conflict between the bulk of the population, which was instinctively, though not professedly, conservative, and which exerted its influence through Congress, and a liberal "establishment," which controlled the federal government's executive and judicial branches. Currently, he contended, the more aggressive of the two liberal power centers was the Supreme Court, "the partisan agent of a fashionable ideology, set on accomplishing by judicial edict what the ideology could not achieve through legitimate political channels." Under Chief Justice Earl Warren, the court's "controlling purpose" was "to give legal sanction . . . to the political judgments of the Establishment," a gross violation of the judiciary's constitutional function.

Yet the widespread conservative calls for Warren's impeachment were ill considered, Brent believed. For the chief justice had done nothing the Constitution viewed as grounds for impeachment, and in any case, guilt lay not with a single individual but with "a usurper branch of government." The best way to solve the problem was for Congress to apply the Constitution's Article III, Section 2, which authorized the lawmakers to restrict or even abolish the Supreme Court's appellate jurisdiction. If that seemed too drastic, a less radical way of bringing the justices to heel would be a congressional censure resolution against the court.[3]

Increasingly, the subject of the court came to absorb Brent, supplanting internal security as his main concern. Henry Regnery, however, kept urging a book on McCarthy. This time he suggested that Brent write about the private McCarthy, the little-known figure behind the public image. There was certainly "much to be said about 'McCarthy the man,'" Brent agreed, "but it is not all flattering. In the light of my very close association with him and with Jean, I really do not feel at liberty to go into those aspects of the question. Maybe some day, but not for a very long time."

Brent had been planning a book on United Auto Workers boss Walter Reuther and the union he headed (to Brent's mind, the epitome of organized labor's monopolistic, coercive, and thuggish tendencies). But his worries about the Warren Court—his belief that in cases such as *Brown v. Board of Education* the court had overstepped its boundaries, usurping a right the Constitution had left to the states and assuming the power to amend the Constitution in the interest of liberalism—led him to put the Reuther book aside. Instead, he told Regnery, he would write about the court. He then plunged into what would become several years of research for the volume, which he tentatively titled *The Warren Court: A Dissenting Opinion*. Regnery showed a mild interest in the new project. In 1960 he asked Brent for a look at the manuscript "if you are not committed elsewhere." But the publisher's perennial hope refused to die. Even as he asked to see Brent's court manuscript, he put in a plug for a book about "McCarthyism" and the "hysteria" McCarthy had caused in the liberal camp.[4]

For *NR*, Brent also devoted much column space to the Eisenhower administration and to the factional tension that wracked the GOP. *National Review* abominated Eisenhower. It expected a Republican president to "roll back" both the New Deal and the USSR's imperial frontiers, and Eisenhower did neither (though his CIA did briefly attempt a "liberation" strategy in Eastern Europe, with little success). Like most of his *NR* colleagues, Brent blamed the president's inaction on naiveté and a soft spot for liberalism (not recognizing that the former general hid his toughness behind a bumpkin's vacant grin).

Eisenhower was "a liberal president," Brent wrote bitterly, and the liberal hold on his administration was "complete and unchallenged." As result, he said, the administration was keeping the country "almost exactly as it found it" in both foreign and domestic policy. Many Republicans, Brent complained, accepted this state of affairs, swallowing a Roosevelt-style, cult-of-personality presidency.

The president treated Democrats as his "de facto allies," Brent asserted, and regarded the GOP's conservative wing as his greatest enemy. How should conservative Republicans respond? How were they to advance their beliefs and aims? They could succeed within the existing, two-party system only by winning elections, but their electoral victories promised to be few. Their best bet, Brent concluded, probably lay in a third party, which they could work with the southern Democrats to establish.

A third major subject of Brent's column was a long-standing Bozell concern: the menace of communism. It was the only issue, he wrote in 1956, that "really matters."[5] This was a judgment he would soon modify, if not in theory then at least in practice. He would continue to treat communism as a serious threat, but only as one among several (and not always the gravest). He seems also to have become less concerned about internal security than he had once been. Now when he wrote about communism, he wrote mainly about the USSR, its military power, and the Cold War (which, like his *NR* colleague James Burnham, he called "the Third World War") rather than about domestic infiltration, espionage, and subversion.

The Cold War, he predicted, would end in Soviet victory. His pessimism stemmed partly from his reading of the historical moment. The world was moving toward "the Soviet, or collectivist, concept, not ours," he argued, and there seemed no way to reverse this long-term trend. What was more, American traditions were hobbling the country's Cold War efforts. Thanks to their moral and cultural heritage, he argued, Americans were "inherently incapable" of matching the enemy in political warfare. But above all, Americans no longer worried about communism, no longer harbored a sense of the peril it posed.[6]

Sad to say, he observed, U.S. policy was making things worse. Baldly stated, Eisenhower was a disaster. After three years of the Eisenhower regime, the United States had become "a flaccid, feckless, indifferent nation that believes, if it believes anything at all, that peace is the highest value" and nuclear war "unthinkable." Accustomed to hearing that war was "peace," concessions "firmness," and enemies "competitors," Americans could hardly be blamed for their insouciance. Trade deals and cultural exchanges with the Soviets only encouraged the attitude. At bottom, America seemed stricken with "a sickness of the will," caring about winning much less than the Soviets did. Hence the depressing spectacle of America as "the hopeless, tormented Colossus of the West."

Eisenhower, Brent wrote, saw the key to victory in beating the Kremlin in a race to end world poverty and win over "world opinion." In fact, for the president world opinion seemed more important than national security. But this obsession with global approval made no sense. "Liberals"—presumably including Eisenhower—identified "world" opinion with opinion in the Third World, which they envisaged as holding "the 'swing vote' in the world election contest." But this was a contest America could never win, not because America was evil, but because it was rich and white, and therefore hateful to the

Third World. Nothing could come of the Eisenhower strategy but failure.[7]

Brent was outraged by Eisenhower's failure to aid the 1956 anticommunist rising in Hungary—especially in view of the president's simultaneous pressure on U.S. allies France and Britain to pull out after they had occupied the Suez Canal Zone, nationalized by a seemingly pro-Soviet Egypt earlier that year.

But no instance of Eisenhower's diplomacy angered him more than the president's 1959 invitation to Soviet leader Nikita Khrushchev to visit the United States. His revulsion was acidly expressed by *National Review*'s cover the week of the visit, a drawing that pictured Eisenhower, a fatuous smile on his face, shaking the blood-soaked hand of his Soviet guest. When Buckley organized an antivisit protest rally at Carnegie Hall (complete with a Bach-playing organist and Jean McCarthy), Brent took part as one of the principal speakers. He also decried the visit in his column, complaining that Eisenhower's responsiveness to the visitor's caviling (Khrushchev sometimes grumbled about his treatment in America, and Eisenhower paid polite attention to his petty griping) made it look as if communism were now "the ascendant world force." In reality, Brent argued, Moscow had greater reason to fear war than Washington did. For philosophical materialists, the prospect of the planet's destruction posed the ultimate terror, because in their view this world was all there was. But people who believed in "a purpose outside of history" (that is, Americans, most of whom, Brent assumed, believed in an afterlife) had no such fear. The possibility of a global catastrophe, an event the Soviets would see as the end of everything, was therefore "*our* weapon."[8]

Not content to protest through *National Review*, Brent also worked on his own to advance the cause. Working from a small Washington office he rented for the purpose, he issued antivisit press releases and worked on protest plans with Capitol Hill friends. Trish became his partner in this enterprise. Assisted by volunteers from Brent's circle of young followers (his "entourage," Trish called this eager group), she sent black armbands far and wide across the country, to be worn during the Soviet leader's stay. As Khrushchev prepared to return home, the Bozells thanked their volunteer helpers by throwing a party. The gathering's formal purpose, the invitations read, was "TO CELEBRATE THE IMPENDING DEPARTURE OF THE MONSTER." The evening's centerpiece was a rented coffin, surrounded by oversized candles, in which lay a man (a local elevator operator from Eastern Europe) who bore a startling resemblance to Khrushchev. Using a homemade compound of face powder and ashes, Trish made him a convincing replica of a corpse.[9]

In one respect, Khrushchev's visit may have struck Brent as useful. In a letter to Buckley, Whittaker Chambers, a fellow *National Review* senior editor, reported hearing Brent say "something to the effect that: Now we will see what kind of conservatives we are, or who's conservative now, or something in that vein."[10] Checking reactions to the president's invitation to the tyrant made it possible to separate conservative sheep from pseudo-conservative goats.

Although he worked hard for the cause, Brent thought conservatism's prospects looked bleak. So, too, he believed, did the long-term prospects of the country. In twenty years' time, he predicted, people would be trying to explain how a country that had once enjoyed limited government and a free-market economy had come to adopt unlimited majoritarian rule and socialism; how a once sovereign nation had fallen under "One World" rule (Brent's World Federalist days now lay far behind him); how an anticommunist country had so often been bested by communists. The answer, he speculated, might simply be that "U.S. leaders ... were unintelligent, myopic, and gutless."[11]

Like an Israelite prophet, Brent foresaw national doom. America seemed to be sailing toward catastrophe, caught up in the pitiless currents of modern history, to which the softheaded Eisenhower's policies were adding momentum. Yet like a believer in predestination who nevertheless strives mightily to save his soul, Brent behaved in ways that belied his grim prognosis. For example, despite his repeated assertions that the Cold War was lost, he thought it urgent that American nuclear testing in the atmosphere continue, calling it "indispensable for perfecting existing weapons and developing new ones." When the Kennedy administration signed a treaty with the USSR banning atmospheric testing, he agreed to chair the National Committee against the Treaty of Moscow (an *NR*-inspired lobby opposing Senate ratification of the treaty). Similarly, in the late 1950s he and fellow *NR* editor Frank Meyer coauthored a piece that implied the desirability of a preemptive strike against the USSR, a long-standing pet idea of Brent's. But again, such a strike would be pointless if America were already defeated. (Buckley killed the article.)[12]

Although Brent's views usually jibed with those of his fellow editors, he sometimes broke ranks. One occasion for this was an *NR* editors' statement called "Why the South Must Prevail," which defended the white southern practice of keeping blacks from exercising their right to vote. Blacks had advanced too little culturally to be qualified to vote, the statement warned. Should they come to power in areas where they formed the majority, existing cultural standards would be threatened. Nor would it be amiss to deprive some whites of the vote, it added, for backward whites were as big a danger as backward blacks.

Brent attacked the statement. Conservatives constantly accused liberals of ignoring the Constitution whenever it forbade undertakings liberals thought socially desirable, he pointed out in *NR*'s next issue. Yet here were conservatives up to the same kind of mischief, justifying violation of the Constitution on the ground that it stood in the way of a social good. How could conservatives credibly do battle with liberals when they gave the law of the land the same short shrift? Following a double standard did no one credit.[13]

Brent also objected to *NR*'s treatment of a papal encyclical. Issued by John XXIII in 1961, *Mater et Magistra* (Mother and Teacher) delivered a social sermon couched in soft-left clichés, the kind of message that set *NR* editors' teeth on edge. The encyclical "must strike many as a venture in triviality coming at this particular time in history," the magazine sniffed. Two weeks later *NR* mentioned the encyclical again, this time flippantly. "Going the rounds in Catholic conservative circles," it reported, "Mater si, Magistra no" (a play on a pro-Castro slogan of the day, "Cuba si, Yanqui no"). Brent shared *NR*'s impatience with the encyclical and in private spoke of it scathingly. Indeed, in the same issue of *NR* that ran the "Mater si, Magistra no" quip, he published a long article called "The Strange Drift of Liberal Catholicism," which tore into the mind-set from which the encyclical had issued. But he also took offense at what he viewed as irreverence toward the papacy and felt called upon to protest. When, however, he revealed his unhappiness to Buckley, the latter only laughed. Brent remembered the episode as his first serious disagreement with his friend.[14]

Brent was immovable once he had made up his mind on an issue, especially when he saw a moral principle at stake, and never pulled his punches in debate. He could be amiable nonetheless. Whittaker Chambers found his psychology complex. "Brent is likeable on sight," he wrote to Buckley, voicing an oft-heard reaction to the lanky redhead, "and what we like is what we feel to be an instinct for honesty." Yet Chambers also gained the impression that Brent was in some way "troubled." "I have constantly to correct a surmise," he went on, "that his intransigence is, in fact, an evidence of his extreme uncertainty about various matters." What he thought those matters might be, he didn't say.[15]

Brent had long talked about seeking a career in politics. After their return from California in 1955, the Bozells bought a house (a three-story brick model on a corner lot, with six or seven bedrooms, servants' quarters, and a swimming pool they put in) just outside the

District of Columbia in the Kenwood section of Chevy Chase, Maryland, so that Brent would be able to run for a seat in Congress. Once settled, he became active in the local GOP, joining the Young Republicans and the Republican Conference, and serving as Montgomery County's Republican precinct cochairman. He also joined the county's Conservative Club and in 1957 became its president. His goal was to build himself a solid political base.

He took the plunge in 1958. Winning his district's Republican primary, he ran for the Maryland legislature's lower house with the aim of using a seat there as a stepping-stone to Congress. His platform called for a right-to-work law, a back-to-basics approach to education, and local resolution of racial conflicts in preference to settlements imposed by federal courts. This was a platform straight out of *National Review* (and in its support for local authority over federal, it also echoed his early Jeffersonian liberalism).

His campaign attracted several young volunteers from Washington (the nucleus of Brent's future "entourage"), who eagerly stuffed envelopes, manned telephones, and handed out fliers. Often these young people gathered at Brent's home to plan campaign events and discuss strategy. The home, some remembered, was a warm and welcoming place—a swirl of kids, pets, bikes, toys, shrieks, sobs, and laughter, with Trish at the piano wrestling with a Chopin piece and Brent dryly describing some Capitol Hill horror. Brent was a pleasure to work for, one recalled, a man full of high spirits and good humor.[16] The campaign received contributions from some veteran anticommunist hard-liners, among them China lobby chieftain and McCarthy ally Alfred Kohlberg and retired general Albert C. Wedemeyer, who also chaired the campaign finance committee.

Brent lost the election, but he took his defeat in stride. He had entered the race knowing his chances were "limited," he wrote to Kohlberg, and his loss wouldn't keep him from future efforts on behalf of conservatism. "For while we may not save our country," he explained, "neither can we abandon it."[17]

FIVE

Ghostwriter

Brent wasn't the only Republican to fare badly in the 1958 elections. On the national level the GOP lost thirteen seats in the Senate and forty-eight in the House. "As *an organization capable of carrying a political doctrine*—any political doctrine—*to national power*," Brent wrote in a postelection article, "the Grand Old Party is recognizably a corpse." The problem, he thought, stemmed from the party's lack of an organization able to take on that of the Democrats. But this weakness could be traced to a deeper problem: the Republican leadership had adopted "the *same* program and philosophy" as that of the Democratic leadership, leaving most GOP regulars no reason to work for victory. The party had made Eisenhower "its high priest in exchange for its soul"—and Eisenhower had led the party to ruin.

As for conservatives, the article went on, they should scuttle the notion that there was a large mass of conservative voters who would come to the polls if the GOP gave them conservative candidates to vote for. This supposed stay-at-home conservative bloc was a myth. In reality, Brent wrote, "a conservative electorate has to be created out of that vast uncommitted middle—the great majority of the American people. . . . The problem is to reach them and to organize them." Success in this task could produce a Republican renaissance—or a third party, made up of conservatives drawn from the two major parties and from independents.[1]

One Republican who won reelection in 1958 was Arizona senator Barry Goldwater. Heir to a Phoenix department store fortune, a jet pilot in the Air Force reserve, and a conservative of libertarian stamp, the trim, silver-haired Goldwater had won his Senate seat in 1952, defeating the Democratic incumbent, Senate Majority Leader Ernest McFarland, in a state where Democrats heavily outnumbered Republicans. The 1952 elections had been a Republican landslide nationally, but now Goldwater had beaten McFarland again even as many of his fellow Republicans went down to defeat.[2]

Goldwater's victory gave a boost to his party standing. When the new Senate met, he was chosen to head the GOP's Senatorial Campaign Committee. His victory also increased his standing among conservatives, as was strikingly evidenced when he addressed a 1959 meeting of the Western Republican Conference in Los Angeles. A boisterous welcome accompanied the senator to the podium. Outbursts of applause greeted his calls for individual self-reliance, balanced budgets, and a downsized government. In contrast, New York's governor, Nelson A. Rockefeller, himself a 1958 Republican winner and a pillar of the party's Eastern Establishment, fell flat with a speech calling for "moderate" positions.

Goldwater's Los Angeles triumph brought him a new outlet for his views. Impressed by his success at the conference, the *Los Angeles Times* invited him to contribute a column. He accepted the invitation, handed over the writing to his aide Stephen Shadegg, and donated his fee to various charities. Called "How Do You Stand, Sir?," the column appeared three times a week, by 1962 was running in dozens of papers, and equipped the senator with a powerful publicity machine. But one more powerful still would soon arrive.[3]

Prominent among conservatives interested in Goldwater was Clarence Manion, a onetime professor of constitutional law at Notre Dame, for many years the dean of the university's law school, and a tireless advocate of free markets, limited government, and hard-line anticommunism. Since 1954 he had hosted *The Manion Forum of Opinion*, a weekly radio program featuring political interviews and discussion.

Manion was also politically active off the air. Deeply concerned about the 1960 race for the White House, he believed that it had to include a conservative candidate. At first this led him to consider a third-party entrant, to be backed by conservatives from both sides of the aisle. Nothing would please him more, he told a friend, than a ticket headed by Senator William Jenner, an Indiana Republican hardliner, with Senator Strom Thurmond, a South Carolina Democrat (and 1948 Dixiecrat presidential candidate), as his running mate. But he soon abandoned his third-party thoughts as impractical and turned his attention to the GOP. He sought a conservative alternative to Vice President Richard M. Nixon (once popular among conservatives but now suspect for his apparent conversion to Eisenhower-style "modern" Republicanism) and Nelson Rockefeller (whom many conservatives loathed as the party's chief spokesman for New Deal–style big government).[4] The candidate Manion looked to was Barry Goldwater.

Manion's plan called for the creation of a massive draft-Goldwater movement—such a movement, he wrote, "might start a 'prairie fire'"—that could force the 1960 Republican convention to nominate the senator. But when Goldwater learned of the scheme, he showed little interest. He himself would support Nixon, he told Manion. Still, he didn't close the door completely. He had no way of blocking Manion, he added, and though he wouldn't endorse a draft movement, neither would he disown one. Finding in this statement all the encouragement he needed, Manion set out to accomplish his Goldwater strategy.[5]

The plan also called for Goldwater to write a book. In addition to publicizing the senator's conservative views, such a volume, Manion calculated, would furnish conservatives with a platform for the 1960 race and help put some distance between Goldwater and Nixon (to whom Manion worried his man had become too close).[6] Needing a title for the book, Manion came up with *The Conscience of a Conservative*. When he could find no publisher willing to bring out the book, he set up a publishing house of his own, Victor Publishing, whose sole publication would be this single work. Goldwater, while still not ready to embrace the plan, did approve the book idea and title.

At first Manion meant to distribute the book free of charge. The recipients were to be business leaders, political figures, and other influential persons who looked like potential supporters of a Goldwater candidacy. But this idea called for too few copies to justify a printing, so he increased the envisaged run to ten thousand copies and arranged to sell the book through ordinary bookstores. Publication was to take place in 1960, several months before the Republican National Convention.

Next, Manion needed someone to write the book. Neither he nor Goldwater ever imagined the senator would do it, and Shadegg would be busy with the column and other chores. In Manion's view, then, the obvious choice was Brent. Brent had proved through his *NR* work that he was able to write vigorous polemical prose, and Goldwater, impressed with Brent's speechwriting for McCarthy, had used him as a writer several times. When Manion offered the job, Brent held back, reluctant to take on a task he feared would be boring. But for a man with heavy overhead and a light wallet, Manion's proposal of a $10,000 fee proved hard to resist, and when Goldwater personally requested his help, Brent gave in.[7]

He took the job in July 1959 but then dragged his heels. The labor he faced doesn't appear terribly daunting: he had Goldwater speeches (some of which he himself had written), columns, and interviews to mine for material, and by now he was thoroughly familiar with Goldwater's thinking. But his lack of enthusiasm for the project, abetted by a tendency to procrastinate, kept him idle. It wasn't until November that he finally got to work.

According to legend, he then produced in a week or so (and in some versions of the story a mere weekend) a finished manuscript of about 120 pages, which Goldwater approved after giving it barely a glance. In reality, Brent spent six weeks or more on the draft. When he finished a chapter, he would bring it to the senator for perusal. Goldwater would read the chapter and return it, sometimes with marginal comments for Brent's guidance. Completing the manuscript in late December, Brent mailed it to Goldwater, who was spending the Senate's Christmas recess in Arizona, for final approval. Goldwater read the draft through, made a few minor changes, and sent it back with his imprimatur.[8]

The question of authorship was a sensitive one for Goldwater. For years he resisted admitting that the book had been ghostwritten. On one occasion he said that Brent had been "the guiding hand" behind the book, on another that "L. Brent Bozell and others" had helped him with the writing, and on yet another (now edging closer to the truth) that the book was based on Brent's "adoption" of material from Goldwater speeches and on Brent's "own research." But many years later he finally acknowledged the truth, telling an acquaintance that Brent hadn't just written the book but had supplied "all the ideas" as well. As for himself, he said, "Well, I read the book. I even agreed with parts of it."[9]

Brent, for his part, said little about his authorship. He didn't deny writing the book, but in Trish's telling, as the years passed and his political thinking changed, he became increasingly unhappy with his work and finally in effect disowned it.[10] His most widely read book was the one that pleased him the least.

F. Clifton White, onetime political scientist at Cornell and later the force behind a second draft-Goldwater movement, once described *The Conscience of a Conservative* as "an accurate distillation of Goldwater's past statements and speeches liberally spiked with pure 200-proof Bozell."[11] Read decades after its first appearance, the book seems to rise to the level of a canonical text. Brent had cast in definitive form the creed that held sway among conservatives in the postwar era.

The book began with a question that had long bothered Brent: "Why should the nation's underlying allegiance to Conservative principles have failed to produce corresponding deeds in Washington?" "Over-sensitivity" to criticism from the liberal-dominated mass media might be part of the answer, the book conjectured, but the puzzle remained. In fact, the puzzle was the reason for writing the book, whose aim was "to show the connection between conservative principle, so long respected, and conservative action, so generally neglected."[12]

What followed, however, showed no interest in solving the puzzle. Instead, it focused on defending conservative values, especially "freedom" (the signature word of the postwar conservative movement), and exposing the dangers that freedom allegedly faced. Thanks to the mushrooming growth of federal power, the booked warned, America was nearing totalitarian rule. To lessen the danger, the federal government must give up undertakings lying outside its constitutional mandate, such as "welfare programs, education [which a constitutional amendment should entrust exclusively to the states], public power, agriculture, public housing, urban renewal, and all the other activities that can be better performed by lower levels of government or by private institutions or by individuals." The time had come "to enforce the Constitution and restore the Republic."

Beyond specific policy changes, reducing the danger to freedom demanded a concept of governance different from the one now prevailing. A conservative statesman might convey that concept this way:

> I have little interest in streamlining government or in making it more efficient, for I mean to reduce its size. I do not undertake to promote welfare, for I propose to extend freedom. My aim is not to pass laws, but to repeal them. It is not to inaugurate new programs, but to cancel old ones that do violence to the Constitution, or that have failed in their purpose, or that impose on the people an unwarranted financial burden. I will not attempt to discover whether legislation is "needed" before I have first determined whether it is constitutionally permissible. And if I should later be attacked for neglecting my constituents' "interests," I

shall reply that I am informed that their main interest is liberty and that in that cause I am doing the very best I can.

Social values played a critical part in upholding freedom. A society that fostered individualism weakened the threat. This was a matter of culture more than of law, and it took such forms as promoting an ethic of personal responsibility, supporting a market economy over collectivism, encouraging the spirit of self-reliance, seeking racial equality through persuasion rather than force, resisting coercive action by labor unions, and rejecting "progressive" theories of education.[13]

Finally, freedom faced danger from without as well as from within, from "alien forces" as well as from homegrown liberalism. "Our national existence is threatened as it was in the early days of the Republic," the book asserted, "[and] we are in clear and imminent danger of being overwhelmed." The defense of freedom required a revolution in U.S. foreign policy. Current policy, "desperately" trying to "appease" the USSR, had to be scrapped. America must take the offensive in the Cold War, replace containment with a liberation policy, strike at the enemy through political and psychological warfare, and make victory rather than peace its overall goal. If Washington rejected this strategy, freedom would be lost.[14]

The vision the book projected was a chilling one, more characteristic of Brent than of Goldwater. America found itself standing at the edge of an abyss, the book suggested. If liberalism prevailed, freedom would surely expire. Only conservatism would enable freedom to survive.

The Conscience of a Conservative can be read in many ways: as a sermon on the creative power of individualism; as a tocsin summoning citizens to a stauncher patriotism; as a symptom of incipient paranoia; as a revivalist call for fidelity to strict constitutionalism; as a rhetorical tour de force that through apocalyptical language restored freshness to long-standing conservative complaints. But to read the book as a restatement of old-fashioned conservatism raises a problem.

For while echoing that brand of conservatism on many counts, on one important count it struck a new note. Its implicit endorsement of the bipartisan Cold War foreign policy launched little more than a decade earlier—which had led to America's assumption of global security commitments, a string of permanent military alliances, the stationing of U.S. troops around the world, and futile efforts at what would one day be known as "nation building"—marked a break with the conservative policy of Washington and Hamilton, which had lasted with few interruptions for a century and a half. On this count, *The Conscience of a Conservative* gave conservatism the gate.

Liberals predictably greeted the book with derision, scorning its antiwelfarism and Cold War militancy. "This is not conservatism, and not reaction," but "nihilism," wrote the *New Republic*'s reviewer. No state that rejected a national welfare system could survive, and in the Cold War there could be "no such thing as victory." Just as predictably, *National Review* acclaimed the book. Reviewing for *NR*, Frank Meyer lauded its firm libertarian orthodoxy and its will to seize the initiative in the Cold War.[15]

But the public response was one nobody could have predicted.

Manion published *The Conscience of a Conservative* to increase its nominal author's political visibility. But neither he nor Goldwater nor Brent foresaw a big sale. Hence the modest first printing (expected to be the only printing) of ten thousand copies and the payment to Brent of a flat fee, with no provision for royalties. To everyone's amazement, the book became a bestseller when it came out in April 1960. By June a paperback edition was in the works, with a planned first printing of 100,000 copies. By 1964 total sales stood at 3.5 million copies, making Brent's slim volume the biggest political blockbuster in American history. In the early 1960s it was almost impossible to find a place where paperbacks were sold—bookstores, bus stations, drugstores, airports—and not see *The Conscience of a Conservative* in the bookrack.[16]

Brent and Goldwater did receive royalties for paperback sales, but since they had agreed on a fifty-fifty split of a 2 percent royalty, neither came anywhere near collecting a fortune. That the book was bringing him surprisingly paltry proceeds puzzled Goldwater. "The only comment I can make on the paperback," he complained to Manion in September 1962, "is that for the seeming hundreds of thousands that have been sold, the returns have been rather meager." Four months later he raised the point again, telling Manion that he found it "a bit odd . . . that a book that was supposed to have sold [by that date] upwards of 750,000 copies should have produced so little." His own take for the second quarter of 1962, he grumbled, was only $364.57 (though a few months later he received a check for more than $10,000).

Brent, however, seemed satisfied with his royalty payments, at least in the early period of the paperback's success. In November 1960 (by which time the book had sold more than 400,000 copies), he confessed confusion to Manion about the paperback contract's royalty provisions but added that any arrangement Victor Publishing worked out for a new contract "is OK with me." (Manion undoubtedly paid what the contract called for. His correspondence with the recipients attests to his bona fides, as does a surviving file of endorsed royalty checks.)[17]

Just as Goldwater's 1958 electoral victory and smash hit performance at the Western Republican Conference raised him to Republican stardom, so the stunning success of *The Conscience of a Conservative* raised him to national stardom. He was now "Mr. Conservative," the acknowledged leader both of the GOP's conservative wing and of American conservatism as a supra-party movement.

Brent, too, experienced a rise in status. Thanks to his coauthorship of *McCarthy and His Enemies* and his work as an editor and columnist at *National Review*, he already enjoyed high standing among conservatives. But when word leaked out that he had written the Goldwater book, which was now part of the movement's holy writ, he entered conservative stardom's upper tier.

When shipments of *The Conscience of a Conservative* began arriving at bookstores, the leading contenders for the 1960 GOP presidential nomination were still Nixon and Rockefeller. Among Republicans in general, Nixon had the edge, but Rockefeller, the Eastern Establishment's choice, posed a clear threat to him. Neither enjoyed much favor among conservatives (though Nixon seemed less objectionable than his New York rival). Goldwater, for all his popularity on the Right, looked like a long shot, since he faced entrenched resistance from party moderates.

Manion, however, refused to give up his hopes. A month or so before the convention met, he formed a group called Americans for Goldwater and set up its headquarters in that year's convention city, Chicago, to keep the Goldwater option in the delegates' minds. He also decided to open the door to compromise: while keeping his sights on the ticket's top spot for the senator, he was ready to settle for the vice presidency if that seemed necessary.

Brent doubted that Goldwater could win the presidential line in 1960 and opposed a vice-presidential nomination that he feared would move the senator from the stage to the wings. But to ensure that conservatism survived *"as a recognizable political alternative"* in the GOP, Goldwater must stay in the race through the first ballot, he argued, and conservative delegates must give him "complimentary" first-ballot votes. A first-ballot presence would strengthen his hand in platform negotiations and make him a natural contender in 1964.[18]

But suddenly the basis of Goldwater's convention leverage, the Nixon-Rockefeller rivalry, collapsed. Just days before the convention was scheduled to open, Nixon and Rockefeller, meeting in New York at the latter's Fifth Avenue triplex, made a deal the media labeled the "Treaty of Fifth Avenue." Under its terms, the governor agreed to support the vice president for the nomination in exchange for a promise to make the platform more liberal on civil rights and choose a figure from the Eastern Establishment as his running mate. Now able to bank on the votes of the Rockefeller delegates, Nixon had rendered himself invulnerable to conservative pressure. Upon hearing the news, conservatives exploded in rage. Goldwater denounced the deal as "an American Munich."[19]

When the delegates convened and the nominating process began, Arizona's governor entered Goldwater's name in the running. Conservative delegates put on a rapturous floor demonstration, and South Carolina and Arizona promised their first-ballot votes. But by this time, the senator's anger at Nixon had cooled. Loyal to the Republican Party before the conservative movement, he went to the podium and took his name off the ballot, urging conservatives to cast their votes for Nixon. Manion reacted fatalistically, saying, "We led our hero to water, but we couldn't get him to drink." Brent, watching Goldwater's speech on television, felt a twinge of disgust. "The son of a bitch," he snapped as Goldwater withdrew.[20]

As he fumed over what struck him as Goldwater's betrayal of conservatism, Brent made a prediction—a remarkable one, as future events would show—about the role Goldwater might one day be seen as having played. Goldwater might or might not be president someday, he wrote, "but he could well become . . . a kind of John the Baptist against the day the U.S. returns to national sanity."[21] (Did *NR* reader Ronald Reagan ever see this column?)

Having made his deal with Rockefeller, Nixon won the 1960 nomination without a fight. But he lost the November election to John F. Kennedy, and after an eight-year absence, the Democrats returned to the White House. Brent refused to vote for either candidate. For a time he urged the creation of a conservative third party but, like Manion, soon gave up the idea. To have any hope of future victory, he contended, the GOP would have to change its ways, freeing itself from the state of "intimidation" that had seized it during the Roosevelt years and transforming itself into "an effective vehicle for the country's potentially dominant conservative tendencies"—even if the effort cost it some elections in the short run.[22]

Conservatives, Brent believed, faced a major challenge. At present, they lacked the votes to win the presidency. Their future depended on "educating, inspiring, and capturing the Republican Party organization; on rigorous concentration on the potentially conservative geographical areas [the Midwest and West, but not the industrial Northeast]; on the infinitely exciting possibilities of Goldwater salesmanship." A major target should be conservative young people, such as those who had been building beachheads on college campuses. Nixon's defeat had freed conservatives from Republican control, Brent went on, and conservatives should take advantage of this newfound freedom. From now on, they must act as a unified bloc whose ties with the Republican Party could be cut in a flash to disabuse the Republican leadership of the notion that conservatives had nowhere to go but the GOP. Lastly, conservatives must offer *"a substantive vision"* of a free society, answering the question "Once we secure our freedom, what will we do with it?"[23]

Brent soon got over his exasperation with Goldwater. He still agreed with the senator on the major questions, including the direction Republicans and conservatives should take. To win, Goldwater contended in a postelection interview with Brent, the Republicans must highlight, not minimize, their "great differences" with their opponents. Conservatives, for their part, should operate inside the GOP and work to take over the party, lock, stock, and barrel. Victory for both lay in making the party conservative.[24]

Invited to speak at the Air War College on U.S. Cold War policy, Goldwater enlisted Brent to write the speech. Brent's draft, based on the Cold War chapter ("The Soviet Menace") of *The Conscience of a Conservative* and entitled "A Foreign Policy for America," had its first airing in November 1960 and a second in *National Review* the following March. It accused the Soviets of aiming at world dominion and the United States of responding with "the attitudes and techniques of the Salvation Army." Calling the destruction of Soviet communism the precondition for a better future, it went on to lay out a program for reaching that end: overthrowing the Castro regime; taking charge of Africa for an indefinite period to thwart communist ambitions on that decolonizing continent; putting an end to disarmament talks, efforts to please "world opinion," and deference toward the United Nations; and adopting a rollback policy for Eastern Europe.[25]

Brent's draft had a third airing in 1962 when it served as the starting point for a new Goldwater book, *Why Not Victory?*, which elaborated on the senator's thinking about the Cold War. But this time it wasn't Brent who did the writing. His hands already full, he couldn't take on any further work. In 1963 Goldwater made a new request. He had drafted a book with the title *Why Not Freedom?* and wanted Brent to make the manuscript readable. Going through the draft and finding it "pretty awful," Brent answered that he wouldn't be able to perform the rescue.[26] After this refusal, his relations with Goldwater remained friendly, but his career as a ghostwriter for the senator came to an end.

SIX

Magic Kingdom

Out of the blue one day in 1960, Brent proposed to Trish that they move to Spain. He was worried about the slow progress of his book on the Warren Court, on which he had been working sporadically for three years. He could quicken the pace, he thought, if he escaped the distractions of Washington, his *National Review* work, his speaking tours, and such freelance jobs as ghosting *The Conscience of a Conservative*. He had visited Spain in 1948 after attending that year's World Federalist Congress in Luxembourg. Although he hadn't found the country especially attractive, it did afford one enormous benefit: compared with France or England, Spain was wondrously cheap. Free of the need to make a living, he would be able to center his attention on writing his book.

Spain had eager promoters among his friends. Willmoore Kendall, a longtime Hispanophile, touted the country to him, as did Trish's brother Reid, a novelist happily settled in Madrid. Strong encouragement also came from Frederick D. Wilhelmsen, a philosophy professor at the University of Santa Clara, who published an occasional article in *National Review*. All praised the virtues and pleasures of Spanish culture, and all made the point that living in Spain cost little.

Possibly religion influenced Brent's decision. Thirty years later he told an interviewer that he had gone to Spain seeking (in the interviewer's words) "an ideal, integral Catholicism."[1] Maybe so, but this purpose suggests the Brent of a later period rather than the Brent of 1960, and since he isn't on record as speaking this way before the move, he may have read the religious quest back into the past.

A second, nonreligious motive, one of which Brent himself may not have been conscious, may also have drawn him to Spain. In 1960 he had been living the same kind of life in the same place with the same job and the same routines for five years—a long time for a deeply restless spirit. Spain, whatever its other allurements may have been, promised something new.

Trish was stunned by what she called Brent's "bombshell." She knew he tended to make abrupt decisions, but this one came without the slightest warning. She remembered that he had visited Spain twelve years earlier, but until now he had never shown any interest in going back. Moreover, given the family's current circumstances—the Bozells were comfortably settled in their Kenwood home, and their children now numbered eight (John joined the fold in 1957, Aloise in 1959, and Patricia in 1960)—moving to Spain would hardly make life easier. But overwhelmed by Brent's excitement, she said she was willing.[2]

Soon after dropping his bombshell, Brent flew to Spain to have a look around. He got help in his reconnoitering from Wilhelmsen, the most rhapsodic of the country's many boosters at *NR*. Wilhelmsen had caught the Spanish bug as a teenager in Detroit when he had found himself riveted by news of the Spanish Civil War. His fervent Catholicism had drawn him to the Franco coalition and especially to its Carlist component and the latter's militia, the Requetés, who had appeared in recruiting posters put up around Detroit dressed in their uniform of red beret and khaki shirt and armed with rifles, revolvers, and rosaries.

Carlism had grown out of a Spanish dynastic conflict. The death in 1833 of King Ferdinand VII, who had left no son to follow him on the throne, had set off a civil war over the succession, in which partisans of the late king's younger brother, Don Carlos, took up arms against those of his baby daughter, Isabella. Six years of fighting brought victory to the Isabellistas, but Carlism survived as an organized political force, and in the 1870s a second war broke out. This one, too, ended in defeat for the Carlists, but again they managed to keep their cause alive. When the civil war of 1936–39 ("the Third Carlist War" in the movement's parlance) began, they returned to the field once again, allied with the generals who rose against Spain's left-wing republic. This time they finished the war on the winning side, but with their century-old dreams as far from fulfillment as ever.

From the start, Carlists fought not only for the dynastic claim of Don Carlos (and then his descendants) but also in defense of local rights against centralized rule, traditional institutions against liberal modernizing, and the Church's central role in the life of the nation. This religious allegiance echoed in the Requetés' battle cry: "Viva Cristo Rey" ("Long live Christ the King"). Wilhelmsen, a man with a connoisseur's taste in traditionalist lost causes, found the romance of the Carlist epic thrilling.

Wilhelmsen first visited Spain in 1957. He returned often, earned a doctorate at the University of Madrid, and landed an annual summer teaching job at the University of Navarre in Pamplona, a Catholic institution founded by Opus Dei. As it happened, the region of Navarre was a Carlist stronghold, and in Pamplona Carlist partisans were many. Wilhelmsen soon made friends among the rebel traditionalists, and they, in recognition of his enthusiasm for their cause, enrolled him in the Carlist legion of honor, dubbing him a Knight of the Grand Cross of the Order of the Outlawed Legitimacy.

Wilhelmsen found enchantment in Spain, not least because it had succeeded in dodging modernity. "No Northerner," he contended, "can really understand the dark richness of the Hispanic way of life, domesticating tragedy and making suffering part of the pageantry of human existence." Northerners, he thought, lived in terror of failing to be modern. "We lack the courage to let history pass us by."[3] For Wilhelmsen, then, Spain was no ordinary country; it gleamed with the luster of a magic kingdom, a land in which "the Catholic thing" still flourished and a life of medieval "fullness" could still be found.

Spain was also a source of Wilhelmsen's political ideals. Unlike most American conservatives, he didn't champion one brand of political modernism (libertarian individualism) over another (liberal collectivism); rather, he scorned all the political nostrums of modern times in favor of the rule of custom, throne, and altar.

"Fritz," as Wilhelmsen was nicknamed, would grow close with Brent in Spain. "To separate Fritz and Brent in our minds," a former student of Wilhelmsen's once remarked, "is like trying to separate Peter and Paul." Fritz steered Brent in a new direction,[4] much as Buckley had done at Yale. And like Buckley's, Fritz's influence proved to be transforming.

Arriving in Spain in January 1961, the Bozells rented a farm just outside El Escorial, a town thirty miles north of Madrid that Spain's sixteenth-century monarch Philip II had made his command center. Brooding over the town stood the massive structure Philip had helped design, a vast stone pile comprising the monastery of San Lorenzo, a large domed church, and Philip's palace. The complex was laid out in the form of a grid, the fiery bed on which St. Lawrence was said to have been martyred. Brent would come to cherish this majestic building as a symbol of the spirit of Christendom on the march.

Much of the time Brent seems to have enjoyed his life in El Escorial. He devoted long hours to writing. He took pleasure in the exotic qualities of this foreign place. (The Bozells, redheads all, must themselves have presented an exotic sight to the townsfolk.) He loved walking in the rugged Castilian countryside. He admired the dignified manner of the local people. But above all he relished the ubiquity of "the Catholic thing,"[5] which, so much more vividly present than in America, seems to have given him a sense of having come home.

Still, his life was never free of trouble. He didn't have much success in learning Spanish. By a friend's count, his vocabulary never exceeded eight words (whereas Trish, who as a child had been looked after by Mexican nursemaids, spoke Spanish well). He feared he was developing a paunch. He was rocked, as was Trish, by a sudden cigarette crisis. Both addicts, in Spain the two smoked *rubios* ("blonds") because of the mild Virginia tobacco these cigarettes contained. One day, without warning, the state tobacco store stopped selling *rubios*, offering only the harsh, black-tobacco brands most natives smoked, and leaving the Bozells with a painful adjustment to make. And despite a considerably lower cost of living, the familiar cash-flow problem cropped up—and proved to be less quickly solvable here than at home. When, as Brent put it, "the [financial] position had become quite critical," he made use of Buckley's help to sell some stock, and when the proceeds couldn't be collected as soon as he had expected, he fell back on Buckley for an interim loan.[6]

On one occasion, events took a gruesome turn. Loving the gentle, clinking sound of sheep bells, Brent bought some sheep so he could hear their bells in the morning. The sheep looked perfectly normal when they arrived, but they surprised their new owner by leaping over the wall enclosing their pasture rather than crossing on planks laid out as a temporary bridge. A bigger surprise greeted Brent when he woke the next morning and could hear no sheep bells. Going to investigate, he found the sheep scattered outside the wall, all dead. It turned out that they weren't the farm animals he had expected but wild sheep who had leaped back over the wall to regain their freedom, only to fall prey to wild dogs.[7]

Trish wrote of her life in Spain, "I spent most of my time there grumbling at inefficiencies and 'at home *this* wouldn't have happened.'" The stress built up early. Not knowing how long the family would stay in Spain or what she would find upon landing in what she called "the unknown," she brought extra shoes in larger sizes for the children and a supply of toilet paper calculated to last a year.[8] Once settled in Spain, she suffered hardships she hadn't expected. For one thing, as in Brent's student days, she did the bulk of his typing. For another, she had her hands fuller with the children than she had foreseen. The older ones, enrolled in school, "had become so Spanified," she wrote to Buckley, "that their gestures and even facial expressions are quite un-American."⁹ She had had "an awful jolt the other day," she told him in another letter, "when I realized I would have to teach two, and possibly, three children how to read and write English during the summer. And I have NO patience. . . . And I still can't spell worth a darn."¹⁰

With Europe at their doorstep, the Bozells occasionally traveled. Brent took the older children to Rome and Assisi to give them broader knowledge of the Catholic world. One winter, the whole family went to Switzerland to visit the Buckleys, who had come for their annual winter holiday at Gstaad. The Bozells, in turn, had visitors at El Escorial, among them Goldwater, who groused about the skimpy royalties Clarence Manion was paying.

Another visitor was Wilhelmsen, who also played host to the Bozells, serving as their personal guide to *Hispanidad*. In 1962 he took Brent and Trish to the annual Carlist commemoration held in the Navarrese village of Montejurra, site of a battle in the most recent civil war. The Carlist force at Montejurra had included not only Requetés but also boys and old men flying religious banners and wielding scythes and pitchforks. (This kind of thing—simple peasants with improvised weapons defending their religion and their way of life—"always got Brent and Fritz going," Trish recalled several decades later.) The spectacle the Bozells witnessed left them mesmerized. "We were utterly swept up with it all," Trish wrote to Buckley. Montejurra was "one of the most astonishing experiences of our life."¹¹

This was the Spain that became Brent's magic kingdom: not the tourist Spain of flamenco and bullfights, not the everyday Spain of shops, farms, offices, and clattering streetcars, but the half-historical, half-mythical Spain of conquistadors and mystics, crusaders and missionaries, that he saw embodied in Philip II's monastery-church-palace at El Escorial. In his imaginings Brent resembled Don Quixote, another whose Spain corresponded less to objective reality than to a cherished dream. Was it an omen that his mentor at Creighton was named Cervantes?

In Spain, Brent's political views began to change. Spain's Christian social order, he told the historian George H. Nash a decade later, had deeply impressed him. Trish confirmed the seriousness of this statement. "It was in Spain that [Brent's] hunger for a Christian society took seed," she noted. "In Spain he was swept away . . . by the concept of Christendom. Where before he was a dedicated Catholic, he [now] became a Catholic who believed that all thinking, all action, no matter where and when, should be rooted in Catholicism."[12] Although he still found grounds for his beliefs in secular values, increasingly he tended to base them on Catholic doctrine. The mixture revealed where he had come from and where he was going, looking back to the man who had written *The Conscience of a Conservative* and forward to the one who would found the magazine *Triumph*.

Brent first used religion-based arguments in August 1961 in a rejoinder to an article called "How We Look to Others" published in the Jesuit magazine *America*. Written by a priest named George H. Dunne, this piece echoed the familiar liberal plaint that people the world over hated the United States because American businessmen exploited the poor and were indifferent to their suffering. By contrast, revolutionaries such as Castro and Mao won support from the poor because, however objectionable they might be in some regards, they projected a credible rage against oppression. Unless America started fighting injustice abroad, the article warned, the world would end up living under communism.[13]

Reading the article as justifying—and even calling for—Marxist revolution, Brent slammed what he called "the anti-American amoral materialism" of the offending piece. His riposte, entitled "The Strange Drift of Liberal Catholicism," was the first of many broadsides against liberal Catholics. What stands out about the article is the often theological grounding of his criticism. He wrote:

> Here, indeed, is the idealism of the utopianists, of Karl Marx—the notion that human manipulation of man's material circumstances can eliminate misery and social tension. . . . A whole *Weltanschauung* is implied here—one that denies the mysterious ravages of original sin, the relevance of divine redemption, the subordination of matter to spirit. And at some point it must . . . call into question the existence of a good God . . . [a] God who taught, in cautioning against distraction from the affairs of the spirit, that "the poor you will always have with you."

Since Father Dunne had dealt with his subject in the context of the Cold War, Brent did likewise. At bottom, he argued, the root of that struggle could be traced to a spiritual conflict. The Church's task in the battle against materialism was not to end poverty but to lead the Christian West in a "crusade" against the communist enemy, to rouse ordinary people "to *want* to fight for their civilization the way a man fights for his life." The Christian West was asserting "a God-given right," which it saw as a "God-imposed duty, to conserve and spread *its* truth, to judge political and economic and social systems according to *its* lights, to change and improve them under *its* authority." The communists' hatred for the West's "divine commission" drove them to wage their war against the West.[14]

Brent next used this theological mode of argument in March 1962 at a rally for World Liberation from Communism, held by a conservative youth organization, Young Americans for Freedom (YAF), at New York's Madison Square Garden. Invited to give the keynote speech (a sign of his current eminence among conservatives), he flew to New York to join fellow speakers Barry Goldwater (whose speech he helped write) and Senator John Tower of Texas in addressing an eager crowd of eighteen thousand.

Brent's speech, "To Magnify the West,"[15] suggested through its sudden shifts in tone and topic the divergent grounds on which his thinking now rested. The speech began conventionally enough, hailing the growing number of conservatism's successes and protesting liberal charges of "extremism." But then, almost abruptly, it put forward an idea of the political philosopher Eric Voegelin as a way of exposing the inner nature of liberalism. In his book *The New Science of Politics*, Voegelin described modern revolutionary ideologies as secular versions of what he called "gnosticism" (though the creed he so labeled sounds more like millenarianism than like the radical dualist, gnosis-bearing sects of late antiquity the word usually denotes). The gnostics, Voegelin wrote, sought to "immanentize the eschaton"—that is, transfer heaven to earth. At its core, Brent now argued, liberalism was nothing but secularized gnosticism trying to establish a paradise in this world—a fruitless enterprise that always led to ruin.

Then came a new change of topic, a shift from analysis to exhortation. Drawing the audience's attention to "the Christian West" as a civilization founded on Revelation and the Incarnation of Christ, Brent contended that the outcome of the West's worldwide struggle with communism would decide the fate of mankind. The West, he declared, must therefore "magnify" itself, carrying its saving truth across the planet both to vanquish communism and to build a global Christendom. (Was this vision a christened version of Brent's bygone World Federalist dream, or maybe even an unwitting form of gnosticism, to which the Manichean notion of a final, decisive struggle between good and evil had been joined?) This was the mission that God had assigned the West.

Lastly, jumping from matters of vast historical sweep to short-term policy recommendations, he rapped out a list of orders that Washington would issue once it grasped its Cold War responsibilities. This concluding segment made no mention of gnostics or the global tasks of Christendom but resurrected Brent's voice as heard in his *NR* column. The list began with an order to the Joint Chiefs of Staff to ready an "immediate landing in Havana." It went on to instruct the U.S. commander in Berlin to "tear down the Wall." (These words may have inspired those Ronald Reagan uttered in Berlin in 1987. Reagan had written to Brent in 1962 in praise of his Madison Square Garden speech.) Among other orders Brent called for were a command to the chairman of the Atomic Energy Commission to test "every nuclear weapon that could conceivably be of some service to the military purposes of the West" and one to the CIA to back liberation movements in all communist-dominated countries, "including the Soviet Union itself." "And you may let it be known," this last order added, "that when, in the future, men offer their lives for the ideals of the West, the West will not stand idly by."

And then, without formal conclusion, Brent stopped and stood still in the spotlight, looking out at the crowd now roaring with delight.

The speech evoked varying responses. Carol Dawson, who had worked on Brent's campaign for the Maryland legislature, called the whole event "a magic moment" and his performance "stunning." Another happy fan thanked him for the segment attacking "agnosticism," which she agreed posed a truly serious problem. Some, however, thought that segment too complicated. Lines such as "The Christian eschaton is post-human" probably caused more confusion than excitement. For a few, attention gave way to irritation over the speech's length. Fuming as he waited backstage to give his own speech, Goldwater threatened to leave if Brent kept talking.

But the orders that ended the speech brought the house down. This was what the crowd had come to hear. *National Review*'s publisher, William A. Rusher, called the conclusion "electrifying." The historian Lee Edwards, a YAF founder, and his future wife, Anne, agreed that if Brent had called on the audience to "march," all eighteen thousand would have risen as one and marched. "He could have led us anywhere," said Edwards. Its problematical middle section notwithstanding, the speech brought Brent his most dazzling public moment.[16]

The fullest expression of Brent's new political outlook came in his September 1962 *NR* article "Freedom or Virtue?," a piece that revealed a mutation in his theory of government. This essay pitted him against his *NR* colleague Frank Meyer, whom, despite occasional chilly spells between them, he counted as one of his closest friends. Both telephone addicts, he and Meyer had for years conferred, joked, and wrangled on the phone almost daily, sometimes for hours at a stretch. Kendall defined "an emergency call" from Meyer to Brent as "one that interrupts the regular call" from Meyer to Brent.[17] It was Brent who coined the term "fusionism" for Meyer's attempt to combine the Right's chief philosophical branches, libertarianism and traditionalism.

Brent wrote his article in response to one by Meyer, "The Twisted Tree of Liberty," that criticized traditionalists for citing the advancement of "virtue" as government's highest purpose. Though agreeing with traditionalists that virtue was man's supreme duty, Meyer reasoned that since virtuous action required freedom of choice, freedom was the necessary "precondition" of the virtuous society, and upholding freedom was government's primary end.[18]

Before going to Spain, Brent probably would have agreed. (*The Conscience of a Conservative* preached a stoutly libertarian gospel.) But living in Spain had given him a different outlook. He had begun to ponder the purpose of government at length, often while walking in the open country outside El Escorial, where he frequently encountered reminders of "the Catholic thing"—a wayside shrine, the sound of church bells, a crucifix at a crossroad. The result of his ruminations was "Freedom or Virtue?," one of the longest articles ever published in *National Review*. Decades later he claimed to have written the essay with American politics in mind, wanting to suggest "Christian modifications of the freedom ideology" in hopes of influencing conservatives as they geared up for a Goldwater run in 1964.[19] But however true this was, a broader, philosophical purpose clearly took precedence.

Rejecting Meyer's brief on behalf of freedom, Brent argued solely on religious grounds that government should make virtue its leading concern. This was because men's principal end was salvation, an end they needed virtue to attain. But virtue wasn't something easily come by. Weakened in mind and will by original sin, men would often stray if left on their own. God gave powerful help in the form of grace, but further help could come from a supportive community (or "commonwealth," as Brent put it), one of whose major elements was government. Government could make it easier for people to live virtuously—in accord with God's "pattern of order"—by rejecting laws that encouraged disregard of the pattern. For example, Spain didn't have a divorce law. This made it easier for Spaniards to follow God's will. True, a Spaniard wanting a divorce could get one abroad, but the inconveniences that this step entailed would give many people pause. So, thanks to the government, those people would end up staying married and thus living virtuously. Government would have helped these people save their souls.

Brent's concern with the "commonwealth" as well as with individuals further distinguished his views from those of Meyer. Reflecting his libertarian perspective, Meyer tended to see people as autonomous units, social atoms. Brent, now a traditionalist, tended to see them in Aristotelian fashion as communal by nature (here again, Kendall's influence may have been present), bound together by communal life, and shaped in thought and deed by communal mores. Hence, in Brent's eyes, communities had great importance as agents of virtue, restraining their members' ability to ignore God's will and fostering through their culture and organs of authority (among them, government) the virtuous life that opened heaven's gates.

Brent didn't stop there. He turned a critical eye on freedom. Political and economic freedom, he insisted, were good not in themselves but only insofar as they furthered the practice of virtue. The demand for freedom for its own sake expressed at its core the wish to be freed of God. The pursuit of this wish was modern history's leitmotif and the source of a centuries-long process of Western decay. If the process continued, it would end in the victory of communism. In short, "the story of how the free society has come to take priority over the good society is the story of the decline of the West." Libertarianism, no matter how noble its formal principles might sound, was the source of the rot.

Yet even a long decline could be reversed. A "Christian commonwealth" would achieve this reversal by fostering virtue, thereby reconnecting the West with God's pattern of order. Such a commonwealth would also resume the mission of expanding "Christendom," or "magnifying the West," with the goal of building a worldwide Christian civilization. This would fulfill Christ's final instruction to his apostles: "teach all nations, baptizing them in the name of the Father, and of the Son, and of the Holy Ghost."[20]

Meyer replied in *NR*'s next issue, maintaining that the virtuous acts of people not free to reject virtue weren't truly virtuous. Despite Brent's good intentions, he warned, the ideas Brent held would lead straight to tyranny and theocracy.[21] Brent, having said his piece, made no reply, and the debate ended. But it stands out as one of the pivotal events in his life: "Freedom or Virtue?" announced his break with his libertarian past (though shreds of that past would linger) and his departure toward a very different future, in which religious and theocratic ideas would mold his thinking.

For a time, the Bozells weren't sure when, or even whether, they would go back to America. In December 1962 the family welcomed its ninth child, William, and soon thereafter they made up their minds to return. February 1963, when the lease on their farm would expire, seemed the best time for Trish and the younger children to go. The older children and their father would rejoin the others in America once the school year ended.

Decades later, talking with an interviewer, Brent and Trish attributed their return home to a sense of duty (as they would one day attribute their going to Spain to Brent's search for "an ideal, integral Catholicism"). They had considered it their moral obligation, they said, to work for the cause of Christendom in America.[22] But in fact, just as religion played little, if any, part in their move to Spain, neither did it prompt their decision to move back home. (It would be two years before religion resurfaced as Brent's driving concern.) The return to America seems to have sprung from other causes.

Before Spain, both Brent and Trish had been conventional "social" drinkers. Although Trish had sometimes caused Brent to worry that she drank too much, neither seemed to be drifting into alcoholism. In Spain, however, both began to go overboard. Trish, perhaps under heavier stress than Brent, suffered graver consequences than he did. On New Year's Eve 1962, Brent wrote in distress to Buckley, painting a somber picture of Trish's (and his own) condition. "The most urgent factor" in the situation, he said, was "the purely practical factor of [alcohol] control . . . in the twofold sense of controlling the amount of Tish's consumption, and of taking care of Tish after she passed the barrier." The implications of the problem, he went on, were "pretty far reaching"—though they might not be, he acknowledged, "with someone more stable emotionally than I am at the moment." He concluded that the issue was "helping to wreck me here, and certainly would in the U.S." (Why he would be worse off at home he didn't explain.)

He planned to keep track of Trish's drinking, and limit it, "but not to the extent of keeping myself in the house every night to do it; and if she begins taking too much, in the doctor's opinion, for the good of her physical health, she will have to go to an institution." When he wasn't at home, he would have a nurse on hand, nominally to look after the children but in reality to see that Trish got to bed safely. The doctor thought they needed "a change of ambience" and advised them to go back to America.

It was true, Brent added, that much of his hesitation about leaving Spain could be traced to his own "falling apart" because of "the Tish business," but he also referred to (but didn't identify) problems "of my own making." In America, he feared, his condition would only grow worse "unless I could find an expedient for separating myself from the Tish trouble."[23]

Brent's life in the magic kingdom was falling to pieces. His worry about Trish, his resentment over the problems she was causing him, and his guilt over his own failing were blending to form a poisonous psychological brew. Whatever the perils that awaited him in America, it was time to go home.

In February 1963 Trish flew from Madrid to New York with the younger children. One of the older children, eleven-year-old Kathy, went with them to lend a hand, as did Mercedes, a servant in the Bozells' El Escorial household. Since tenants were renting the Kenwood house until June, the group spent the next few months with Trish's mother in Sharon, putting up in an old barn on the Buckley property that had been converted into living quarters for guests.

Brent, meanwhile, stayed on in El Escorial, moving with the remaining children to an apartment in town. When the school year ended, they, too, flew to New York, but first they visited Paris and Berlin. In Berlin, Brent took the children across the wall into the city's eastern sector to give them a glimpse of life's bleakness under communism. As they moved through run-down, war-scarred East Berlin, he told them of the vices and failings of the communist system, undeterred by the constant presence of an East German guide. At the end of the tour, in a nod to his libertarian past, he addressed some words to the guide on the virtues of freedom.[24]

As he flew toward New York, Brent was entering a new stage in his life. Although he may not have realized it at the time, the curtain was coming down on the present stage—the "Buckley stage," it might be called: the time of his close friendship with Buckley, his conversion to conservatism, his *National Review* articles and columns, his writing for Goldwater. Only two important features of his past political outlook remained (both of which predated his friendship with Buckley): his affection for the Tenth Amendment and his hard-line anticommunism. The next stage—the "*Triumph* stage," it might be called after the magazine he would found in 1966—had only begun to take shape, though its philosophical foundation, thanks to "Freedom or Virtue?," was clear. For the present, he was working his way through a time of transition. Accordingly, it was also a time of ambiguity, in which remnants of the Buckley stage and portents of the *Triumph* stage somewhat awkwardly coexisted.

SEVEN

Pulling Up Stakes

Brent's fear that disaster awaited him at home proved unfounded. For a time Trish's drinking problem persisted, sometimes leading him to judge her condition hopeless. But by 1964 she had begun to show signs of recovery, even if an event such as her sister Maureen's sudden death could briefly shake her "control."[1] In some respects she left her life before Spain behind. A serious pianist since childhood, she now decided to give up the instrument. She possessed "a certain technical ability," she confided to Buckley, but no talent for interpretation. In place of the piano she took up painting, driving to Baltimore several days a week for lessons. She had long since given up riding. "I couldn't ride," she once explained to a visitor. "I was always pregnant." In 1966 she gave birth to her tenth and last child, James, but she never got back on a horse.[2]

Reversing feelings she had expressed in El Escorial—exasperation with backward Spain, approval of efficient America—she now compared America unfavorably with Spain. Driving to Baltimore, she wrote to Buckley, "I marvel at the degree of ugliness in the American scene." The approach to Baltimore offered an array of "car dumps, smoke stacks, rubbish, smog, unending brick, identical square houses surrounded by no lawns but mountains of litter." In such an environment, she wondered, "How can a human [aspire?] to anything greater than just getting along?" Spain, in contrast, had "no machines—so no drabness; no television—so they have their feast days which they make fine by their spirit and laughter. No social security—so they take care of their own."³

Trish lengthened her list of American shortcomings after several Bozell children returned to Spain for schooling. Home on vacation from her school in Ávila, Kathy told Trish of the school's course in politics. It stressed "the hierarchical order of the family," Trish noted approvingly, "the woman's place therein, and [made] the comparison between the family unit and the political unit. That is, the rich, or upper class, owe a duty toward the lesser orders, as do units of government, but all within the context of freedom and the limitations on it imposed by a transcendent law." Kathy's report, she concluded, was "a crushing commentary . . . on the utter junk our children are being forced to swallow here at home."⁴

Brent, for his part, settled back into his old life—or so it appeared. He reentered the inner circle at *National Review*. He made another attempt at winning public office, this time setting his sights on a seat in Congress. He labored away at his study of the Warren Court, a work expressing his views of the 1950s. He gave active support to familiar conservative causes, including a hard-line anti-Soviet policy, the resumption of nuclear testing in the atmosphere, states' rights, and the election of Goldwater to the presidency. But this seeming continuity with his pre-Spain life was deceptive, for religious concerns held an ever greater place in his thinking.

Back in America, Brent resumed his debating and lecturing, mostly before conservative groups and college audiences. He would do so, he told Buckley toward the end of his stay in Spain, partly for the money (for example, after deducting $400 for airfare, he calculated, he would net $950 for a six-lecture tour out West), "and, well, because I ought to."⁵ In an *NR* ad, he declared his willingness to debate all comers on any topic within his sphere of competence.⁶ A sortie of

January 1964 took him to California to debate Robert Maynard Hutchins—president, first, of the University of Chicago, then of the Ford Foundation, and now of the liberal Center for the Study of Democratic Institutions. Their topic was the constitutionality of *Brown v. Board of Education*, the Supreme Court's 1954 decision banning racial segregation in public schools. Hutchins defended the decision as constitutionally valid. Brent disagreed. Despite the claims put forward by judicial supremacists, he replied, Supreme Court decisions shouldn't be treated as "something like Stalin's," entitled to universal and unquestioning obedience. The justices could only interpret, not command. Although the debate's transcript shows Brent skillfully making his case, he came home dissatisfied. His performance, he told Trish, had been no better than "fair."[7]

Among his lecture topics, Brent listed such secular-sounding subjects as "The Warren Court," "Liberation or Surrender," and "A Conservative Looks at His Party," all staples of his column in the 1950s. But he also included "To Magnify the West," in which he characterized the West not in his libertarian way as the bastion of freedom but in his religious way as the bastion of Christendom (or at least what was left of Christendom). Another topic, "The West's Real Role in the Cold War," may also have focused on the Christendom theme (the words "Real Role" perhaps signifying a Western duty to spread the "Christian Commonwealth").

For a while it looked as if Brent might again work for Barry Goldwater. Like many conservatives, he shuddered at the thought of Nelson Rockefeller as the 1964 Republican presidential nominee and hoped the nod would go to the Arizona senator. In 1961 Republican political consultant F. Clifton White had joined with Ohio Republican congressman John Ashbrook and *NR* publisher William A. Rusher to launch a campaign to put Goldwater at the head of the ticket.

Goldwater, however, disclaimed any interest in running. To his aide Stephen Shadegg he insisted in 1961 that he didn't want the nomination and wouldn't even discuss the possibility of seeking it.[8]

Yet to Brent, Goldwater showed signs of a different attitude. Shortly before the Bozells set off for Spain, he told Brent "confidentially" that he planned to "avoid making any kind of Presidential noises" at least until after the 1962 elections, at which time he would see how the ground looked. To say anything before then, he explained, would cost him the chair of the GOP's Senatorial Campaign Committee and much of his influence with the Republican National Committee.[9]

In the two years that followed, Goldwater consistently wavered. After the 1962 elections, he told Shadegg that he didn't know whether to seek the presidential nomination or run for reelection to the Senate. In January 1963 he told F. Clifton White that he didn't intend to go after the nomination. In September, Shadegg told Brent that he doubted whether Goldwater had made up his mind.[10] Still, at that point Goldwater seemed to be leaning toward running. He had assembled a team of Arizona friends that looked like the core of a national campaign apparatus. In fact, this group would soon turn into a Goldwater for President committee, at which point the White-Ashbrook-Rusher group dissolved.

Many conservatives were eager to aid the new committee, among them Brent. Though no longer drawn to Goldwater the libertarian, Brent still supported Goldwater the hard-line anticommunist. John F. Kennedy struck Brent as weak, no better a Cold War president than was Eisenhower. The country needed a leader who would take off the gloves, he thought, and of all the candidates in sight, Goldwater seemed the one most likely to do so. Moreover, Kennedy looked beatable. As president, he hadn't accomplished much, and he bore the stigmas of the Bay of Pigs and the Berlin Wall. But the road to the White House wouldn't be smooth, Brent warned Shadegg. On the way, there would be "an awful lot of pits not to fall into."[11]

Thinking about how they could best aid the Goldwater effort, Brent and Buckley came up with a plan for a campaign brain trust, a group of conservative intellectuals and academics who would furnish the senator with an arsenal of policy ideas. In September 1963 they outlined the plan to a Goldwater confidant, Jay Hall, who invited them to his suite at Washington's Hay-Adams Hotel to discuss it further. When the two arrived at the hotel, they were surprised to find not only Hall but also William J. Baroody, founder of the conservative think tank the American Enterprise Institute (AEI), and Denison Kitchel, a Goldwater friend and adviser who now headed the Goldwater for President committee.[12] As the visitors described their idea, Baroody and Kitchel listened impassively. The meeting broke up with vague talk of considering the plan, but Brent felt that he and Buckley were getting the brush-off. A few days later the *New York Times* reported, "The Goldwater-for-President ship has just repelled a boarding party" from the extreme Right. Buckley and Bozell, the paper alleged, had "cornered" some Goldwater campaign workers and tried to break into the campaign "on the policy planning level" but had been chased off.[13]

Miffed, Brent asked Goldwater who had planted the *Times* story. "Well, you don't think I did it, do you?" the senator answered. Brent then called Shadegg, who also disclaimed all knowledge, saying, "I'd hate to venture an opinion." White suspected Kitchel, speculating that the latter feared Brent and Buckley's presence in the campaign would give Goldwater an "extremist" image. Shadegg later decided the evidence pointed to Baroody, head of an organization devoted to public policy research. Goldwater biographer Lee Edwards shared Shadegg's belief. Fear of an extremist image, he wrote, was probably a tale meant to hide Baroody's tracks. The AEI chief had wanted to shield his own brain trusters from competition. Goldwater himself eventually accepted this explanation. In his 1988 autobiography, *Goldwater*, he wrote that Baroody, unhappy at the thought of sharing power, had concocted the *Times* account. Goldwater said that he "would have welcomed [Brent and Buckley] into the campaign with open arms" and that when he learned how they had been treated, he was "heartsick." "But what could I say? What could I do?" he asked. "It was too late."[14]

After President Kennedy was assassinated in November, Goldwater reconsidered running, doubtful whether any Republican could win. But his retreat was brief. Feeling that he couldn't let his partisans down, he announced his candidacy in January 1964.[15]

Brent supported Goldwater's run for the White House even as he stood aloof from the campaign after the Hay-Adams rebuff. At first he believed the senator had a real chance of winning. "Who would have thought during JFK's first year that Barry Goldwater would be within an ace of the Presidency in 1964?" he wrote to Buckley in May of that year. "Things *are* going our way; and at a far faster pace than we had reason to hope." As time passed, his optimism faded. But if he came eventually to expect Democrat Lyndon B. Johnson to win, he didn't foresee the Johnson avalanche the election produced. He was "devastated" by its crushing size, Trish recalled. Furious that some moderate Republicans had given Goldwater purely nominal support and that others had gone over to Johnson, he urged conservatives to give up on the GOP and get to work forming a party of their own. But when few conservatives embraced the idea, he dropped it.[16]

Brent would never again do any work for Barry Goldwater. A key connection with his pre-Spain past had ended.

Brent had another reason for remaining apart from the Goldwater campaign: he had his own race to run. By early 1964 he had decided to run for a seat in the U.S. House of Representatives. He would try to wrest the GOP nomination for Maryland's sixth congressional district from the incumbent, Charles Mathias, an Eastern Establishment Republican, the living image of a type that Brent detested. Since Mathias was a good fit for the moderate-to-liberal sixth district and well funded to boot, a challenger would face a steep uphill struggle. But friends believed that Brent could win by sheer force of personality, and he himself was eager to run, seeing the race as a stepping-stone toward grander things: the Senate when Maryland's next senatorial contest came along and then, maybe, the White House.

Another motive seems to have been present as well, one not in evidence in his earlier run for office. His chief aim, he told Kathy, was to act more effectively for "the Catholic cause." If he made it to Congress, the family would stay in Kenwood, and he would focus his political career on aiding the Church. If he lost, the Bozells would move, and he would find a different way to serve the cause.[17]

In February, two days before publicly announcing his candidacy, Brent revealed his plans to Buckley. He didn't seem to have thought much about organizing his campaign, hadn't as yet even picked someone to manage it. So a few days later, Buckley proposed a recent Yale graduate named Neal Freeman. He had met Freeman at Doubleday, where the latter was working as an editor, and soon after invited him to dinner. When dinner was over, the story goes, Buckley had had to give Freeman a job at *NR*, since that seemed the only way to get the young man to go home. He had assigned Freeman to a variety of tasks and found him versatile and energetic, someone with the spirit to manage Brent's campaign (though Freeman had no experience in that line of work). Brent, too, took to Freeman upon meeting him and hired him as both campaign manager and press secretary. Despite Freeman's youth and inexperience, the decision proved a good one. Trish later described his campaign work as "invaluable."[18]

Each morning at the campaign's Bethesda headquarters, Brent and Freeman plotted strategy. Also attending these sessions at least some of the time were the campaign's three "advisers": Kendall for domestic affairs, Wilhelmsen for foreign affairs, and CIA veteran and future Watergate villain E. Howard Hunt, who seems to have lacked a clear-cut sphere of activity. Kendall, mastering his tendency toward crankiness and taking a serious view of his responsibilities, furnished Brent with a wealth of practical advice. Wilhelmsen, with no expertise in foreign relations, didn't have much to offer in his formal role. But his willingness to take on chores others avoided and his Old Regime talent for sociability made him a welcome presence in the campaign.

Hunt, often absent or lurking silently in the background, tended to go unnoticed.[19] Also on board was a longtime friend of Brent's, General Albert C. Wedemeyer, who had raised money for the candidate's 1958 campaign and now did so again. Partly through Wedemeyer's labors, Brent collected $20,000 from 250 donors (including several Buckleys) for a campaign that ended up costing $36,000.[20]

Alongside Brent's old comrades-in-arms appeared a new one. A New Yorker studying law at Catholic University and a fan of *National Review*, Michael Lawrence saw a report in the *Washington Post* that Brent had entered the Maryland sixth district's GOP primary. Volunteering for the campaign, Lawrence spent most of his time serving as Brent's driver, which afforded him frequent opportunities to chat with the candidate. Soon a friendship developed between the two that contained an element of the mentor-pupil bond. As Lawrence drove Brent between campaign events, he learned from his passenger to question such commonplace notions as "the Middle Ages was a time of darkness followed by the light of the Renaissance"; "there is, ever was, or ought to be 'a wall of separation' between Church and state"; and "Scotch whiskey is superior to bourbon."[21] The friendship proved to be lasting. Lawrence would work with Brent for years to come.

Brent ran against Mathias as the "real" Republican in the race. He was "A Republican Who Will Vote Republican" in Congress, read one of his campaign handouts, whereas Mathias turned into a liberal Democrat whenever he crossed the state line into Washington. Mathias, Brent charged, backed appeasement of the USSR, expansion of the welfare state, compulsory racial integration, and the Warren Court's efforts to "usurp" the power to legislate. Brent stood for "true Republicanism": victory over communism (a cause that should be furthered by demonstrations of American will, such as freeing Cuba from communism), integration through the conversion of "minds and hearts" rather than through federal bayonets, and the breaking of the government's "stranglehold" on the economy. (Despite his college courses in economics, Brent seems to have known little about the subject. His stump speech warned of a depression if people like Mathias won the coming elections. When a reporter asked him whether he didn't mean a recession, he is rumored to have answered, "Recession, depression—what's the difference?") He also made school prayer one of his central issues, vowing to fight to restore it if he were sent to Congress.[22]

By and large, Brent's positions echoed those of his 1958 campaign and rarely expressed his more recent, traditionalist views. Although he sometimes alerted his audiences to the peril of gnosticism, on the whole he ran a conventional conservative race. Also conventional was the Mathias campaign's response. Taking a leaf from the GOP moderates' playbook, Mathias charged Brent with being a "radical rightist," a man with "extremist" ideas. Meanwhile, a third contender attacked from the opposite flank. Harry Simms, an eccentric who enjoyed running in Republican primaries, denounced Brent as a "comsymp" (short for "communist sympathizer"), a word coined by John Birch Society founder Robert Welch. Brent should come clean about his ties with *National Review*, said Simms, since the magazine was packed with people who had communist backgrounds (as indeed it was: Meyer, Burnham, and Kendall, to name just a few).[23]

Brent loved campaigning and did it with endless zest. He loved ranging over the district, giving speeches, trading banter, shaking hands. His excitement before giving a speech could grow so great that he would have a drink or two to calm down. His high spirits, Mike Lawrence recalled, made him fun to be with. People were taken with his approachability, his friendly manner, his shiny, tooth-filled grin, his fiery red hair. The hair became his leading campaign trademark. "Bozell for Congress" bumper stickers were colored a fluorescent orange and showed a mop of bright red hair above a large right ear. A flyer announced that Brent and Trish had nine children, ages one to thirteen and "all redheads." A campaign photo showed all eleven redheads formally posed in the Bozells' living room—a perfect portrait of a perfect American family.

Brent campaigned all over the sixth district, from rich, suburban Montgomery County to the Maryland panhandle's Allegany County, hardscrabble country much like neighboring West Virginia.

Here, too, he did well, assuming a credible homespun persona for the small-town folk, whose attention he could hold even when lecturing on gnosticism. On one occasion, he let his audience determine his message. The campaign had a sound truck that cruised around the district broadcasting a campaign theme chosen for the day. On this day the theme was better race relations, and the sound truck blared, "Achieve racial harmony without violence." Suddenly realizing he was driving through a black neighborhood, Brent switched without missing a beat to "Freedom now!" Looking back from the vantage point of more than four decades in politics, Freeman pronounced Brent the greatest natural campaigner he had ever seen, better even than the superlative Ronald Reagan. "When Brent was in good form," said Freeman, "he was the best."[24]

But if Brent couldn't be bested on the hustings, he could be bested at the polls. People liked to see him, hear him, and meet him, but when it came to vote getting, Mathias had the edge. With the advantages of incumbency, much more money, and a better ideological stance for the sixth district, he couldn't be toppled by force of personality alone. All the same, Brent polled respectably against this powerful opponent, winning close to eleven thousand votes, or roughly a third of the total. "And this, surely, is not a bad beginning," he told Freeman, a comment implying an interest in running again. To Buckley he voiced this interest explicitly. "The personal conclusion I draw from the campaign is that I shall stay in politics," he wrote, still humming with the excitement of the experience. "I know of no better way to serve our cause [that is, conservatism, not the Catholic cause]." But Freeman saw a less positive response to defeat. "He took it personally," Freeman remembered. "He took it as personal rejection."[25]

Despite his letter to Buckley, Brent never again ran for elective office. Political ambition, a defining trait of the Buckley stage of his life, had begun to yield to a different aim. In the past he had seen his first duty as defending the nation; now he had begun to see it as defending the faith.

The 1964 Goldwater debacle left many conservatives in shock. To ensure the Right's survival, they agreed, rebuilding the movement should begin without delay. Ever since Eisenhower's victory over Taft for the 1952 GOP nomination, conservatives had talked of forming an organization that would draft conservative policy proposals, publicize conservative positions, and spearhead conservative lobbying both inside and outside the party. After Kennedy's victory in 1960, Meyer had urged the creation of such a group, which he wanted to model on Americans for Democratic Action, a source of policy ideas for liberal Democrats.[26]

Revived by the 1964 disaster, this idea now became a reality. In December 1964 the *St. Louis Post-Dispatch* reported (in language suggesting the unmasking of a right-wing plot), "About 100 top ultra-conservatives met secretly in Washington today to form a new political organization." The meeting gave birth to the American Conservative Union (ACU), which, according to an inaugural statement, was committed to "a mobilization of the moral, political and intellectual resources of the American conservative movement."[27] Among those present at the Washington meeting (which was held in broad daylight at the Capital Hilton Hotel) were several people prominently linked with *National Review*, among them Meyer, who was one of the gathering's principal animators; Buckley, who delivered the after-lunch speech; and Brent, who chaired a panel on "Foreign and Military Policy" and was appointed to the ACU's board of directors.

But all too soon the ACU ran into trouble. Part of the problem, many thought, lay with the board's chairman, Donald C. Bruce, a three-term GOP congressman from Indiana who had once hosted a radio talk show in Indianapolis. Bruce had been chosen not by a founders' vote but by a small group of insiders—chiefly, Congressman John Ashbrook of the 1961 Goldwater for President committee, indefatigable conservative publicist Marvin Liebman, and YAF founder and congressional aide Robert Bauman—who were looking for a figurehead chief. Bruce had the qualifications this trio desired: a solidly conservative congressional voting record, a knack for public speaking, and a willingness to fill a post no one else wanted. Soon, however, the three realized they had made a mistake. Bruce wanted to rule as well as reign. To make things worse, he lacked the ability to compromise, growing rigid and truculent when others questioned his preferences. Nor did he get along well with the *NR* people, who constituted a weighty presence on the board. Meyer, Bauman recalled, came to write Bruce off as "a dolt." The quarreling eventually reached such a level of rancor that the very people who had picked Bruce for the chairmanship now asked him to resign. Bruce, no happier with the situation than they were, did so, and in September 1965 Ashbrook took his place.[28]

Critics also regarded the organization as structurally lopsided, claiming that its headquarters and staff had, in Liebman's words, "started off too big." At the outset, said Liebman, it would have been better to keep costs down and concentrate on publishing and fundraising rather than accumulating personnel.[29]

During the ACU's first year, Brent was an active member of the board. He attended many of its monthly meetings and spoke out in favor of aggressive antiliberal projects. At the July 1965 meeting, for example, he proposed commissioning "a major study of the life and political record of John V. Lindsay," a liberal Republican congressman from Manhattan and favorite conservative bête noire, who was running for mayor of New York City against a Tammany Hall Democrat and the Conservative Party's candidate, Buckley.[30]

Like Meyer, Liebman, and others, Brent lamented the way the ACU was evolving. Bruce's resignation hadn't saved the day. To salvage the ACU, further change seemed necessary. The key step, Brent and his fellow critics believed, would be to create a new, action-oriented executive position, to be filled by David R. Jones, an ACU founding member, YAF's executive director, and in Bauman's words "every organization's dream." Endowed with strategic imagination, managerial skill, and limitless energy, Jones called for an ACU-YAF alliance, which would aim at gaining control of the Republican Party (in Jones's words, "the primary target") and then launch "Operation '72," the recruitment of "a veritable army of campaign workers" determined to win the 1972 election. Jones embodied the driving spirit Brent thought was needed.[31]

In February 1966 the critics took action, demanding a special meeting of the board to resolve "unsettled questions" bearing on the ACU's future. Held on March 2, the meeting provided the framework for a coup, in which Meyer, the journalist Ralph de Toledano, and Brent took turns moving, seconding, and securing the passage of a list of resolutions designed to make the ACU a dynamic force. The key resolution proposed a new post, "executive coordinator," with the power to hire and fire all salaried personnel. The post was at once entrusted to Jones, who emerged from the coup the ACU's day-to-day boss.[32]

There was now "a small flicker of hope" that with good leadership the ACU could survive, Brent told Ashbrook a week later. But "whatever happens," he added after another few days, "I wish the ACU all good fortune."[33] This last sounds like a farewell message, and so it was. After helping found and then save the ACU, Brent became absorbed in other plans and quietly slipped out of the organization, thereby cutting one more tie with the conservative mainstream.

Compared with his involvement in another group born of the Goldwater ferment, Brent's fifteen-month stay in the ACU looks lengthy. Founded in 1964, the Philadelphia Society aimed at fostering discussion among conservative intellectuals. Brent spoke at the society's first national meeting, held in Chicago in February 1965, on the topic "A Purpose for Our Foreign Policy." His speech, as summarized in *National Review*, voiced his perennial gloom about the future of the West, warning that "the West as a self-conscious embodiment of Christian truth has forgotten its identity." But he never spoke at the Philadelphia Society again, leaving only this meager trace of his fleeting presence.[34]

After his return from Spain, Brent's principal tie to the mainstream Right, his *National Review* connection, began to wither. In 1960 he had written sixteen "National Trends" columns for the biweekly magazine. In 1963, 1964, and 1965 he wrote only three, two, and four, respectively. At the end of 1962, while still in Spain, he told Buckley that he would no longer be able to work for *NR* "on a regular basis" because he needed to give "single-minded attention to whatever new thing I decide to do in the future." He suggested, therefore, that his name be dropped from the magazine's masthead. Perhaps worried that Buckley might sense coolness in the letter, he closed, "My affection for you and *NR* remains . . . absorbing and without limit." Unhappy at the thought of a masthead without Brent's name on it, Buckley persuaded his friend to stay on board, though he agreed to move his name from the masthead's "editors" section to its less prominent "contributors" section.[35]

As Brent's presence at *NR* grew faint, the focus of his writing changed. Between January 1956 and January 1961 he had published twelve articles and book reviews, none of which chose a religious issue as its subject. Between August 1961 and December 1965 he published sixteen more, ten of which concerned religion subjects and upheld a traditional Catholic point of view. Of his last six articles and book reviews, five concerned religious subjects and defended traditional Catholic teachings. Among the purposes that drew him to his typewriter, arguing for familiar Catholic doctrine and practice, especially against the criticisms of liberal Catholics, was clearly becoming the one that engaged him the most.

Declarations of affection notwithstanding, Brent began to argue with Buckley more strenuously than he had in the past. In 1962 he had backed Buckley's decision to run an editorial condemning the John Birch Society's Robert Welch, who, in his privately circulated book, *The Politician*, had gone so far as to accuse Eisenhower of being "a conscious agent of the communist conspiracy." But in 1965, when *NR* denounced not just Welch but the Society *en bloc*, Brent flared up. Most Birchers didn't share Welch's eccentricities, he protested in a letter to *NR*. They weren't crackpots but well-meaning people who hoped to restore "the traditional values of the Republic." When Buckley refused to publish the letter (explaining that if he did, he would have to repeat all his anti-Birch arguments in his reply), Brent's indignation grew. If the letter wasn't published, he answered, he would demand that his name be removed from the magazine's masthead. Buckley then proposed that Brent meet with the editors to discuss the matter.[36] What happened next isn't clear. Although Brent's letter remained unpublished, the name "L. Brent Bozell" nonetheless stayed on the masthead.

Much more acrimonious was a clash between the two over abortion. In an April 1966 column Buckley observed that the Second Vatican Council's Declaration on Religious Liberty seemed to contradict the insistence of some Catholics that abortion continue to be banned for everyone, including people who, in cases of abortions performed "under certain circumstances," opposed the ban. If the Church continued to exert "an undue leverage on civil policy," Buckley warned, it risked provoking resentment that could lead to greater evils than a limited right of abortion.

Shocked by what he considered a kind of apostasy, Brent fired a furious blast at Buckley's comment. The column "reeks of relativism," he protested, and could equally well serve to justify euthanasia or genocide. Buckley sounded as if he had "never heard of the natural law." Indeed, "not even the tipsiest representative of the Catholic New Breed has been driven to this bit of recklessness." A reference to Buckley as "my friend" did nothing to soften the letter's hostile tone.

Shocked, Buckley drafted an even more furious response. Brent's letter, he wrote, was "pompous," "conceited," and "a venture in fanaticism." It proved that Brent had lost "a sense of personal proportion," since he seemed to see himself as "the only conscience left in the Catholic world." But then Buckley thought better of sending the letter. Instead, he ran Brent's missive on *NR*'s letters-to-the-editor page, followed by a brief, dry retort.

Brent also cooled off, but not completely. In a letter to Buckley after a meeting between them in New York, he wrote that given "the differences that are emerging between us," he "must allow for the possibility of future rows." Referring to their recent argument, he commented, "Your position and especially the cavalier manner . . . in which you have come to it, strike me as outrageous, and as gratuitously harmful to the Church. So I reacted as one outraged." Because future "spats" might be "unavoidable," *NR* should "quietly" drop his name from its masthead to "rid ourselves of a situation where the demands of dissociation come into play."[37] But again Buckley held back, and the masthead remained unchanged.

In October 1965 Brent pulled up stakes. On top of moving away from long-maintained ties and ambitions—his *NR* senior editorship, his hope of political office, his attempts to put Goldwater in the White House (soon to be followed by his departure from the ACU and the Philadelphia Society)—he sold the family's house in Kenwood, and after a decade of living in a Washington suburb, the Bozells moved seventy miles west to Huntly, Virginia, a small town at the northern end of the Blue Ridge Mountains. Their new home—a farm, with chickens, pigs, horses stabled for neighbors, and a swimming pool—looked out on a rustic landscape of mountain and forest, the primeval kind of countryside Brent loved. Although backwoods Virginia bore little resemblance to Navarre, the name they gave their new home was "Montejurra."

EIGHT

Defender of the Constitution

Immediately after the assassination of John F. Kennedy, Brent came up with an idea for a book on how liberals would exploit the crime for partisan ends. He intended to argue that liberal protests against supposed right-wing "violence" and "fanaticism" would be purely political, that liberals would invoke the assassination to justify gag laws, and that these laws would be used to silence conservative critics. But he couldn't get the project off the ground. Publishers disliked his plan to devote an entire chapter to liberal ideology. They were also checking up on him, he came to believe, and once they had identified him as a right-winger, they would turn him down.[1]

Meanwhile, he continued to work on his Supreme Court book. By the time he returned from Spain he had grown sick of the project, but having spent so much time and effort on it, he felt compelled to complete it. So he slogged on. Henry Regnery, who had read part of the manuscript, seemed willing to publish it, though he feared that the spring of 1964, the publication date Brent had in mind, would require "rushing." But that date soon ceased to matter, for when the spring of 1964 arrived, Brent was busy running in the sixth district's GOP primary. He put the unfinished manuscript aside, though a campaign press release informed the public that the candidate was planning to publish "a two-volume work . . . this fall." Brent spent the summer revising the manuscript—a job his perfectionism turned into a lengthy process—with the help of his erstwhile campaign aide

Mike Lawrence, whom he hired to work on the volume's footnotes and index.[2]

Despite this assistance, progress remained slow. *The Warren Revolution: Reflections on the Consensus Society*, as the book was now titled, didn't come out for another two years, and when it was finally published in the fall of 1966, the publisher wasn't Regnery but Neil McCaffrey. McCaffrey, an editor at Macmillan in the early 1960s and an ardent conservative, had founded the Conservative Book Club in 1964. Finding a bigger market than he had expected, and with too few titles to satisfy demand, he had decided to bring out books as well as sell them. In 1965 he launched the publishing firm of Arlington House. He also brought on Neal Freeman as a senior editor. Freeman began urging McCaffrey to publish Brent's book.

Brent had known McCaffrey at least since 1958, when the publisher had contributed to Brent's campaign for the Maryland legislature. Both took their Catholicism as seriously as they did their conservatism, and having a common worldview, they became fast friends. All the same, when Freeman urged McCaffrey to bring out *The Warren Revolution*, the publisher held back. Aware that Brent was advancing very slowly, he wondered whether the book would ever be finished. If Brent had a contract, he would finish, Freeman maintained. He would feel morally bound to make good on a formal commitment.[3] Eventually persuaded, McCaffrey offered Brent a contract. Brent signed and, as Freeman had predicted, completed the book.

Why Brent switched from Regnery to McCaffrey isn't clear, but he may have been thinking of publishing's business end. Considered a publisher with a first-rate eye for manuscripts, Regnery was also reputed to be short on marketing drive. Brent had felt that to be the case when Regnery published *McCarthy and His Enemies* in 1954, finding it necessary to give tips on marketing strategy. More recently, after the *New York Times* had panned a Regnery title, James Burnham's *Congress and the American Tradition*, Regnery had called a halt to promoting the book, convinced a successful sale was now out of the question. Regnery also struck some as too casual about business matters. He would accept a submission but then fail to draw up a contract, ran a common complaint, leaving the author uncertain whether he would be published. In the past, when Regnery had been the major (and almost the only) conservative publisher, conservative writers had had to put up with such vagaries. But now an attractive alternative had appeared on the scene in the person of the Bronx-born, business-wise McCaffrey.[4] Brent, who seems to have had no formal contract with Regnery, may have taken the initiative in going over to his old publisher's new rival, though it's equally possible that Regnery got cold feet about *The Warren Revolution* and decided not to publish it.

Freeman tackled the job of editing Brent's sprawling manuscript—an effort that tested his editing skill to the utmost—and pruned it down to manageable size. Another Arlington House editor, Aaron Brown, then took on the manuscript.[5] The book finally came out in the fall of 1966, but only as volume one of the two-volume opus promised in Brent's campaign literature. Volume two, the first volume announced, would arrive in due course.

Brent began his book with the claim that during Earl Warren's tenure as chief justice the country had been writhing in the toils of a constitutional crisis. A series of perverse Supreme Court rulings stemmed from a poor understanding of the court's authority and of the American constitutional order as a whole. Contrary to popular belief, the United States had not one constitution but two. The first, drawn up by the Founding Fathers in 1787, and changeable only through the amendment process spelled out in its text, could be called the "written" or "fixed" constitution. The second, a set of social understandings, values, and mores—broadly put, the American way of life—could be called the "unwritten" or "fluid" constitution. (Echoes of Willmoore Kendall still sounded in Brent's thinking.) The fluid constitution was amended not through a formally prescribed procedure but through "organic processes"—the evolution of old agreements on political, social, and cultural norms into new ones under the pressure of changes in the country's socioeconomic structure.

Under the Warren Court, Brent went on, the distinction between the two constitutions had eroded. Ignoring the slow-moving organic processes through which the fluid constitution was amended, and operating on a faulty understanding of judicial review (the court's power to declare laws "unconstitutional"), the justices had been amending the fluid constitution through rulings from the bench, which they treated as having the force of fixed-constitution amendments. As a result, Brent concluded, "*a Supreme Court decision has become equivalent to a provision of the fixed constitution.*"[6] Dealing with the fluid constitution in this fashion meant acting in the absence of a supporting social consensus or in the teeth of an opposing consensus—a sure-fire recipe for social disorder. Examples of court decisions that Brent thought defective were *Brown v. Board of Education* and the Schempp-Murray cases—*Abington School District v. Schempp* and *Murray v. Curlett*, two consolidated cases in which the court banned required group prayer or Bible reading in public schools. His detailed analysis of these and other major decisions formed the bulk of the book.

Without legal warrant, Brent charged, the Supreme Court had remade itself into a standing constitutional convention. The kind of government the Founding Fathers had envisaged was giving way to a radically different kind, a judicial dictatorship, in which the court decreed changes in the law that once could have occurred only through the fixed constitution's amendment procedure. In this way the court was reshaping American society along lines the country's liberal elite desired (but the mass of ordinary citizens often opposed). That elite could thus steer clear of possibly recalcitrant legislatures and turn to federal judges to produce the laws it wanted. At this point, the only way to end government by judicial fiat would be to amend the fixed constitution or persuade the court to stop usurping power. (Brent knew that the Constitution did, in fact, furnish a way to solve the court problem. In an *NR* piece of 1961, he had pointed to Article II, Section 3, which empowered Congress to limit or even abolish the court's appellate jurisdiction. But now as then he seemed to regard this provision as nonfunctional in practice, doubting whether it could ever be successfully applied.)[7]

According to Brent, the court had usurped power through an interpretation of judicial review that gave the justices the last word on the constitutionality of laws as well as broader authority to enforce their rulings. Now only the court could decide on the Constitution's meaning, which amounted to making the famous words of Chief Justice Charles Evans Hughes ("The Constitution is what the judges say it is") the law of the land. If Hughes's words were true, then judicial review had to mean judicial supremacy, and American government would rest on straightforward "judicial despotism."[8]

But the words weren't true. American history offered little evidence that judicial review had been so understood in the past. Eighteenth-century court cases cited as supporting an expanded power of judicial review usually, when closely examined, turned out to do the opposite. The Constitution made no mention of judicial review, nor was the concept debated at the Constitutional Convention. Hamilton and Madison wrote ambiguously on the subject. But the idea was clearly at odds with the overarching constitutional scheme envisaged by the Founding Fathers and Hamilton and Madison's *Federalist*—that is, an ensemble of checks and balances designed to keep any one branch of the federal government from having the last word.

Moreover, if any one branch had been so empowered, it would have been Congress, which the Founders thought the most important of the three. They would never have chosen the Supreme Court over Congress (or over the states, for that matter) as the ultimate, unanswerable interpreter of the Constitution.[9] The Constitution was intended not to smooth the way for change but to block change until the states and all three branches of the federal government had reached a consensus in favor of change—a design incompatible with judicial review construed as judicial supremacy. The notion that the Supreme Court had from the beginning enjoyed sole authority to interpret the

Constitution and impose its interpretation on Congress, the executive branch, and the states was nothing but nonsense, Brent argued.

What, then, of the ruling of the first chief justice, John Marshall, in *Marbury v. Madison*, which gave birth to the Supreme Court's power of judicial review? Marshall did gain for the court "a somewhat larger role in interpreting and enforcing the Constitution than the Founders had contemplated," Brent conceded. "But even the blanket prerogative asserted by Marshall of refusing to enforce any legislation the Court deemed unconstitutional would not establish the Supreme Court as the 'final arbiter' of the Constitution—in the sense that its decisions would determine not only the rights of litigants, but also of sister departments of government." The latter claim came not from the Marshall Court but from the Warren Court. The Marshall Court's conception of judicial review—more leeway for federal courts to interpret and enforce the law—fell far short of the Warren Court's, which put forward a clear-cut claim to judicial sovereignty in ordering that school desegregation take place "with all deliberate speed."[10] How Marshall's doctrine was alchemized into Warren's would be the subject of his book's second volume, Brent told his readers.

Almost always, the author of *The Warren Revolution* sounded more like the Buckley-stage Brent of the 1950s than like the Brent who had discovered a better world in Catholic Spain. The book dealt with a wholly secular issue, the constitutional legitimacy of the Warren Court's jurisprudence, and did so from a wholly secular point of view, even when criticizing the court's ruling in the school prayer case. But the voice of the new Brent also came through, if only briefly. At one point, for example, wishing to place his subject in broad historical perspective, he moved from American judicial history to the evolution of the West. "The decisions that have determined Western fortunes for the past half century," he wrote, "perhaps for the past half millennium [that is, since the end of the religion-oriented Middle Ages], appear in the reckoning to have been wrong." Their wrongness he blamed on what he called "the Western sickness," whose cause he diagnosed without elaboration as "probably theological." Some two hundred pages later, he offered a second brief comment on the course of Western history, speaking darkly of "the collapse of Christendom conceived as an organic community beholden to an authority beyond itself."[11] Thus, although *The Warren Revolution* should be classified as a Buckley-stage book, Brent's emerging *Triumph* stage had a preview in its pages.

Brent drew his evidence from a wide array of sources ranging from early American judicial thinking and practice (including the records of pertinent colonial trials, cases tried in the courts of the newborn republic, the Constitution itself, and the writings and debates of the framers) to key Warren Court cases. Given the abundance of this material and the care with which he explored it—his work brings to mind his painstaking treatment of congressional hearings transcripts in *McCarthy and His Enemies*—it's easy to see why the book was nine years in the making. But this voluminous documentation and the detailed study he gave it, if necessary for defending a thesis as heretical as his, probably dampened the book's prospects for commercial success. Too scholarly and technical for some readers, too contrary to the zeitgeist for others (the book charged current ideological fashion head-on), *The Warren Revolution* found few readers when it finally appeared in print. Sales figures are no longer available, but Freeman recalled that the book fared poorly in the marketplace. And the modest sales it did have were "optically enlarged," he added, by its inclusion in packaged offerings from the Conservative Book Club.[12]

Reviews were too few for *Book Review Digest* to take note of them. *The Warren Revolution* "didn't cause much of a ripple," Mike Lawrence remembered. Buckley spoke admiringly of the book and went out of his way to promote it. He had ordered three hundred copies from Arlington House, he told Brent, and had directed McCaffrey to send a copy to anybody Brent thought should have one. He also planned to keep copies at *National Review* for visitors "who might profit" from having one, he said, and intended to make the book the subject of a column. But he sadly acknowledged that the book had received little notice.[13]

Professional journals and liberal reviewers ignored *The Warren Revolution,* perhaps because they dismissed Brent as a "right-wing extremist." But three conservative academics, all writing for conservative magazines, did review it, and all mixed words of praise with pointed criticisms. *NR* ran a long review by Martin Diamond, a Claremont University historian of American political thought and institutions. Brent had "pushed his arguments too far," Diamond contended, and "obscured and distorted" his attack on judicial supremacy by including an "unconvincing" treatment of judicial review. What was more, in his theory of constitutional change and social consensus, he had come "dangerously" close to endorsing a "sociological jurisprudence he otherwise detests"; indeed, he had stopped just short of claiming that the Constitution should mean whatever a social consensus wanted it to mean. Brent's unacknowledged wish, Diamond concluded, was a populist constitution, strong on states' rights and leaning toward congressional supremacy.

A milder yet still critical review came from James McClellan, a professor of constitutional law and American government at a succession of southern universities. Writing in Russell Kirk's quarterly, *Modern Age,* McClellan taxed Brent with exaggerating the Warren Court's derelictions. Although these were by no means trivial, he agreed, McClellan claimed that some earlier Supreme Courts hadn't been much better. And he disagreed that judicial review was the problem Brent thought it was. Since all of the Warren Court's controversial decisions stemmed from cases it had heard on appeal from state court rulings, the root of the current court uproar lay less in the doctrine of juridical review than in the Fourteenth Amendment's first section, which enabled the court to impose its wishes on the states.

George Carey, a Georgetown University professor of government (who frequently collaborated with Kendall), viewed the book more favorably than Diamond and McClellan had but found in it what he considered an important error. Contrary to Brent's belief, he wrote, the Founding Fathers didn't envisage the court as part of "the 'consensus' machinery" the book described. Rather, they probably regarded the court's main role as ensuring "a fair administration of the laws."[14]

Yet to some readers the book came as a revelation. One told Trish that he had been reading for nearly six decades and now almost never encountered an unfamiliar idea, but that on reading *The Warren Revolution* he had found something new. The idea of judicial review, when treated as being synonymous with judicial supremacy, did indeed clash with the idea of a constitution in which no branch of government enjoys superiority over the others. The contradiction was glaring, yet hardly anyone seemed to notice it.

Many years after the book came out, former *National Review* senior editor Joseph Sobran told Trish, "Brent had the genius to see the simple key to everything, the thing so obvious that the rest of us didn't see it. The super-obvious I call it. He was so undistracted!" Sobran didn't stop there. "Brent's book on the Warren Court changed my life," he continued. "He was a genius! He made it impossible to think in accustomed ways."[15]

Brent didn't seem upset about the book's failure to gain notice, nor did he comment on the criticism it received. His dominant feeling may have been relief that he had finally finished the project. Trish found him utterly uninterested in *The Warren Revolution*'s fate. She had "no knowledge" of his feelings about the reviews, she told an inquirer, which probably meant "that he was at least satisfied with them." But it was also possible, she noted, that because he was now so wrapped up in his magazine (the first issue of *Triumph* came out only weeks before the book did), he didn't care at all about the book's reception.[16]

The Warren Revolution, begun in 1957, could be called the swan song of the old Brent. Not only did the new Brent fail to write the book's promised second volume; in February 1968, less than a year and a half after the first volume's publication, he repudiated the entire work on religious grounds and with it the Constitution he had so recently and zealously defended.[17]

NINE

Defender of the Faith

In the 1950s and early 1960s many Catholics lamented the lack of a conservative Catholic political magazine. They usually envisaged such a magazine as a conservative Catholic equivalent of the liberal Catholic weeklies *Commonweal* and *America*, or in Brent's words as "a Catholic *National Review*."[1]

No Catholic complained of this lack more vehemently than Brent. In his article "The Strange Drift of Liberal Catholicism," he called for a Catholic journal of opinion that wouldn't feel "an overriding vocation for social work" but would see its "supreme duty" as serving "the Christian West." After *America* attacked his claim that the West was "God's civilization" and should be defended in just those terms, and then refused to publish his rejoinder, he renewed his call for a Catholic *National Review*. Liberals formed "a clear oligarchy" in Catholic political journalism, he wrote to *NR* from El Escorial, and conservative Catholics had no means of challenging the oligarchy. But help was on the way, he happily reported. Weary of "Liberal summonses to open-mindedness," he and Fritz Wilhelmsen were planning to found such a magazine. Lest anyone mistake their intention, they were going to call their publication *La Inquisición*.[2]

While in Spain, Brent did talk with Wilhelmsen about starting a magazine. He had become "increasingly alarmed" by the rise of heresy in the Church, he later told a *Washington Daily News* reporter, especially by Dutch theologians' questioning of the divinity of Christ.[3]

His talks with Wilhelmsen, however, never got past café chat, yielding nothing that could properly be called a plan of action.

Back in America, Brent seemed to lose interest in the magazine idea. His aim was to act more effectively for "the Catholic cause," he told his daughter Kathy during his 1964 primary race. If he lost, he would find another way to serve the cause. After his defeat he told Robert Bauman and Bauman's wife, Carol, that he had grown tired of politics, that all he cared about now was "the Catholic cause."[4] But neither to Kathy nor to the Baumans did he mention a magazine.

In the summer of 1964 he went back to work on *The Warren Revolution*, but all the while his thoughts kept turning to the religious arena. Still on hand was Wilhelmsen, who stayed on in Maryland for a time after the primary, sharing with Mike Lawrence the apartment Brent had used as his campaign headquarters. Night after night, in a haze of cigarette smoke and bourbon fumes, the three talked. Conversation, Lawrence recalled, ranged "from Maritain to *Marbury v. Madison*, from Carlism to Chesterbelloc, from Goldwater to Gnosticism." But the subject they took up most often was the Second Vatican Council and the commotion it had let loose in the American Church. The Church's situation had become perilous, Brent maintained; preserving Catholic orthodoxy would require a struggle.

Prompted by this worry, talk of a conservative Catholic magazine became part of the discussion, and it was then, Lawrence later told an inquirer, that the talk became "real."[5] Again, however, no concrete plan took shape. Wilhelmsen returned to Spain and Lawrence to law school, while Brent, stunned by Johnson's crushing defeat of Goldwater, went back into politics by way of the ACU.

But the thought of starting a magazine kept gnawing at him. Liberal Catholics weren't just politically harmful. More than ever, he feared, they were doing harm to the Church. Under cover of Vatican II's aim of "updating" the Church, they were working toward goals long sought by the Church's enemies. Brent identified those goals in a May 1965 essay in *National Review*:

Consider the fresh ideas, still unanointed to be sure, that now blow freely out of the editorial offices of the Catholic press and down the corridors of the seminaries: population control and planned parenthood via contraceptive artifacts; mixed marriages with parents invited to slug it out over the children's souls, on an equal footing; proscription of capital punishment; a "dialogue" with homosexuals; nuns dressed like all the other ladies; priests as family men; religious liberty, meaning, concretely, an Open Door policy for Spain; racial equality as the age's transcendent moral demand . . . ; accommodation as the relevant mode of dealing with Communists; the preeminence of the social gospel (the Catholic twist: a holy war on poverty); the possibilities of constructing a theology on a study of fossils. These are the principal items of the current diet, pejoratively stated perhaps.

Further liberal Catholic goals might be noted, he went on, such as lowering the Catholic liturgy "to the meeting house level." But whether or not the liberal agenda was desirable, all its entries originated in "a world that has always viewed itself as laying siege at the walls of Rome." Liberal Catholics sought peace with this world by accepting its wishes, by embracing secular norms and Protestant tastes. But their ultimate purpose, he argued, went deeper. Like the libertarians he had explained in "Freedom or Virtue?" as wanting at bottom to free themselves from God, liberal Catholics yearned "to be liberated from the constraints imposed by a specifically Christian apostolate." This yearning portended a chilling future. "I doubt," he concluded, "whether one can exaggerate the trouble the Catholic Church is in."[6]

Yet it would be wrong to ascribe his wish to start a magazine to hostility toward the Vatican II reforms (or, better, misappropriation of the reforms: he objected not to the English Mass as such but to the bishops' virtual banning of the Latin Mass and their imposing of what he viewed as poorly translated texts and a humdrum liturgy). His hostility didn't launch his publishing ambition but only fed it.[7]

Above all else, he responded to a sense of calling. His duty, he felt keenly, was to serve "the Catholic cause." Twenty years later he wrote:

> I was forty years old when *Triumph* magazine began to appear in 1966, plenty old enough to have done something with my life. It was a life that had been, in some sense, Catholic . . . but nothing measurable had been accomplished along that line (besides fathering a lot of children). What I had done instead was to contribute certain writings, talks, agitations and political campaigns to the cause of secular conservatism, a cause that I then imagined had a close connection with Catholicism.[8]

But then he decided the connection wasn't so close after all, that he needed a different way to pursue his mission (which in the future he would usually call his "apostolate"). He must work to save the Catholic Church in America and bring America into the Catholic Church.

Other motives also drew him forward. For all its (rare) balking at current Vatican pronouncements (*"Mater si, Magistra no"*), *National Review* had never criticized traditional Catholic teachings. (Indeed, *NR* was seen by some as a Catholic journal.) But by 1965—even before his row with Buckley over abortion—Brent may have begun worrying that *NR* was going wobbly.[9] He wouldn't have found reassurance in a Buckley column of 1965 that took up the issue of birth control and the danger Buckley saw of an overcrowded America. Birth control was "not exclusively a moral issue," Buckley wrote, but also one related to society's general well-being. Although he stopped short of formally endorsing birth control, he welcomed the Vatican's decision to review its prohibition and obviously hoped that the Church would lift the ban. If it didn't, he warned, America would become a new India.

Four months later, *NR* senior editor (and former Jesuit seminarian) Garry Wills weighed in on the subject with a long article called "Catholics and Population." Not only did Wills find birth control morally acceptable. He also claimed that the Vatican's most authoritative statement on the question, Pius XI's 1930 encyclical *Casti Con-*

nubii, failed to meet the requirements for infallibility and therefore lacked the power to command assent.[10]

Brent strongly opposed birth control, seeing in it a wedge separating sex from love and the creation of life.[11] He couldn't have agreed with Buckley's column, but he did not criticize it (at least not in print). Wills's article was a different story: denying *Casti Connubii* binding force seemed to rile Brent even more than declaring birth control morally permissible. In a rebuttal called "The Open Question: Mater si, Magistra si!" he defended the pope's authority to decide the question, citing evidence that he thought proved *Casti Connubii* infallible.[12]

Brent's worry about *NR*'s dependability on Catholic issues stemmed also from the magazine's willingness to publish a positive view of what he saw as chaos in the Church. Once again the offending writer was Garry Wills. In an article called "On the Present Position of Catholics," Wills expressed amazement and delight at what he termed the "effervescence" in the Church. It was "about time," he wrote, that religious "renewal" had come. Conservative Catholics had nothing to fear, he insisted, for this was "a conservative reform"—"not a dissolution of the unchanging original Church, but the breakup of a temporal crust over the ancient vitality of the Faith."

Along the way Wills also took a poke at liberal Catholics, noting that the same people who championed Church reforms, more variety in worship, more attention to the feelings of the grassroots Catholic population, and more local decision making in Church affairs showed exactly the opposite attitude toward liberal political authority. There, liberal Catholics favored centralized power, authoritarian rule, and elite imposition of progress on the backward masses.[13] If Wills intended this comment to reassure his conservative readers, he got nowhere with Brent.

Upheavals in the Church, Brent's growing concerns about *NR*'s trustworthiness on Catholic issues, his own defeat in the congressional primary, the Goldwater rout—all these factors were pushing Brent to leave the political battlefield for the religious one and start his own magazine. But another factor was in play: his relationship with

Buckley. In 1991, after interviewing Trish and Brent, the historian Patrick Allitt wrote that Brent "had been and felt himself to be in the shadow of his celebrity brother-in-law" and that this situation was a key to the magazine's founding. Brent thought Allitt's idea contained some truth.[14] His connection with Buckley had affected his life profoundly, and by the mid-1960s it had turned into a problem for him.

Buckley tended to engulf people he took to, binding them to him as something like protégés. Thus had things gone in his friendship with Brent, at least to a degree. It was Buckley who had converted Brent to conservatism, encouraged his marriage with Trish, invited him to coauthor *McCarthy and His Enemies*, introduced him to McCarthy, and made him an editor and columnist at *National Review*. Writing the book with Buckley had led Brent to writing speeches for McCarthy, which had led to his employment by Goldwater, for whom he had written America's top political bestseller. Buckley had even found him a campaign manager. These were favors Brent couldn't repay, and wasn't expected to. But his status as a Buckley beneficiary over the years—it seemed as if his post-Yale life had been founded on Buckley—had eroded his original status as Buckley's peer.

Nor did Brent escape the Buckley magnetism. Like many other people close to Buckley, he acquired some of the latter's trademark mannerisms. The journalist Farley Clinton, who worked for both men, thought Brent had made himself into a Buckley "carbon copy." Brent's son Chris noticed that his father had adopted a red-ink pen of the kind Buckley famously used. Garry Wills (who himself was engulfed by Buckley for a time), on first meeting Brent, heard Buckley's voice in Brent's, which, he wrote, "makes broad sweeps and veers" just like Buckley's.[15] (Buckley, for his part, showed no sign of imitating Brent.)

Yet Brent harbored a fiercely independent spirit, as evidenced by the battles he had fought at *National Review*. He had never backed off from a fight, never hesitated to differ with Buckley on any issue, never bowed to Buckley's opinions when they clashed with his own. His pride, moreover, ran as deep as his need for independence and pushed him to compete with a man some thought he aped.[16] But he hadn't succeeded in keeping abreast of his rival, and his self-consciousness over the gap between them had begun to ache. The disparity found expression in various ways: for example, the growing media practice of identifying Brent by noting that he was Buckley's brother-in-law. (No one ever identified Buckley by mentioning his tie with Brent.) If being the child of a famous parent can be stressful, being the friend of a celebrity with whom one had once—but no longer—stood on an equal footing may be worse.

People who knew both men recognized Brent's problem. William A. Rusher once observed that Brent was "a proud personality" who "must have found it difficult to live comfortably in Buckley's shadow." Willmoore Kendall thought the Buckley link had done Brent harm. "Brent should never have got himself absorbed into the Buckley empire," he remarked to Wills. "If he had gone back to Nebraska he would have become a very distinguished United States senator." To Brent, Kendall criticized Buckley in bitter terms, appearing to see Brent and himself as Buckley victims. "The Buckleys," he said, "consume people like a furnace consumes coal."[17]

What the forty-year-old Brent wanted after twenty years of Buckley was a feeling of independence from—but also the return of his old equality and intimacy with—a man who had evolved into something like his patron. As Trish put it, Brent needed to catch up with Buckley, needed to escape the embarrassment of falling behind, needed to be free of the fear that he was pitied.[18] Publishing a magazine of his own might help him fill these needs. At the same time, however, it would put him in competition with a man now far ahead of him—and so leave him more than ever in Buckley's wake.

Before Brent could start up a magazine, he had to raise money. This he set out to do through the Committee for a Conservative Catholic Magazine, which he and Trish set up in the summer of 1965. Its members included Brent and a group of traditionalist conservatives: Wilhelmsen, who had just joined the faculty of the University of Dallas; Thomas Molnar, professor at Brooklyn College and prolific writer on political and religious subjects; Francis Graham Wilson, a political scientist who had taught the young Willmoore Kendall; and Russell Kirk. Kirk, who had recently married a Catholic and become one himself, took a keen interest in the project, discussing it with Brent as "our undertaking" and proffering advice on how to get it going.[19] Also on hand was Mike Lawrence, who had just finished law school. Instead of taking the bar exam, he had resumed work for Brent as the committee's business manager.

In September 1965 the committee sent out its first fund-raising letter. Drafted by Brent, the letter repeated familiar conservative complaints. Liberal Catholics, it charged, were "pecking away at the free market system, . . . downgrading the Communist threat, and . . . insinuating that the conservative political position is, somehow, un-Christian." Once widely recognized as a bulwark of conservative thinking, the Church now seemed to speak "almost exclusively in left-wing accents, and often in revolutionary tones." The need for a conservative Catholic magazine had never been more pressing, the letter went on, and $100,000 would make it possible to start one—a modest sum "in terms of the stakes," which it identified apocalyptically as "the survival of the Christian West."

Addressed to "Dear Conservatives," not "Dear Catholics" or "Dear Catholic Conservatives," the letter referred only to political issues (communism, big government, the welfare state). The closest it came to religious issues was its reference to the charge, often voiced by liberal Catholics, that Catholicism and "capitalism" stood as moral opposites. In tune with its secular emphasis, the letter described "the Christian West" largely in political rather than in religious terms—as characterized by individual freedom (rather than, for instance, social policy based on Catholic teachings) and therefore the opposite of the tyrannical USSR (rather than, for instance, the atheistic USSR).

Speaking for "the conservative cause" rather than "the Catholic cause," the letter gave the impression that the (as yet unnamed) magazine would bear a marked resemblance to *National Review*. Just what made the magazine "Catholic" was far from clear. Not surprisingly given its stress on secular politics, the letter explicitly urged non-Catholics to subscribe, declaring that the magazine should have the support of "the *entire* conservative community," not just Catholics.[20] Brent's deepening immersion in religion notwithstanding, the man who had invented (or at least perfected) Barry Goldwater was still alive and could still crank out the old conservative line.

Two weeks later Brent sent out a second funding appeal calling for $100,000, this time "in the next few weeks." He also mailed a four-page "Preliminary Report" (stamped "Confidential, Please") that told more about the magazine's aims. Now the emphasis turned decidedly Catholic, perhaps because the first appeal hadn't attracted a sufficient response. Besides advancing a conservative Catholic outlook, the report stated, the magazine would indict modern, secular society and work to transform American life by "portray[ing] the configurations of a religiously conceived and motivated social order, including proposals for its achievement." Put another way, the magazine would seek to convert America to Catholicism and the kind of society that Brent had discovered in Spain.[21]

A brochure announcing still more goals followed the report. The magazine would take on the "joyful challenge" of rescuing "the churches," the brochure announced (sounding an ecumenical note that would soon fall silent). It would also work to rescue the American polity, since the "barbarians," in addition to rending "the fabric of Christendom," were "even now pulling down the foundations of the Republic." (The admiration for "the wisdom of the American tradition" would soon vanish as well.)[22]

As the weeks passed, money began to arrive. The influx was slow, the checks small, the contributors mostly conservative Catholics of modest means who found the tumult of the 1960s alarming. Brent and Trish also lent a hand, donating a hefty chunk of family money,[23] and that winter Brent reached his financial goal.

Toward the end of 1965 Brent finally named the magazine. The editors, he wrote in an announcement, had decided to call the magazine *Future* because they "assume that the full realization of the Christian vision lies ahead." (According to Lawrence, the name also mounted "an anticipatory defense" against a criticism liberal Catholics were bound to make: that the magazine grew out of a longing to restore the past.)[24] Brent settled on a monthly publishing schedule (instead of the weekly or biweekly schedule at first envisioned), since this would lower production costs and pressures. Four senior editors would top the magazine's masthead: Brent, Wilhelmsen, Molnar, and John Wisner, like Brent a convert disturbed by Church disorder and the country's downward course. Lawrence became *Future's* business manager. (He would later move to the magazine's editorial side). *Future* also acquired a fixed physical location, office space Brent rented in downtown Washington.

The post of managing editor went to Trish. To learn the trade, she spent two months apprenticing at *National Review* under her sister Priscilla, *NR*'s managing editor. Ahead of her lay a decade of demanding work that included not only the chores that went with her job title but also contributing an occasional article or review. If the magazine's crew had been a tribe, Brent later wrote, then Trish would have stood in the forefront as its "head squaw."[25]

Trish appeared to thrive in her new career. She was "in splendid shape," Brent wrote to Buckley. This was mostly true but not entirely, for she worried about squaring her job with her maternal duties. "My conscience where the children are concerned is always queasy," she told Buckley early in the magazine's life, and the passage of time did little to ease her qualms. "I found leaving home yesterday quite heart-wrenching," she confessed in 1969, "particularly leaving Willie and Jamie [her two youngest]. There is something about little children that tugs at the heart."

To fill both roles, she adopted a grueling schedule. Rising at 3:30 a.m., she set out in the dark for the ninety-minute drive to Washington, began work at 6 a.m., and left the office for home at 3:30 p.m. to make sure she would have some time to spend with the children. The commute was hard, but she said she didn't mind it. It was "well worth it for the glorious place we had amidst the Blue Ridge Mountains," she wrote to an inquirer, and the schedule spared her the horrors of the Washington rush hour. (Brent, for his part, set out at 6:30 a.m. and got back home at 8 p.m., or sometimes later.)

After Washington's 1968 riots, the Bozells rented a burned-out Trailways bus station near the office and remodeled it into a comfortable, two-bedroom apartment. Both usually stayed at the apartment on Monday night, and Brent occasionally did so all week long. Trish found the place a godsend when the strain of work and commuting grew too great.[26]

By the middle months of 1966, the prospects for the magazine looked bright. According to Brent's figures, as of May 1966 five thousand subscribers had signed up,[27] a number not far from the one *NR* had begun with. Moreover, Catholic writers were starting to show an interest. The eminent English historian Christopher Dawson agreed to contribute a piece to the maiden issue, news that left Trish bubbling with delight. The archbishop of New Orleans arranged a meeting between a group of his fellow bishops and Brent, who delivered a full-throttle pitch on behalf of *Future*. "The response appeared quite favorable," Brent wrote to Kirk, "and I am hopeful that some very strategic bishops will be helping us directly or indirectly, once the proper avenues have been established."[28]

As usual Buckley came forward offering help. He wanted to take out a hundred subscriptions, he told Lawrence, and asked where seventy or eighty might most profitably be sent. Lawrence suggested Catholic college libraries, but Buckley opposed this on the grounds that such libraries didn't put new magazines on display. "The thing to do now is to see that potentially interested and influential readers, publicists, and donors get the magazine," he advised. Did Lawrence have a list of such people on hand? "Or should I attempt to make one up?"[29]

As *Future*'s first issue took shape, Brent's excitement soared. Lee Edwards's wife, Anne, who was working as Brent's secretary at the time, described the office atmosphere as "electric." Brent throbbed with energy, practically shooting off sparks, and found it hard to interrupt work for lunch. He said he had a good appetite, Anne Edwards recalled, yet coffee and cigarettes made up his entire diet.[30] He had realized his dream: there was actually going to be a conservative Catholic magazine, and it would flay the liberal Catholic intelligentsia, the secular Left (whose approval liberal Catholics seemed to crave), and the on-the-fence Catholics, too timid and mannerly to resist the left-wing tide.

Yet clouds occasionally dimmed the sun-filled sky. In June 1966 the Junior Chamber of Commerce, which published a house organ called *The Jaycees' Future*, protested the name *Future* as too closely resembling that of its own magazine and threatened to take Brent to court if he didn't change it. At first Brent derided the Jaycees' demand as absurd, but his scoffing soon gave way to anger. Exploding on the phone one day with the Jaycees' attorney, he warned that if the Jaycees persisted in their nonsense, they would be "embarrassed in various syndicated columns" he unleashed on them. But the Jaycees stood firm. By this time Buckley had entered the fray, writing in sneering tones to a Jaycee official that he "would appreciate any details explaining how anyone would confuse a Catholic monthly with your own publication." When the official answered this query with a cutting response, Buckley mailed him a list of instructions on civilized manners.[31] In late August, however, a week before *Future*'s first issue was scheduled to appear, the Jaycees filed the lawsuit they had been brandishing. Brent felt sure he would win the case in court. But unwilling to spend *Future*'s money on a legal battle, he decided for the good of the magazine to give in.

In September 1966 the former *Future* made its debut as *Triumph*. He had chosen that name, Brent told Kirk, because it conveyed "the same forward vision and confident mood regarding Christianity's ultimate destiny" that the word *future* had.[32] But he may also have had a further motive in mind. *Triumph* suggested the attitude known as "triumphalism"—exaltation of the power and glory of the one true Church combined with disdain for the Church's midget rivals. Liberal Catholics hated this arrogant stance, judging it offensive to modern religious good manners, the ideal of interfaith harmony, the ecumenical spirit, and other liberal Catholic desiderata. Therefore, calling his magazine *Triumph*, Brent well knew, would be like thumbing his nose in the face of liberal Catholicism. Whether such thinking influenced his choice of the name isn't clear, but given his love of provocation (*La Inquisición*), it certainly may have.

No sooner had Brent put the Jaycee affair behind him than new trouble struck. Gathered at the printer's to watch *Triumph*'s first issue appear, the editors were making a final correction on the last page proof when lightning, ripping through the building, disabled the press. "Naturally, we paused, wondering if we had just been notified of the pleasure of the Holy Ghost," Brent wrote to Kirk. "But a friend soon reminded us that lightning bolts are part of Lucifer's traditional equipment."[33] After a five-day delay the printing took place, and *Triumph* arrived at the post office ready for mailing. But there trouble erupted for the third time as postal workers mislaid much of the delivery. A month later, some subscribers were still awaiting their copies.

In the face of these mishaps, Brent managed to maintain his morale, and after a while light broke through the clouds. "Response to *Triumph* has been most enthusiastic . . . and our circulation is 7,000 and building at a minimum of 500 more per month," Lee Edwards, who had signed on as *Triumph*'s advertising director, informed a potential advertiser in November.[34] Having surmounted a daunting succession of unforeseen obstacles, Brent had finally made it all the way to the battlefield. He now charged forward, armed and eager to fight.

TEN

The Cutting Edge

In the world of Catholic journalism, *Triumph* stood apart, and not just because of its combative conservative stance. In several ways the newcomer presented an anomaly. For one thing, few of the *Triumph* editors were cradle Catholics. (Sometimes the magazine suggested a haven for converts who had entered the pre–Vatican II Church and wanted to stay there—*Mater si!*) For another, few had the Irish ancestry so common among American Catholic journalists. For a third, as sometime *Triumph* editor Farley Clinton once pointed out, few were personally familiar with everyday Catholic America.[1] Among *Triumph*'s higher-ups, only Mike Lawrence—an Irish-American cradle Catholic from Queens and a graduate of Jesuit-run Fairfield University and Catholic University's law school—came from that world. For a fourth, few knew much about publishing magazines. Brent himself—a convert, ethnically hard to place (but not Irish), only moderately acquainted with ordinary Catholic life (though he had gone to a Catholic high school, he hadn't grown up in a Catholic family or neighborhood), and only thinly versed in the work of magazine publishing (his sole previous experience being his two-issue, four-page Yale newspaper, *The Conservative View*)—perfectly embodied the *Triumph* type.

Nor could *Triumph* in its fledgling stage boast many well-known conservative contributors. Except for Brent, only Willmoore Kendall and Russell Kirk could be thus described, and neither stayed close to the magazine for very long. In the grip of one of his signature choleric eruptions, Kendall stormed off after his first *Triumph* article was published, ordering Brent to "get my name the hell off the masthead of that rag."[2] His death soon afterward made his departure permanent. Kirk left peacefully and incompletely, agreeing to do a book review now and then. Nevertheless, in November 1966 he too asked Brent to remove his name from the masthead of a magazine he had once called "our undertaking." He explained that since he wrote for many magazines, it would be "imprudent" for him to identify himself too closely with any one of them. Besides, he added, he had refused *NR* permission to put his name on its masthead, so he would be "unkind" if he now granted that right to *Triumph*.[3]

Triumph was very much Brent's personal property. It was he who wrote most of the key editorials, handled most of the fund-raising, and made all the final decisions. Among his colleagues, only Wilhelmsen (whose intellectual influence over him was still great) stood a chance of approaching something like equal status. But Wilhelmsen lived in faraway Texas, had regular teaching duties to attend to, lacked the time to go out and scare up money, and visited *Triumph*'s Washington office only every other month. He was doomed by these circumstances to serve as a junior partner.

Triumph's function, Brent told Kirk in the magazine's second year, was to act as a "cutting edge into the great heresies of our age." The enemy he identified as "the technocratic, materialist, self-seeking, thoroughly un-Christian culture of the West."[4] *Triumph* attacked with unshakable faith in its own ideas, the editors explained, because these ideas were based on Christian knowledge. But a further reason bolstered its self-confidence. "I am now convinced," Brent wrote years later, ". . . that if they were sound ideas, they had some outside origin that led to a truer position than was held before. By 'outside' I mean a human source other than self, or a divine source—call it an inspiration or intuition—that becomes self." Added guidance came from a set of axioms he codified as follows: "Politics is deeper than economics. Culture is deeper than politics. The spiritual is deeper than the cultural. The Christian spirit is the true One; all the others are either incomplete (and thus distracting) or false (and thus deadly)." He worked hard to express these ideas with clarity and force. He was "a word lover," said Anne Edwards. "He took pains with his writing, and lavished great care upon it." He also lavished great care on the writing of others. He was a "heavy editor," *Triumph* editorial factotum Gary Potter recalled.[5]

Brent had one further concern in mind: although he had originally called for "a Catholic *National Review*," he now wanted to distinguish *Triumph* from the older magazine. His need for an autonomous identity remained pressing, and to his chagrin he continued to be identified by reference to Buckley. The headline of a *New York Times* article on the founding of *Triumph* read, "Catholics Issue a New Magazine: Conservative Monthly Is Set Up by Buckley Relative." A full four years after the magazine's first issue, Brent had to remind Henry Regnery, one of whose new books identified him as "a frequent contributor" to *NR*, that "there was an easier identification [that is, editor of *Triumph*], to say nothing of the fact that I have not contributed anything to NR for five years." The idea of publishing Buckley gave him pause. He hoped to run articles by Buckley often, he told the latter, but wanted to wait until *Triumph* had had a chance "to emancipate itself from the suspicion that it is the Ecclesiastical Branch of National Review."[6] In the end, Buckley's writing never appeared in *Triumph*, except for some starchy letters to the editor criticizing Brent's views.

Yet in some ways, *Triumph* seemed to mimic *National Review*. To begin with, as Anne Edwards observed, the early *Triumph* saw itself in a *National Review*–like role: standing athwart history yelling, "Stop."[7] Moreover, in *Triumph*'s early days, its secular commentary often jibed with *National Review*'s (though before very long the two magazines would diverge sharply). In addition, many *NR* contributors also contributed to *Triumph*, among them Jeffrey Hart, Colin Clark, Dietrich von Hildebrand, Sir Arnold Lunn, John Lukacs, Gerhart Niemeyer, Farley Clinton, Neil McCaffrey, Erik von Kuehnelt-Leddihn, and Buckley's younger brother, Reid, to name only a few.

The resemblances between the two magazines didn't stop there. Most of the illustrators and cartoonists who drew for *Triumph* already did so for *NR*, and many of the ads the two ran regularly were the same. *Triumph* even used many *NR* type fonts. Some of this sharing of writers, illustrators, and advertisers may be traceable to the dearth of conservatives in these fields in the 1960s. Everyone had to draw water from the same well. But whatever the reason, much of *Triumph* looked like an *NR* clone. Even before *Triumph*'s debut, this resemblance raised eyebrows. When Brent showed Kirk a dummy issue to illustrate the look he had in mind, Kirk commented: "Well, Brent, this is quite impressive, but there is already a magazine just like this. It is called *National Review*." Brent "didn't like that," Kirk recalled. "It was primarily an anti–*National Review* thing."[8]

At the root of *Triumph*'s half-imitative, half-adversarial stance toward *NR* lay Brent's ambivalence toward Buckley: he seemed to want both a *National Review* of his own (though a "higher," more faithfully Catholic *NR* than the original) and an anti–*National Review* that would testify to his separateness from Buckley and to the return of the parity that had once existed between them. *Triumph* was always what Brent consciously intended it to be—a magazine founded to uphold traditional Catholicism. But it was also the product of his struggle with his private demons.

Triumph addressed a multitude of subjects, ranging from the Vatican II reforms to the Irish Republican Army. But it focused mainly on what it saw as the ruinous impact of liberalism on American Catholicism, politics, and culture. Brent seethed at what he considered Church funk in the face of the enemy. As he had once berated the GOP's Eastern Establishment for failing to mount a real effort against New Deal liberalism, so he now berated the American Catholic bishops for failing to crack down on Catholics who had gone astray. It was true, he admitted, that the bishops (like the "me-too" Republicans of the Eisenhower era) were willing to criticize their adversaries. But (also like the Eisenhower Republicans) they didn't seem willing to roll up their sleeves and fight them.

High on Brent's list of grievances stood liturgical reform. Changes in the Mass, the substitution of a dreary vernacular for sonorous Latin, the replacement of altars with Protestant-looking communion tables, the folk-music-style hymns accompanied by guitars, the anti-Marian slant that had come into fashion—all struck him as either sentimental, disrespectful, or vulgar. The Mass should be "a regal ceremony as befits Christ, the King," he told Nicholas von Hoffman of the *Washington Post*. "We prefer Christ, the King, to Christ, the Brother." As for Latin, it conveyed "the majesty and mystery" of the Mass, a feat that everyday English couldn't accomplish. One of *Triumph*'s most incisive articles, a piece by Gary Potter called "The Liturgy Club," traced the means by which English—bad English, Potter thought—had pushed the Latin Mass off to the sidelines despite the fact that in permitting the use of the vernacular, Vatican II hadn't meant to ban the ancient tongue. The process of liturgical change that Potter described involved the transfer of once broad authority into very few hands, failure to follow a decision-making procedure meant to be "open," frequent buck passing, and even subterfuge.[9]

But infinitely worse in Brent's eyes than the aesthetic failings of the new Mass was the possibility that some new Masses might not be Masses at all, that "the celebrating priest does not intend what the Church intends." Still, we must persevere in our fidelity, he told *Triumph* readers. "The Church of Rome, however poor her furnishings, however tawdry her dress, is home. It is Christ's home, who wishes us with Him during the night, as He signals us down these strange corridors into a new day."[10]

Sometimes Brent's protests moved beyond words to action. For example, at Mass one Sunday, coming to the front of their church to receive communion, the Bozells knelt down according to the old form instead of remaining afoot according to the new. Challenged by this defiant brigade of redheads (arranged in a horizontal line—a battle line—in order of size), the priest obeyed their silent but thunderous command. Instead of placing the host in their hands, as the new liturgy ordained, he bent down and placed it on their outthrust tongues.[11]

Horrified by the new Mass (she called it "the hootenanny Mass"), Trish feared that the Church's Liturgical Commission would take authentic Catholicism out of the service. "For the first time," she confided to Buckley, "I've come to look on the hierarchy, some of it, with distaste, with the kind of suspicion that presupposes that they are dishonest. And that is a terrible thing to do."

When the pastor of the Bozells' parish church moved statues of the Blessed Virgin and St. Joseph from their customary places near the altar to the back of the building, Trish exploded. The move, she stormed, was an insult to the mother of Christ. Fearing such changes might endanger the faith of her children, she wrote in furious protest to the bishop of Richmond, in whose diocese the parish lay, accusing him of failing to perform his episcopal duties. If the old ways weren't restored by a given date, she put him on notice, she herself would return the statues to their proper places, ring the altar bell (which had ceased to be used) at the proper times, and "intone [prayers] loudly and clearly in Latin." She was "deadly serious," she warned. "The scandal which my actions might attract are [*sic*] picayune by comparison with the scandal of a bishop of the Church who treats his religion with such insouciance."

When she showed the letter to Buckley, his response was scolding. "Why don't you question the religious seriousness of the Pope[?]" he asked. "After all, he is far more responsible than Bishop Russell for the deterioration of standards." And how could she and *Triumph* "plead the necessity of order and authority and then announce that . . . you are going to take matters into your own hands?" Brought up short by these questions, Trish decided not to proceed with her plans.[12]

Brent found the new Catholic schools as dismaying as the new Catholic liturgy. A *Triumph* editorial called "Mater No, Magistra No"

(Brent hadn't yet broken free of the *NR* culture) charged Catholic schools with adopting the values of secular liberalism partly in hopes of getting a slice of state aid. Catholic parents were going to have to begin home schooling. (The Bozells themselves never tried this out—the demands imposed by *Triumph* wouldn't have allowed it—though Brent required his children to spend two hours a day in the summer reading books.) Catholic University, *Triumph* complained, had given up Catholicism for "Americanism" (that is, secular liberalism), while the seminaries, having forgotten the difference between "profession" and "vocation," were now graduating "incompetent professionals and unholy priests."[13]

Ever mindful of the religious education of his own children, Brent kept a wary eye on the schools they attended. He gave Kathy, enrolled at a Catholic boarding school in Connecticut, cab fare so that she could go to Sunday Mass in a nearby town rather than be forced to endure what Trish would have called the school's hootenanny Mass. When Kathy told her father she wanted to drop her religion class since she already knew all about religion, he answered that not even the pope knew all about religion. But he also asked to see her religion textbook. The school had replaced the book with mimeographed handouts, and Brent was displeased with the idea of religion these handouts conveyed. He decided to send Kathy to Spain to continue her schooling.[14] Some of her siblings also went to high school in Spain but then returned to America for college, often the University of Dallas, where Wilhelmsen stood fast as guardian and guarantor of Catholic orthodoxy.

In a speech at a banquet in San Francisco in 1970 celebrating the opening of Thomas Aquinas College, he praised the new school for its traditional Catholic philosophy and spoke scathingly of the Catholic colleges struggling to become indistinguishable from their secular counterparts. The Christianizing of the West would have to begin all over again, he told his audience. The still vibrant spirituality of the East, especially the religious spirit pervading India, might help in this work by inspiring the West to revive its own spiritual heritage.[15]

Another Vatican II enthusiasm that drew Brent's fire was ecumenicism. An early mailing from the Committee for a Conservative Catholic Magazine had spoken of defending "the churches" (not just "the Church") against the secular onslaught, but no sign of that outlook could be found any longer at *Triumph*. In practice, the magazine warned, ecumenicism meant fudging Catholic truth to make it appear reconcilable with Protestant error. A *Triumph* editorial described a joint Catholic-Anglican statement on the Eucharist as "one of the most ambiguous formularies" ever written. Because Anglicans feared transubstantiation "like the plague," Catholic negotiators had deliberately sidestepped verbal precision, hoping to project the appearance of doctrinal accord.

Triumph spotted a similar Catholic willingness to ignore essentials, this time in hopes of lowering school costs, in a plan to merge the Catholic schools of Grand Rapids, Michigan, with their Protestant opposites. Participants in the merger would find common ground, said the Catholic bishop of Grand Rapids, in a "basic Christianity... common to all of us." "A 'basic Christianity... common to all of us' may tickle Bishop Breitenbeck," *Triumph* snapped, "but it is not what the Catholic people hold. It is, in fact, simply a way of describing the American Protestant consensus." Ecumenicism, the magazine fulminated in another editorial, meant giving up Christ in exchange for a spurious "unity."[16] But if Brent objected to theological compromise with non-Catholics, he didn't object to working with them on Catholic terms. One of *Triumph*'s editors, Robert Fox, was a Lutheran.

Nothing set Brent ablaze more quickly than the "life issues." "Birth control, abortion, sterilization, dehumanizing pornography and 'sex education,' population-destroying weapons—all are part of a determined secular policy to lay waste the entire Christian teaching on the sanctity of human life," he declared in a 1970 fund appeal letter. "Christians, quite obviously, must respond."[17] And respond he did, especially on abortion and birth control ("life destruction" and "life prevention," in *Triumph*'s parlance). He condemned euthanasia and assisted suicide as well. *Triumph* said relatively little about capital punishment, however. The editors endorsed the death penalty somewhat hesitantly (as long as it was "properly imposed," they noted). The magazine also published the Jesuit priest Thomas J. Higgins's long and carefully argued natural-law defense of capital punishment, "Why the Death Penalty." Still, Catholic University's David Schindler, a friend of Brent's in the 1990s, doubted that the *Triumph* editor had ever made up his mind on the subject.[18]

As the abortion rights movement gained strength in the years before *Roe v. Wade*, *Triumph* devoted more and more space to attacking it. The magazine also attacked the Catholic bishops for mounting what Brent saw as feeble resistance to the trend. This weakness he blamed on the bishops' acceptance of "pluralism," a live-and-let-live attitude, much praised by liberals, that governed relations among the country's religions and moral codes. The bishops feared that they would infringe on the rights of others if they opposed abortion rights too strenuously, he wrote, but they shouldn't so fear. The right belief was: "Religious pluralism, understood as freedom of worship—yes. Cultural pluralism—emphatically yes. But the Catholic people is not at liberty to agree to withhold from anyone the protection of the moral law."[19]

Catholics weren't trying to force their religion on others, *Triumph* protested. Abortion violated not only Catholic doctrine but also the natural law, which bound all people. The "right" to abort might be backed by an electoral majority and swarms of "Herodian" judges, but that simply made the killing "democratic." Efforts must, of course, be made to preserve antiabortion laws where they still existed and to restore them where they had been repealed. But more had to be done. "Christians" (*Triumph* often wrote "Christians" rather than "Catholics," believing that the only authentic Christians were Catholics) must organize to bring women considering abortion the help that might persuade them "to allow their babies to live."[20]

Even worse than abortion, Brent argued, was birth control. For while abortion "merely cuts . . . short a human experience of Life, and so moves it on to a new experience," birth control "blocks the very entrance of Life." (This reasoning shocked some *Triumph* editors, including Trish.) The so-called world population crisis announced by birth-control advocates was a "myth," *Triumph* contended. State financing of birth-control programs amounted to a new, taxpayer-bankrolled Holocaust.[21]

In July 1968 Pope Paul VI issued his encyclical *Humanae Vitae*, reaffirming the Church's ban on "artificial" contraception. Brent exulted. "Great Day in the Morning" sang out his editorial on the pronouncement, which he followed with a graphic two-part piece on the mystical links between sex, love, and child bearing. ("I was embarrassed," said Trish, the mother of ten, to a visitor.) So great was Brent's joy that, eager to declare it to the world, he plastered his luggage with stickers reading "Viva el Papa."[22]

Catholics who had hoped to see the ban lifted were distressed. McCaffrey criticized the Vatican's appeal to natural law, telling Brent that "by definition" that law was supposed to be "accessible to right reason . . . regardless of faith." Yet *Humanae Vitae* rested on "a doctrine that is intellectually convincing to few Catholics and practically no non-Catholics." Nor did *NR* welcome the pope's decision. The encyclical seemed to envisage "'nature' as a kind of sacred machine with which men cannot tamper," the magazine objected. "We think this is one of those many papal statements the Church will come . . . to regret."[23]

Brent denounced disregard of *Humanae Vitae* as rebellion against papal authority (an authority he described in a different context as affording "the only reliable way of knowing what the Church is—of knowing, indeed, whether there is a Church"). Fervently pursuing his mission of defending the faith, he championed the encyclical not only in *Triumph* but also at public debates, forums, and panel discussions. At a meeting of Washington Catholics to discuss the issue, he denied a right to ignore the papal teaching. Those who did, he bluntly insisted, should leave the Church. At George Washington University for a debate on the encyclical, he and Lawrence (who often accompanied him on such sorties) found themselves facing an overflow crowd rather than the small one the evening's sponsors had expected. Asked if they could stay a while longer, Brent answered for both. "Wherever two or three are gathered in His name," he replied, "Mike and I will stay."[24]

On the whole, Brent thought, the near future of Catholicism looked grim. Differences among Catholics over liturgy, theology, and authority struck him as now so wide that it wouldn't be possible to bridge them. The Church, he concluded, was inexorably headed for schism.[25]

Triumph also commented on secular subjects: communism, Vietnam, nuclear strategy, and the epidemic of urban black rioting, among others. Trained on the moral dimensions of the topics it dealt with, its analysis always yielded an indictment of liberalism, in Brent's view the principal cause of America's decay.

Brent's most durable political position, surviving largely unchanged from his days at Yale, was his anticommunism. Rather than a policy of serious resistance to communism, he continued to argue, Washington preferred a policy based on appeasement. Its occasional attempts to "contain" communism notwithstanding, U.S. anticommunism remained a "self-evident joke." True resistance had become an exclusively "Christian enterprise."

If he saw only falseness in "official" anticommunist policy, he found something worthy of praise in the communist enemy. Unlike Americans, he wrote, communists didn't drop principle to promote good feeling. Watching a Polish communist at a would-be ecumenical gathering with liberal Catholics at Vermont's St. Michael's College in 1965, he thought the Pole's unwavering loyalty to his faith "might have pleased St. Michael, if only as a demonstration of manliness." He also noted that the Pole had had a Catholic upbringing and was rumored to have served in his youth as an altar boy. This history, Brent implied, accounted for the man's steely firmness.[26]

The Vietnam War proved American anticommunism's bad faith, Brent believed. The war had begun, in *Triumph*'s reading of events, as an effort by South Vietnam's Catholics to block the takeover of their country by communist North Vietnam and its southern collaborators. The United States had entered the struggle against the communists not in hopes of advancing a Christian purpose but rather in pursuit of its Cold War containment strategy. To promote political cohesion in South Vietnam, Washington had then abetted the murder of the country's "divisive" Catholic president, after which South Vietnam had become more unstable. Unable to win the war, Lyndon Johnson had begun alternating the carrot of bribery (massive development aid for the Mekong basin) with the stick of heavy bombing to force the communists to accept a compromise peace. The agreement Washington sought would require the communists to recognize an independent, noncommunist South Vietnam (at least in the short run, to allow U.S. forces to leave without looking defeated) in exchange for broad communist participation in a South Vietnamese coalition government. Johnson's successor, Richard Nixon, was continuing this policy. Thus, a war once waged to exclude the communists from power was now being waged to *bring* them to power in a way that wouldn't embarrass the American government—which exposed American anticommunism for the farce it was.[27]

Brent also decried the doctrine of mutual assured destruction (MAD) governing U.S. nuclear strategy. Moral principle furnished the basis of his view. "War may—often must—be waged," *Triumph* asserted, "but may not be waged sinfully" by targeting civilians for destruction. No matter how dire the consequences of nuclear restraint might be—and it could lead even to total American defeat— Christianity forbade the deliberate killing of civilians. Hence, no MAD-style strike could be looked on as morally permissible. "Better Dead or Red than Sinful" was the Christian standpoint.

Less objectionable than MAD, Brent reasoned, would be a strategy based on a "thickened" antimissile defense and a counterforce aimed with great precision at the enemy's launching pads. But the best course would be to heed the Vatican and junk nuclear missiles, since such weapons were "*immoral in possession as well as in use.*" After all, an America left open to conquest would fare better than one left open to "the judgment and wrath of God."²⁸ Brent had turned sharply from his position of 1963, when he had headed the *NR*-led effort to block a treaty banning atmospheric nuclear testing.

Grand-scale rioting, looting, sniping, and arson in poor black urban neighborhoods, a major domestic problem of the late 1960s, prompted an oddly romantic interpretation at *Triumph*. Without quite saying so, the magazine seemed to relish these explosions as proof that the liberal state was breaking down. Blacks had no interest in the trash liberals held out to them, the magazine contended, but rather seemed eager to "burst violently through the flesh into the realm of the Spirit." Moved by "a need to find some spiritual value beyond the sterile legal and material satisfactions offered them in the name of equality," they were rebelling against meaninglessness, longing for "contact with the divine." Yet in response liberals were promising them only "the cold technological rationalism of secular democracy." This promise came from a "fatally flawed Anglo-Saxon culture that first enslaved and animalized [blacks], and then attempted to appease [their] wrath by inviting [them] to eat heartily on its rotten remnants." Not surprisingly, blacks didn't respond—or rather, did their responding with Molotov cocktails. The Black Power movement—"with a prudent utilization"—could, perhaps, accomplish America's salvation, *Triumph* suggested. The movement had the potential to "play a leading role in breaking up the secular behemoth, and so restore liberty and human dignity to America."²⁹

The sole cure for social disorder, racial or otherwise, *Triumph* advised in an editorial called "Soul, Brother," was the Christianization of government and society, which would lead to "a social order harmonized with ultimate reality." In Lawrence's opinion, expressed in an article on *Triumph*'s first three years of publication, "Soul, Brother" marked a key shift in the magazine's viewpoint. The editorial represented *Triumph*'s first explicit call for a Catholic theocracy, declaring that the Church must act as "the guiding hand" in public life. But this view entailed a problem, Lawrence admitted. Corroded by its quasi-embrace of liberalism, the Church no longer seemed qualified to play such a role.[30]

During his *Triumph* stage, Brent seldom paid heed to economics—and when he did, he treated market economics with contempt. When he wrote the name "Adam Smith," for example, he usually modified it with phrases such as "moral ass." Economics wasn't important, one *Triumph* editor assured him. The magazine should devote its attention to "higher truths." On the rare occasions Brent discussed the dismal science, he approached economic issues as problems of personal morality, to be dealt with in the light of Christian moral teaching. (Economics, he maintained, was "a Christian subject, which cannot possibly be understood without understanding the Incarnation.") He took instruction from the papal social encyclicals, especially Leo XIII's *Rerum Novarum* (1891), which rejected "socialism" (statist, materialist, hostile to private property) and "capitalism" (ruthlessly competitive, selfishly individualist, profit-crazed) in favor of a private-property-based cooperative economy, heavily leavened with the practice of Christian altruism, that would make its top priority the common good.

Brent was also influenced by the Catholic essayist and historian Hilaire Belloc (the subject of Wilhelmsen's first book), whose work *The Servile State* (1912) opposed capitalism and socialism in equal measure for reducing ordinary people to servile status. To avoid the concentrations of power these systems produced, Belloc advocated widespread small property ownership, in his eyes a major bulwark of personal freedom. He found his economic vision realized in Europe's medieval economy (small-scale, decentralized, communal).

Brent found little virtue, however, in Paul VI's encyclical *Populorum Progressio* (1967), which urged a global redistribution of wealth on behalf of the poor countries. In Brent's eyes, the papal plan exuded utopianism, disdain for property rights, and a totalitarian, communistic tendency, and hence provided a blueprint for further decline.[31]

Judging by *Triumph*'s Letters to the Editor page, reactions to the magazine ranged from delight to revulsion. Many readers rejoiced in the fledgling *Triumph*, which so forcefully voiced their own attachments and resentments. A large number of these fans probably also read *National Review*, and given the similar views of the two magazines in *Triumph*'s early days, they may have regarded the two as in essence really one. Such people were soon to suffer a painful shock.

National Review welcomed *Triumph* "jubilantly" as the journal conservative Catholics had so long pined for. The most prominent Catholic publications were liberal, *NR* once again complained, and their content amounted "to a desacralization of Christendom." But now—"At Last" was the editorial's title—a challenger had entered the lists. Even where some *Triumph* writers disagreed with *NR*, the editorial noted, these differences paled beside those separating the two magazines from their liberal rivals. In this judgment *NR* turned out to be wrong—or right only briefly. Differences, yes; trivial ones, no—as the future would reveal.

After *Triumph*'s third issue, Brent asked Neal Freeman to give his opinion of the magazine. Freeman handed in a mixed review, beginning with praise but ending with pointed criticisms. *Triumph* didn't look "exciting," he observed. "A good layout is the best investment you can make." He also stressed the need for livelier writing, for a style that would brighten the magazine's cheerless tone. "I have the feeling," he said, "that in secret ballot your writers would have opted for [the name] Armageddon rather than Triumph."

One recipient of a prepublication copy of the magazine reacted with disgust. "I hope your magazine will either never appear or very soon be forbidden to appear," wrote the Austrian Catholic baroness Maria Augusta von Trapp of the Trapp Family Singers. "How can grown-up intelligent Catholics be such an obstacle to the workings of the Holy Ghost?" Brent published the letter but didn't append a reply.[32]

Commonweal, one of the two always-cited examples of the kind of magazine *Triumph* was founded to oppose, mentioned it only in passing. Noting the publication of Thomas Molnar's latest book, the liberal Catholic journal identified Molnar as an editor at "the new conservative Catholic magazine *Triumph*." And that was the sum of it.[33] The second always-cited example, the Jesuit weekly *America*, took no notice of its new opponent at all.

A Rockwellian childhood in Omaha

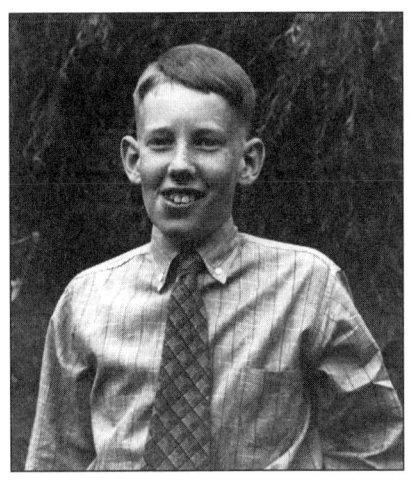

Brent's father, Leo Brent Bozell Sr. (right), nearly converted to Catholicism; the Episcopalian family sent young Brent to a Catholic high school, Creighton Prep (below: Brent is third row, fourth from right)

A formidable partnership: After forming a nearly unbeatable debate team at Yale, Brent and his friend William F. Buckley Jr. (left) partnered to write the provocative book McCarthy and His Enemies. *Here they are at work on the manuscript.*

Brent joined the extended Buckley clan when he married Bill's favorite sister, Trish. (Brent and Trish are standing far right; Bill and his wife, Pat, are standing far left.)

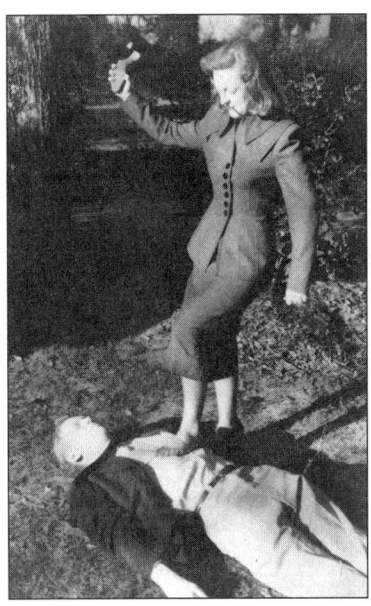

A playful moment for Brent and Trish

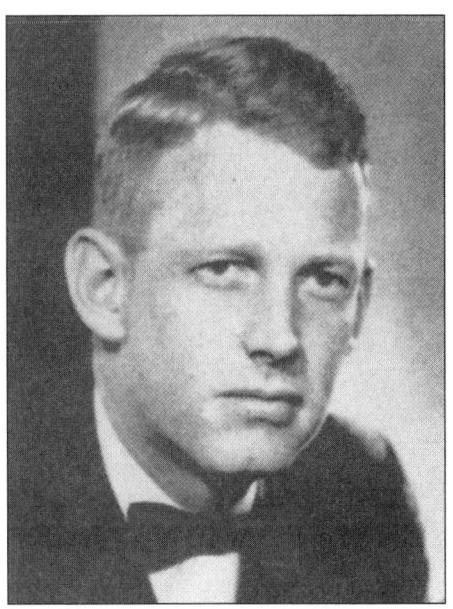

McCarthy, Goldwater, National Review: *rising conservative star*

The Bozells in the 1960s: (from left to right) Brent III, Patricia, Michael, Kathy, William, Trish, Christopher, Aloise, Brent, Maureen, and John. A tenth child, James, was born in 1966.

"The Catholic thing": in starting Triumph, *Brent was dedicating himself to his primary concerns—and, perhaps, trying to escape Bill Buckley's shadow*

With son Michael, a Benedictine monk, in 1979; one of Brent's happiest moments in later years came when Michael was ordained as a priest in 1994

ELEVEN

Autumn in America

"*Triumph* is invariably called a 'conservative Catholic' magazine, but we prefer to be known as 'radical Christian,'" *Triumph*'s editors announced five months after the magazine's first issue appeared.[1] The statement seems strange. Brent himself had routinely spoken of *Triumph* as a "conservative Catholic" magazine. To deepen the mystery, what the editors meant by "radical" wasn't clear. They didn't intend to imply theological novelty: *Triumph* never strayed from the doctrine of the Baltimore Catechism, long used for religious instruction in parochial schools. Nor did they mean a tolerant attitude toward violence, a tactical option that Brent almost always opposed. Rather, they seem to have meant (as evidenced by the contents of *Triumph*) something like taking Catholic doctrine as the rule in all moral judgments, standing by Catholic beliefs now under siege, maintaining fidelity to the faith come hell or high water.

But however the editors understood the term *radical*, *Triumph* was also turning radical in the word's everyday sense, expressing "extreme" opinions in "extreme" language and calling for "extreme" action to achieve its ends. For example, it flayed the bishops (who were accustomed to receiving deference from the Catholic press) for what it considered their treason on abortion, and it did so in language that conveyed its disgust with their behavior. A typical *Triumph* blast declared, "The bishops' abortion statement—calm, measured, reasoned, a debater's brief instead of a crusader's banner—was a contemptible surrender."[2]

Explanations for *Triumph*'s radicalization usually focus on Brent, who alone determined the magazine's outlook and tone. Thomas Molnar thought Brent had succumbed to a kind of "mysticism" that got in the way of attempts at moderation. But Molnar also attributed Brent's radicalism to what he called "a quite serious jealousy" of Buckley, vented through articles (root-and-branch attacks on America, for example) he thought would cause Buckley pain. Changes in the Church's "atmosphere," Molnar added, likewise contributed to making a radical of Brent. Buckley blamed Brent's radicalism on the spirit of the age, writing that the *Triumph* editor had absorbed the "antinomian" ambience of the 1960s, when "formulations *à outrance*" had become the norm. Mike Lawrence, too, cited the pull of the historical moment. Two developments had drawn *Triumph* (that is, Brent) to "new themes," more radical themes: Pope Paul VI's decision to crack down on departures from orthodoxy and a level of disorder in America that foretold the coming collapse of the liberal system. Russell Kirk thought Brent had been seized by "the demon of the absolute," which had lent an extremist flavor to his writings and led him to "look for a dogma in all things." Neal Freeman, remembering Brent's later mental illness, wondered whether the tinder within him that eventually burst into flame hadn't already begun to smolder in the late 1960s.

Despite Brent's radical turn, his new persona had much in common with his old one. Impatient, combative, passionate in his attachment to his principles, and hostile by instinct to compromise, he had long revealed a tendency toward radical rhetoric, as shown by his *NR* columns attacking Eisenhower. The feverish '60s propelled this tendency forward, and a magazine committed to defending tradition and orthodoxy turned into what a later observer called "probably the most countercultural samizdat around."[3]

❖   ❖   ❖   ❖

The year 1968 revealed the depth of Brent's radicalization. That year, he published three articles in *Triumph*—one each on the Constitution, the Catholic Church in America, and the American way of life—that set forth his thoughts on what he saw as the country's pathology and laid bare his estrangement from mainstream American society.

"You did me the kindness of saying kind things about [*The Warren Revolution*] when it came out," Brent wrote to Kirk in February 1968. "I now think you were too kind, which I try to explain in the current *Triumph*." He was talking about an article called "The Death of the Constitution,"[4] in which he announced that he wouldn't continue his Supreme Court book, for which he had earlier promised a second volume. Since Americans no longer wanted a constitutional republic, he said, he saw no point in going ahead with the project. But more important, he had come to realize that the Constitution had never possessed legitimacy. A product of the liberal mentality of an earlier age, it vested final authority not in God, from whom all genuine authority flowed (and whom the Constitution never once mentioned), but in "the people." Hence, it placed no limit on the popular will and furnished no veto if "the people" chose evil over good. "The Constitution has not only failed," he wrote, "it was bound to fail. The architects of our constitutional order built a house in which secular liberalism could live, and given the dominant urges of the age, would live. The time has come to leave that house and head for home."

Coming from the author of *The Warren Revolution*, which had appeared only a year and a half earlier, this reversal was stunning. The Constitution's defender had suddenly become its assailant.

In the second article, "The Autumn of the Church,"[5] Brent exposed more fully than elsewhere in his writings what he saw as the root of the Catholic episcopate's cowardice. After a long period of expansion, he argued, the Church in America had yielded much of its influence to liberalism. Many bishops had rushed to board the liberal bandwagon, waving passes from the major formulator of the pluralist idea, the Jesuit political philosopher John Courtney Murray. (Although *Triumph* published several conservative Jesuit writers, it opposed the liberal outlook of many Jesuits, calling them "workaday renegades.")

In his book *We Hold These Truths: Catholic Reflections on the American Proposition* (1960),[6] Murray called the Constitution's First Amendment provisions regarding religion (no congressional establishment of a national church and no congressional interference in the free exercise of religion) "articles of peace" between the Catholic Church, whose traditional political ideal was a Catholic state, and the religiously neutral American republic. These provisions, enshrining the pluralist principle of religious tolerance, made America a hospitable place for Catholics, who could practice their minority faith there undisturbed. But all coins had two sides: beneficiaries of tolerance themselves, Catholics must in turn tolerate the religions of others and refrain from attempts to impose their own on the country.

This bargain had worked well, Brent commented, as long as the Church and America had seen eye to eye. Until recently, for example, both had forbidden abortion. But that time had passed. On several important issues, the Church and the American government now stood at odds. Yet whenever they differed with "the national secular establishment," the bishops shrank back from taking a forceful stand, unwilling to violate the golden rule of pluralism. "The American Church has married the American State," Brent concluded, and "is thereby committed to its secular values and goals." The bishops wished to be American more than Catholic.

The Church would recover from this flabbiness, Brent assured readers. (Before his Ascension, Christ had promised his apostles that he would be with them "always, even unto the end of the world.") But its near-term future had to be viewed with foreboding. "If she is to protect herself and if she is to abide by her divine mission to teach all peoples," contended a 1970 *Triumph* editorial probably written by Brent, the American Church "must break [Murray's] Articles of Peace; she must renounce the pluralist system; she must forthrightly acknowledge that a state of war exists between herself and the American political order."⁷

In the final article of his 1968 trio, "The Autumn of the Country,"⁸ Brent widened his target from the Constitution and the Catholic episcopate to take in the liberal culture pervading both. "The liberal Republic is coming down," he announced. "It could be a matter of months, at most a few years, before the wreckage is visibly upon us." The proximate cause he identified as a widespread abdication of authority by its customary holders, ranging from government and university officials to parents. Thus, parents raising children knew "nothing of moral and spiritual limitations," he charged, adding, "They haven't the faintest idea of what to forbid, or why." He found the underlying cause of such problems in "the American creed": liberalism. The "central tenet" of this creed—"man is on his own"—"came down to a revolt against God," Brent wrote.

The myriad woes now plaguing the country might have a further cause, he speculated. God might be punishing America to "cleanse and purify" it and to "invite us to try again to renew the world in Christ." But the fulfillment of this purpose lay far in the future. For now, a somber era loomed. If liberalism was Christianity's enemy, and if liberalism also shaped the spirit of America, then Christianity and America must be enemies too. For years Brent had looked upon *America* and *liberalism* as antonyms. Now he decided that they had been synonyms all along.

"Yes, we are patriots; but we are Christians first," *Triumph*'s editors declared in the magazine's maiden issue.⁹ By 1968 the first clause of this statement seemed questionable. America was "a vast moral and spiritual wasteland," *Triumph* thundered. The American credo held that "salvation comes from democracy, education, a nifty standard of living, and a stockpile of nuclear bombs." Catholics (and many non-

Catholics "of good will") were becoming increasingly convinced of "a hard fact: that non-Catholic America is morally disgusting. It is a panorama of evils: gay liberation, women's liberation, pills, pornography, sterility and murdered babies . . . a society based on divorce and consumption, contemptuous of the past because it has none." *Triumph*'s April 1970 cover showed a pregnant Statue of Liberty holding aloft a coat hanger (stereotyped tool of the kitchen-table abortionist) in place of a torch. This, claimed *Triumph*, was the meaning of American freedom.[10]

Brent's anger at Americans wasn't by any means new. He had already lambasted his countrymen during the Eisenhower years for failing to recognize the danger that communism posed. But now he voiced his anger even more bitterly. His anti-Americanism led to division at the magazine. For if his colleagues shared his hostility to "secular liberalism," some, including Trish, thought that when it came to America "in general," he went overboard. Farley Clinton, for example, couldn't abide Brent's assumption that "the US of A was a horrible place, not merely horrible but irredeemable." Lawrence, on the other hand, recently told an inquirer that he couldn't recall dissenting from Brent's writings, which he thought had something to offer beyond hostility. "What *Triumph* was about, most fundamentally," he wrote, was "idolatry." The magazine hoped to "expose the besetting, characteristic idolatry of Americans, which consisted . . . in worship of America." *Triumph* wanted to help Americans to "throw off their bondage to their strange god and to return to allegiance to the Lord our God." Brent tried to teach them that America wasn't their messiah. It was this message, Lawrence contended, and not the "churchy stuff," such as attacks on the new liturgy, for which *Triumph* should be remembered.[11]

While agreeing with some of his criticisms of America, Brent's Buckley-stage friends rejected his overall view. But such differences didn't require the severance of friendships. Frank Meyer happily visited the Bozells at Montejurra, where he and Brent continued their endless duel. William Rusher, perhaps humoring a man he considered a harmless eccentric, replied amiably to Brent's broadsides against mainstream conservatism, and Kirk still favored *Triumph* with book reviews. Earnest, forthright, and, for all his dark portrayals of America, often in high spirits, Brent in person remained as hard as ever for conservatives to dislike.

But one friend admonished him. Neil McCaffrey, whom Lee Edwards described as "a firebrand Catholic" and who was eager to see more conservatives in Catholic journalism, had invested a wealth of hope in the newborn *Triumph*. Soon, however, McCaffrey began to fret. "I want to register some disquiet about the course [*Triumph*] is taking," he wrote to Brent in November 1967. "Must the defense of orthodoxy involve alienation from American values?" Was it credible that America headed "Satan's Empire"? Why did Brent seem to "rejoice" in the country's troubles? And why did he treat conventional conservatives so harshly? McCaffrey noted that he had heard about a colloquy of Catholic journalists where Brent had urged his colleagues to "vomit out of your mouth and being the word, approach, and mood of 'Conservative.'" Did such talk make sense? There was also a practical matter to bear in mind. Probably everyone who subscribed to *Triumph* was a conservative. Was Brent wise to tell his readers he despised them?

Brent answered by reiterating that those in the *Triumph* circle "are patriots and hold the usual prejudices in favor of the fatherland." But he quickly added that "our calling is to assert Christianity, not Americanism, and the two . . . are not always compatible." American values that clashed with Christian values were "spurious." The American Church was collapsing because it was trying "to be more American than Catholic." The Church's faith shouldn't be confused with the nation's.

Brent told McCaffrey that his article "The Death of the Constitution" "was written to you." McCaffrey read the piece at Brent's request and found its assertions extreme. He also heard a utopian note in the article that put him in mind of what Brent had decried as "gnosticism." He warned in a letter to *Triumph* that, like liberals,

"Mr. Bozell needs reminding . . . : His kingdom is not of this world." Commenting on the two "Autumn" articles, McCaffrey seconded their criticisms but not their "apocalyptic" tone or "hand-rubbing glee over our troubles." "The way to save society," he instructed the magazine, "is not to dismantle it, then hope to reconstruct it by saying the rosary. This is utopian, and irresponsible." As a penance, Brent should spend a year reading "friendly yet candid" Church histories, especially Ronald Knox's *Enthusiasm*, a history of heretical extravagances in the Catholic Church.[12]

Brent almost never granted anything to his critics. But he did once admit that when angered he might go too far. The occasion was a *Triumph* article by James K. Fitzpatrick, a columnist for *The Wanderer* and a New York area antiabortion activist. Called "Dear Triumph, Do You Really Mean It?" the article took Brent to task for unbalanced criticism. "Dammit," Fitzpatrick protested, "the country just isn't that sick." Brent replied that he loved the American people ("which, because they are my people, I prefer in the main to any other") and the American landscape ("because it is mine," and because God had "showered upon it an inordinate amount of his beauty"). It was America's spiritual pretensions that *Triumph* scorned. But he conceded that *Triumph*'s reputation for anti-Americanism was partly "of our own making," that "the tone and possibly the rhetoric of some things we have written in the past—and perhaps still write—have needlessly contributed to the impression." Tone came from feeling, he added, and he felt "quite angry."[13]

In July 1969 Brent received a subscription renewal check from a Sister Isabel, a Maryknoll nun and devoted reader of *Triumph*. Calling down God's blessing on his work, she also implored him, "Please do not quarrel with WILLY BUCKLEY for he is my friend."[14] Her plea came too late. By this time, the Brent-Buckley friendship was faltering badly.

Much of the trouble seemed to stem from Brent's religious views. As Buckley later put it, "Brent went further than I would do in pressing the demands of our Church in the secular realm." But there were other sore points. *Triumph's* anti-Americanism, sounding to Buckley "as hostile to the American ethos as any revolutionary organ of the hard Left," added to the tension growing between them. In addition, Buckley criticized *Triumph* without pulling punches. Asked by the acutely sensitive Brent what he thought of the article "Soul, Brother," *NR*'s editor replied that he found the piece "impossibly diffuse," truly dreadful in its wordiness and sprawl. Buckley also reacted to "The Death of the Constitution" with dismay, mourning Brent's "derogation of [*The Warren Revolution*]" and dismissing the *Triumph* piece as a mere "act of piety." *Triumph* (that is, Brent) was "adamantly naive" to suppose that the Constitution would never have fallen "if the Lord had been explicitly invited to serve as [its] initiator," he wrote to the magazine. Even if the framers had founded "a God-oriented America," within weeks the country would have been "racked with the conventional secular anxieties."[15]

Yet despite the tension between them, the two still seemed to be friends. In their private correspondence, they continued to call each other "Will" and "Butch," nicknames preserving the memory of happier times. Brent praised a Buckley column on American Catholicism, and Trish told her brother how much Brent had liked an article he had written for *Commonweal*. When Buckley came close to punching the novelist Gore Vidal before a national television audience at the 1968 Democratic convention and then felt depressed about the incident, Brent, hoping to lift Buckley's spirits, applauded his rage.

Meanwhile, Brent continued to benefit from Buckley's assistance. When he needed help finding another hand for *Triumph*'s office, he turned to Buckley, who came up with one. When he landed in what he described as "a very rough" financial squeeze, he borrowed the money that bailed him out from Buckley. When he needed an extra car, he bought a used one for ten dollars from Buckley. "Thanks again," he wrote to Buckley in August 1968, "for the continuing help with Chris' schooling" (for which Buckley was footing the tuition bill).[16] Trish's status as Buckley's favorite sister may have offset any embarrassment Brent felt about this ongoing stream of favors. Outwardly, at least, he seemed comfortable with the pattern.

Yet for all his appearance of equanimity, Brent hated the strain that burdened his relations with Buckley. He linked the problem with differences over religious issues. But he also sensed that its root lay in something deeper, something emotionally much harder to come to grips with: the divergence in status between two close friends who had started out as equals. Once, they had been perfectly relaxed in each other's company; now they felt awkward, even embarrassed. Everything had changed, but they had to pretend that it hadn't.

Longing to put an end to the tension, Brent decided to make an all-out effort to do so. The Buckley-Vidal incident may have inspired the decision, since it revived for a moment his earlier intimacy with Buckley, exactly the kind of bond he hoped to restore. Toward the beginning of autumn, he proposed to Buckley that they meet to discuss their relationship. Buckley (to judge by a follow-up letter he received from Brent) replied with suggestions for a meeting place and an agenda. But Brent thought both of these wrong for what he had in mind. "You misunderstand me completely," he wrote back.

> I don't want to discuss your soul. . . . Neither do I want to talk about Humanae Vitae or such like. . . . I want to renew our friendship. I don't want to become "acquainted" with you, which is a silly foundation which ignores how deeply you and I continue to penetrate each other after twenty years. I want to resume our friendship, step by step if necessary, so that we can somehow find ourselves captured by our former intimacy. Miami or Bermuda races are not right for this. [An avid sailor, Buckley seems to have suggested that they hold their meeting during a regatta he had entered.] We need 24 undistracted hours to relax and be serious and laugh, as nature moves us. I very much want this.[17]

In the end, they met at Buckley's home in Stamford, Connecticut, where they talked for hours beside the swimming pool. Brent appears to have been desperate to succeed. In his reply to Buckley's letter, he had even proposed that if religious disagreements impeded a renewal of their friendship, then he wanted to "exclude those subjects" from the talk. But despite his efforts, the meeting failed.

The reason for the failure can't be confidently explained, since neither participant left an account of the meeting. But probably both shied away from any mention of the problem's root—not disagreement over birth control or abortion or the proper role of the Catholic Church in American life or the right tactics for promoting Catholic interests but rather their painful uneasiness with the status gap that had separated them in recent years.

If the Stamford failure came as a blow to Brent, it probably came as an equal blow to Trish, who feared the prospect of a break between her husband and her brother. Right after the meeting, she wrote a long letter to Buckley "to bring Brent's attitude toward you into understandable focus." But dissatisfied with what she called her "flailing attempt" to explain Brent, she made a fresh attempt a few days later. In her first letter, she wrote, she had used words such as "'envy' and 'jealousy' as being formerly between you."

> That's so inexact. Before *Triumph* [Brent] felt caged by being put (by himself as well, perhaps) in an eternal position of comparison vis-à-vis you. It was a competition neither one of you looked for or wished, and his awareness of your embarrassment at being "ahead" made him set up a defensive barrier against your own—your near pity, your overwhelming sensitivity and niceness to him which he sensitively and rightly perceived as compensatory, and therefore unnatural, in the sense that your and Brent's friendship has always presupposed an equal respect.

But after that period, she continued, Brent had changed. He had finally discovered what he wanted to do with his life—defend the faith—and so had founded *Triumph*. At that point he had lost "his fear of appearing pitiable." He was able to see Buckley's goodness to him as kindness rather than pity. Moved by "love and gratitude . . . too long suppressed," he had gone to meet with Buckley

> not just to save your soul, but to re-establish the former, deeply missed rapport. He wanted to present himself as once more being in a position to help you, should you ever need it or wish it. He wanted to say, "I'm well again, sure again, and between us there is something that doesn't boggle at talking about ultimate things even though in disagreement. Let's stop staying away from each other as persons. There are too few in each of our lives not to make a separation, one from the other, a deeply felt hole."[18]

Trish's diagnosis hit the bull's-eye in some respects but not all. The time she associated with Brent's healing—the start of the *Triumph* era—was too early. The day was coming when the Buckley spell would evaporate, but in 1968, let alone 1966, it hadn't yet arrived. (How Buckley replied to Trish is no longer known.)

After the Stamford meeting, the Brent-Buckley relationship remained in a rut. Sometimes letters between the two conveyed a sense of closeness. In January 1969, for example, they discussed Chris Bozell's chances of getting into Yale, wondering how much Brent's "legacy" might affect the odds. After Meyer's death in 1972, Brent contributed a eulogy to a collection in *National Review* and sounded right at home in his old milieu. But at other times, their exchanges were sheathed in ice. Planning to publish an anthology of modern conservative thought, Buckley sought Brent's permission to include excerpts from *The Warren Revolution*. Brent turned him down, replying, "It would be good discipline for you to write your own books," to which Buckley riposted, "I marvel at the behavior of someone who would lead others into Christian habits."[19] (Soon after, however, Brent granted the desired permission.) And all the while, Brent attacked Buckley's stand on abortion, denouncing it as formalistic and anemic.

In reality, the Butch-Will relationship was dead. No single event can be cited to date its demise, but from the early 1970s to the mid-1980s direct contact between the onetime friends ended, and Trish became their sole remaining link. At this stage Brent escaped the Buckley spell, letting go of the moribund friendship, recovering his freedom, and ceasing to fear that others might view him with pity. The only continuing reminders of his Buckley trauma were occasional anti-Buckley flare-ups.

In March 1969, six months after the Stamford meeting, Brent published a piece called "Letter to Yourselves"—"Yourselves" being his former comrades of the mainstream Right.[20] Lawrence later described the article as Brent's "decisive severance of himself and *Triumph*" from conventional conservatism. Farley Clinton characterized it more pungently as Brent's spitting "right in the eye of William F. Buckley Jr." Brent himself explained it more companionably as an attempt "to encourage a common advance toward political wisdom."[21]

As a political statement, "Letter to Yourselves" offered nothing new. Brent had already aired its message in "Freedom or Virtue?," "The Autumn of the Country," and other articles. This time, however, he fixed his sights less on liberalism than on what he called "secular-conservatism," for which "Letter to Yourselves" served simultaneously as a death certificate, an obituary notice, and an autopsy report.

Conservatism had died with the Goldwater debacle, Brent wrote. Its death became indisputable in 1968 when the victorious Nixon, whom conservatives had supported, paid them back by giving them the brush-off. Proof of the movement's death was easy to find. The liberal order had collapsed, but conservatives weren't responsible for bringing it down, and no one was asking conservatives to supply a replacement. Moreover, although liberals had just suffered a defeat of historic proportions, they had never yet lost to conservatives in a critical fight.

Two illusions were blinding conservatives to the reasons for their failure. First, they believed conservatism differed from liberalism in its very essence, when in fact the two movements were branches of the same tree. Both were descended from nineteenth-century classical liberalism, and both had inherited their ancestor's highest ideal: individual self-fulfillment. Today's liberals, looking at life from a largely material standpoint, saw economics as the key to self-fulfillment. Conservatives, like their classical liberal ancestors, saw moral discipline as the key to self-fulfillment and the unaided individual will as the source of moral discipline. But here conservatives were taking leave of reality, for only an elite possessed such force of will. To maintain moral discipline, most people needed the help of Christianity, while the Church, for its part, had to have public support. Yet conservatives, true to their liberal lineage, favored a fully secular public realm.

Here lay secular conservatism's second illusion: the idea that "politics—the ordering of the public life—can proceed without continuing reference to God." True, many on the Right were not only friendly to Christianity but were also practicing Christians. Yet most of them treated religion in the liberal fashion, as something purely personal, and denied Christianity its place in the public realm. They hadn't acknowledged "the Christian teaching that the proper goal of the orderers of the public life was to help open men to Christ." Their blindness to this truth had led to conservatism's failure, since as long as its principles made it the right wing of liberalism, conservatism had little hope of achieving success. With this restatement of his familiar theocratic outlook, Brent concluded his graveside reflections on the mainstream Right.

But more soon followed. A month later Brent published a companion article, "Politics of the Poor,"[22] which elaborated on positions he had taken in "Letter to Yourselves." "The public life," he repeated, "is supposed to help a man be a Christian." The "poor" (the mass of ordinary people) needed the supportive environment of a formally Christian society to receive and retain the Christian message. Here Brent quoted his anti-Murray, the French Jesuit scholar Jean Daniélou, who wrote that it was *"practically impossible for any but the militant Christian to persevere in a milieu which offers him no support."* Hence, to fulfill its most important function, that of helping people to be Christian, the public authority would have to set up *"sensible signs of the divine"*—for example, plenty of Christian art in public places. In such an environment the Church's importance would grow.

The sketch of a Christian polity in "Politics of the Poor" drew heavily on Brent's experience of Spain, always his model of an explicitly Christian society. (In 1970 he began writing a column called "Near to the Escorial," telling readers that Philip II's church-monastery-palace complex was "a place which I do not find it good to be far away from for too long a time.")[23] But for all its Spanish Catholic inspiration, his vision also suggests that of today's Muslim militants (though without religious violence and persecution)—that is to say, a society unified by a common revealed religion supported by the civil power, which sees its main purpose as promoting the faith, enforcing God's will, and aiding the progress of its people toward the joys of paradise.

"Letter to Yourselves" and "Politics of the Poor" received criticism from several regular *NR* contributors, who in measured tones denied the death of conservatism and warned against staking the future on Christendom's rebirth. But *NR* itself—which is to say, Buckley—reacted with weary scorn, replying that "to dismiss even contemporary America as one vast plot against the survival of our eternal souls is Manichean and boring."

Brent shot back. "*Triumph* is 'anti-conservative'?" he asked. "Okay. Boring? Well . . . Manichean???" *Triumph* was trying to bring God back, "visible and resplendent," into public life, rather than keep Him shut up out of the way in churches. This might be boring, but it wasn't at all Manichean.[24]

Brent worried about how "Letter to Yourselves" would strike conservatives, fearing it might cost him some old friends. Right after the article's publication, he sent a copy to Rusher with a request for comments. "I run the risk of offending you," he told *NR*'s publisher. "I am most anxious not to do that." Rusher replied equably. Perhaps seeking to humor Brent, whose feelings he seemed to want to spare, he ignored the article's theocratic core, quietly affirmed conservatism's long-term promise, and applauded the clarity with which Brent had set forth his opinions (this last a tried-and-true way of bestowing praise while at the same time withholding approval). But this even-toned answer failed to reassure Brent. "He's now disgusted with himself for what he thinks is a sanctimonious aura he gives the piece," Trish told Buckley. He had had such an essay in mind for quite a while and wanted to get everything "just right." But now that he had done the job, he thought he had botched it.[25]

According to a 1969 *Triumph* survey, 88 percent of the magazine's subscribers identified themselves as Catholics, and 50 percent as Republicans, of whom 44 percent considered themselves "moderately" conservative. But 65 percent of the entire sample had voted for Nixon in 1968, which implied that most subscribers were opposed to liberalism. Seventy-two percent had college or postgraduate degrees, and 45 percent called themselves professionals. Forty-six percent fell between the ages of thirty-five and fifty-four, but only 55 percent were married, which may mean that many subscribers belonged to the clergy. About half recommended *Triumph* to their friends. Twenty-eight percent subscribed to between six and ten other magazines, but a discouraging 95 percent of this group said that if asked to pick their favorites, they would name as their fourth choice or better a magazine other than *Triumph*.[26]

The number of *Triumph* subscribers is hard to gauge. Records are no longer extant, and when they were, subscribers' names often lingered on the magazine's mailing list long after their subscriptions had run out. Brent noted in a letter to subscribers that in the magazine's first year of publication (September 1966 to September 1967) their number had risen from four thousand to more than sixteen thousand. Estimates of the peak figure run as high as thirty thousand. But however high the number actually was, it soon started falling, eventually reaching estimates as low as three thousand. Warren H. Carroll, a major figure at *Triumph* in the 1970s, later wrote that for most of the magazine's history its readership declined.[27]

Triumph's first few months were unusually promising for a magazine of its kind. "I do believe we can survive financially—at least we are determined to try—without asking our friends for charity at this time," Brent wrote to subscribers in the spring of 1967, a time when the six-month-old *Triumph* was adding subscriptions. But the tide soon turned. In October 1967, when *Triumph*'s deficit had reached $100,000, he wrote again, this time with an urgent request for contributions, explaining, "We have been driven to the wall." Only a month later, with the deficit still mounting, he wrote yet again, now "to beg your immediate help to save *Triumph*."[28]

The source of the problem isn't hard to find. From the outset, *Triumph* had rested on a narrow base. As Freeman once remarked, *NR* had only "a sliver" of the country's magazine readership, and Brent, aiming at *NR*'s conservative Catholic readers, was targeting "a sliver of a sliver." *Triumph*'s shift from "conservative Catholic" to "radical Christian" disappointed (and often angered) such people. Learning of *Triumph*'s founding from *National Review*, and envisaging the new magazine as a second *National Review*, they had subscribed—only to find articles attacking their bishops, their country, and conservatism. Trish put the difference between the two magazines this way: "*NR* was read by Americans who were also Catholics; *Triumph* was read by Catholics who were also Americans." True, perhaps, but she might have added that *NR*'s editor seemed to love America, while *Triumph*'s frequently expressed disgust for the country. Molnar thought Brent would have taken his radicalism even further had he not feared losing all his conservative readers.[29] If Molnar was right, then Brent practiced restraint with too little zeal, for conservative Catholic subscribers fled *Triumph* in droves, taking its hope of financial stability with them.

As subscribers vanished and financial pressure mounted, Brent was forced to devote more time to shaking the alms bowl, a chore he hated. *Triumph* "urgently needs $125,000 to stand off present creditors," read a typical fund-raising appeal, sent out in January 1969. The appeal brought in more than $100,000, a sum later supplemented by Brent's long-faithful supporter General Wedemeyer. But such sums didn't cover the relentlessly rising deficit, and the scramble to keep *Triumph* going went on and on. Three months later *Triumph*'s publisher, Donald G. McClane, sent out a new cry for help, this time to the magazine's "special friends." "It would be less than honest to represent *Triumph*'s path as anything but difficult," he wrote. "Month to month survival continues to occupy our time and attention to a large extent."[30]

Red ink, however, doesn't seem to have dampened Brent's spirits, or at least not for long. For as *Triumph*'s prospects declined, his dreams expanded.

TWELVE

Phantom Empire

Toward the end of the 1960s Brent's recurrent restlessness returned. He loved *Triumph* as much as ever, but he hated the drudgery that magazine publishing entailed. Besides, grander ambitions now beckoned. Through *Triumph* he had hoped to reshape the Church in America. The time had come, he now decided, to pursue a larger goal: to make America, and eventually the whole world, Catholic. He would turn *Triumph* over to Mike Lawrence, he told his daughter Kathy, and from headquarters at El Escorial he would lead an apostolate designed to achieve that goal. In 1969 he summarized his aims in *Triumph*: "to preserve the orthodox Christian Faith in the Church, and make [that faith] once again the guiding light of our nation and the world." *Triumph* would act as the apostolate's "advance guard and . . . spokesman."[1]

Making a start in early 1970, he gathered his lieutenants at a monastery near Berryville, Virginia, where they combined a retreat with discussions on building the apostolate.[2] At the center of their planning stood *Triumph*, but the magazine now gained a supplement, an eight-page, biweekly newsletter called *Catholic Currents*. Focusing on Church affairs, the newsletter presented what it called an "unabashedly pro-orthodox" viewpoint against the "biased reporting of the diocesan press."[3] The apostolate's media plans also called for founding a publishing house, the Escorial Press; a Christian Commonwealth Book Club; a film production company; and direct-mail campaigns (the first of which would be called "Stop Immorality on TV") to spread Christian values among the American public.

Further projects thronged Brent's drawing board. One of these, Americans United for Life, he envisaged as a national lobby against the legalization of abortion. Among the apostolate's many projected components, this one alone would recruit an ecumenical membership, although its platform would be based on Catholic teachings. A Youth Division (with a uniform modeled on that of the Carlist militia) would give young Catholics an "activist" group that would be "neither right, nor left, but Christian."[4] A "new center of Christian learning," suited to "the post-modern era," would be founded to replace liberal Catholic University, and apostolate-linked "cells" would serve the cause on other campuses. In addition, since increasingly secular-minded parochial schools could no longer be trusted, a pilot elementary school would be established as a model for Catholic primary education throughout the country.[5]

To improve their chances of influencing American society, apostolate participants would form a national network of "guilds," which Brent described as "the cornerstone of our efforts to form Catholic apostles to the public life." Comprising about a dozen members each, the guilds would rally Catholic opinion against birth control, abortion, and secularist trends in Catholic institutions. They would also perform what the Church called "the corporal works of mercy"—for example, providing food, clothing, and shelter for the needy.

In 1971, while laboring over his blueprint for the guilds, Brent visited Robert Welch, the founder of the John Birch Society. He sought tips on recruiting and organizing guild members, and he also hoped for donations from well-healed Catholic Birchers. He came home, he reported, with some possibly useful advice but without any money.[6]

The apostolate's most successful component—indeed, its only successful component—was born of a brainstorm. Nostalgic for El Escorial, Brent and Trish decided in the late 1960s to rent an apartment there for use on future visits. An apartment would also be handy if Brent were to make the town the apostolate's world headquarters. Excited, he flew to Spain to start apartment hunting, probably in the fall of 1969. He headed for Avila, where Kathy was now at school. Suddenly appearing at her door, he startled his daughter, who had no idea he was coming. She happily agreed to go with him to El Escorial, but she was puzzled by something about him she couldn't pin down. Although she was used to surprises from her father, this time he struck her as somehow "a little bit different," she later recalled.

In El Escorial Brent found a suitable apartment, but also something more. As he and Kathy strolled through the town one day, he noticed a building across the street from Philip's palace and stopped before it, transfixed. The building, it turned out, housed a school that could be rented during the summers. Instantly, Brent visualized it as a place where he could set up a summer school—one perfectly located for training Catholic militants. That the building had immediately and inexplicably riveted him seemed a sure sign that God approved of his plan.[7]

The summer school, which opened in 1970 and held classes for the next five years, operated as a branch of another of Brent's creations, the Christian Commonwealth Institute (CCI). Its annual eight-week session enrolled about fifty students, most of them college-age Americans. They took courses in theology, history, metaphysics, and politics to gain—as an ad in *Triumph* put it—"insight into the public life proper to a Christian." And an extracurricular benefit also lay at hand, the ad pointed out: the opportunity to experience "the organically Catholic life style" still surviving in Spain.[8]

Many participants responded enthusiastically to the summer school, among them Kathy's future husband, Cyrus Brewster (who would become the director of Brent's guild network), and Chris Bozell's future brother-in-law, Joe Baker (who would become a priest, as would about seventy other alumni of the school). Others, however, found some fellow students abrasive. "I can only say it was grim," wrote one participant to Buckley, "like the prose in *Triumph*—where every phrase is a funeral." This writer found especially grating the chronic anti-Americanism of some of his classmates, who seemed compulsive in their attacks on the Constitution, *NR*-style conservatives, and American life in general. Baker later spoke of the quarreling these attacks provoked.[9]

Some students also heaped abuse on the Franco regime of Spain. Disciples of Fritz Wilhelmsen denounced Franco for naming as Spain's future king the Bourbon pretender rather than his Carlist rival and for paying too little heed to the needs of the Church. The indiscreet chatter of the American Carlists attracted the attention of the police, and one of the critics was ordered to leave the country.[10]

Despite the presence of discord, the school flourished, and when the rest of Brent's apostolate collapsed, it managed to survive. In 1977 it was revamped into a four-year liberal arts college, renamed Christendom College, and relocated to Front Royal, Virginia, only a short distance from the Bozells' Blue Ridge farm. The college flourishes to this day.

But if the school did well, the rest of the CCI languished. It tried to run programs of various kinds in the United States—lecture series, conferences, and weekend institutes for group study and discussion—but none came close to matching Brent's Spanish success.

Over this array of components—the existing ones (*Triumph*, the summer school), the semiexisting ones (the guilds, the CCI domestic programs), and the ones doomed never to exist (the Escorial Press, the film production company)—Brent placed an umbrella organization, the Society for the Christian Commonwealth (SCC). Set up in 1966 simultaneously with *Triumph*, the SCC had been idle ever since (though *Triumph* had sometimes mentioned a Lecture Bureau of the Society for the Christian Commonwealth). The reason for this idleness, Brent told Neil McCaffrey, was that he had never had funds to give the SCC a function. But at Berryville, the SCC at last received one: in Brent's words, it would lead the effort to "instaurate the sovereignty of Christ in the social order," or as CCI chief Warren H. Carroll put it, it would work to make America a "confessional state—a nation publicly committed to the Catholic Faith."[11]

What would an officially Catholic America look like? This was a question that *Triumph* almost never raised, and when it did, never answered in much detail. But in a 1970 article dealing mostly with other subjects, Brent drew a sketch of the Catholic America he dreamed of:

> The first citizen of the city [as Brent here called his imagined Catholic America] would of course be the Church. She would not govern directly . . . but she would be the anchor for the whole public thing. Her articulation of divine and natural law would be the constitution of the city, with which any human legislation would be expected to comport. Her ceremonies and feasts, her penances, would set the rhythm of the public life. Her art and music would fill the streets of the public life. Her compassion for sinners and for suffering would shape the soul of the public life.[12]

After the Church, society would rest on the family. Hence the law would provide no formal procedure for divorce but would include penalties for the private dissolution of marriage. To strengthen the sacred bond between "life and love," the manufacture and distribution of contraceptives would be banned, and severe punishment would be visited upon abortionists. Third in importance in an officially Catholic America would be the school system. Public education would become explicitly Catholic. Children would be free to attend non-Catholic schools, but these would have to depend on private financing. All social arrangements would be designed to help people lead Christian lives and thereby assist them in their effort to attain salvation. A Catholic foreign policy would seek this end throughout the world by pursuing the conversion of all countries to Catholicism, thus obeying Christ's final instruction to his apostles—preach to all nations, baptizing them in the name of the Father, and of the Son, and of the Holy Ghost—even if non-Catholic governments raised objections.

A Catholic America would also practice censorship, Brent added in a different article. For example, it would prohibit the circulation of writings that attacked marriage and the family or called for legal abortion. Sometimes his views, if not voiced, could be inferred. For example, his admiration for Carlism, which *Triumph* described as favoring "decentralized self-government," implied that his Catholic America would be organized along decentralized lines—not a surprising preference for an old Jeffersonian.[13] (Yet his views on Church government ran in the opposite direction, for on this score he leaned toward centralized, papal power.)

Such were the political goals of the SCC, and such was the machinery Brent envisioned to achieve them. But it became clear as SCC components multiplied that few enjoyed more than a token existence; that while growing on paper, the apostolate lacked substance; that unlike the genuine empire of Philip II, a phantom empire was burgeoning under Brent.

In one instance other than the Spanish summer program, Brent made a dream come true: he mounted what was probably the country's first antiabortion protest rally. A few weeks after the 1970 Berryville retreat, a court decision legalized abortion in Washington, D.C. Brent concluded that if an abortion case ever reached the Supreme Court, abortion would be legalized across the land. The Catholic bishops' response to the threat was to "cut and run," sneered *Triumph*. Purely verbal opposition had led nowhere, the magazine concluded; "all we have left is action."

In May 1970 Brent met with a handful of like-minded Catholics to plan an event he called an Action for Life, a protest rally to galvanize the foes of abortion. This demonstration, he would claim many years later, was "the grandfather of proper Catholic resistance to the abortion protected by the American state."[14] It was also the event that ruined his chances of becoming a noteworthy force in Catholic affairs.

On May 28 Brent sent registered letters to Washington area hospitals known to perform abortions, asking that they refrain from doing so on June 6 or, failing that, at least allow aborted fetuses to be baptized and removed in a "decent and orderly manner" for Christian burial.[15] As his demonstration site he chose George Washington University Hospital's clinic. He expected a few hundred people to attend the rally: lone individuals, informal groups, and also a uniformed troop of traditionalist Catholics, a band of young activists known as the Sons of Thunder.

Set against the background of everyday American politics, the Sons of Thunder stood out as exotics. The troop's name came from the Gospel of St. Mark, in which Jesus refers to the Apostles James and John as "the sons of thunder." About twenty students at the University of Dallas (Chris Bozell among them) formed the core of the group, with a periphery of a few dozen more scattered around the country. The Dallas leaders had earlier belonged to Young Americans for Freedom, but at YAF's 1969 national convention they had been repelled by what they saw as an obsession with economics, market theory, money, profit, mammon. "It was awful," they reported to Wilhelmsen once back in Dallas. "[The YAFers] worshipped the dollar like a false God."

The students felt the need to "do something because of the way things were going in the country," one of them later told an inquirer, and hoped to "draw attention to the moral issues of the day." Some of the students turned to Brent and Wilhelmsen for advice. To have any impact, Wilhelmsen told them during a meeting at Brent's farm, they would need to "do something dramatic," something visual enough to get media coverage. For this, a catchy name and a uniform would help. St. Mark supplied the first of these, and Brent and Wilhelmsen the second: the martial garb of the Carlist Requetés—red beret and khaki shirt, a rosary worn around the neck, and on the shirt a patch bearing the image of the Sacred Heart. Catholic activists all over America, Brent hoped, would adopt the red beret as their movement's badge.[16]

The Sons of Thunder held their first demonstration, a Valentine's Day protest against contraceptives, at a Planned Parenthood center in Dallas. Wilhelmsen, with whom they kept in touch by telephone, made his home the group's "communication center." Joined by several dozen nonmembers, the Sons carried anti-birth-control signs and knelt down inside the building to recite the rosary while security guards tried in vain to get them to leave. Once satisfied that they had sufficiently dramatized their protest, and seeing that the police were about to start making arrests, the demonstrators ended their "kneel-in" and withdrew. Their fusion of radical form and traditionalist content won them the media attention they had hoped for. A photograph of one of their leaders, Michael Schwartz, appeared on the front page of the *Dallas Morning News* the next day, and Schwartz was later a guest on a nationwide talk show.[17] Now the Sons were heading for Washington to team up with Brent.

On the morning of June 6, several hundred antiabortion protesters attended a Mass of the Holy Innocents at a church within walking distance of the George Washington University Hospital clinic. (Trish wasn't among them, she and Brent having decided that with small children to care for, they couldn't both risk going to jail.) The Mass began with Spanish-style trumpet blasts. A black, a Chinese, a white, and a Mexican priest concelebrated the Mass, and Wilhelmsen supplied appropriate Bible readings. (Brent, who eleven years earlier had staged the Khrushchev "wake," never discounted the value of symbols and theater.)

After the Mass, the demonstrators (seventy to eighty by the *Washington Post*'s count, three hundred by *Triumph*'s) carried tall processional crosses, papal flags, and antiabortion signs to a small park across the street from the clinic. Inside the park they listened to a succession of speakers, including Son of Thunder Michael Schwartz; Lawrence's plainly pregnant wife, Mary Jo; and Wilhelmsen. Dressed in his Carlist regalia and brandishing a foot-long crucifix, Wilhelmsen read thunderously from Revelation and ended with the Carlist war cry, "Viva Cristo Rey." He looked utterly furious, recalled Son of Thunder Joe Baker, who feared that his philosophy teacher might have a stroke.

After the speechmaking, the time for action arrived. Most of the demonstrators stayed in the park, kneeling in prayer, while Brent, pulling on a red beret, holding up a five-foot wooden cross, and shouting, "Viva Cristo Rey," led a small group across the street to the clinic to deliver his request for permission to baptize fetuses. Seeing them coming, clinic security guards locked the main entrance. But one of the protesters, the six-and-a-half-foot-tall Brad Evans, raced around the corner of the building to a side door and jammed his cross between its leaves before the guards could shut it. In the scuffle that broke out as Brent's cohort pushed into the building, an interior door made mostly of glass was shattered. A few minutes later, the Washington police arrived, clubs at the ready. The cry "Viva Cristo Rey" seemed to alarm them. Some thought the language was Latin, others weren't sure. "I don't know what it was," one cop told a *Washington Post* reporter, "but it didn't sound good." Clubs now swinging, the police soon subdued the protesters. Brent, his face bloody from a blow that glanced off his forehead, was forced to the floor, arrested and handcuffed, and hauled off for booking on charges of assaulting a police officer (which he denied doing), unlawful entry, and destroying property. His trial was set for October.[18]

The next day, without directly saying so, Brent conveyed his intention of leading more Actions for Life. "We can't just save our own lives and mind our own business," the *Washington Daily News* quoted him as telling reporters. Nor would he forswear resorting to force. "Sometimes the use of the sword may be necessary," he said. "Yes, I think Christ would want that in some cases." A few days later he warned, "America is going to have to reckon with its Christians, like it or not." June 6 should be taken as a foretaste of things to come.[19]

In October, at the time of his trial, he published a blistering anti-abortion op-ed piece, "Encouraging Murder," in the *New York Times*.

America was embarking on "a rampage against life potentially far more extensive, and already far sicker, than any of the great genocides of history," the article charged. Such words could have served as stage setter for a second rally, but none was forthcoming. Instead, Brent formed another SCC group, Action for Life, through which he aspired to give "coordination, direction, and impetus to the growing pro-life movement."

But this bid to put the SCC at the head of the country's antiabortion forces came to nothing. His attempt to hold an ecumenical National Right to Life Congress in Washington in April 1971 foundered when the bishops, fearing further violence, refused the group's support.[20] The June 6 protest, then, probably sealed Brent's fate, for the bishops' rejection doomed his prospects as a Catholic leader. He might still have organized rallies on a local scale, but he never did so.

The reason, Kathy later told an interviewer, was that at his trial he was suddenly "hit by reality." Found guilty of unlawful entry and damaging property, he received a suspended sentence and five years' probation. Future violent protests (even if he did nothing to stir up violence) could land him in prison. Concerning imprisonment, he wrote in 1972:

> The rule of thumb is given to the individual Christian who has any reasonable doubt that he is obliged in conscience to risk jail. The rule is, don't. A true command of conscience is unmistakably compelling and comes to a man alone, in the simple company of God. He must heed it. But to heed a dubious command is not only presumptuous: it is to leave a battle in which he may be needed (the lone jailbird is not long remembered) to make a more effective monstration.[21]

Lawrence, however, had a different explanation for Brent's inaction. Once Brent had satisfied his urge to lead a protest rally, Lawrence told an inquirer decades later, he wanted to move on. The June 6 rally, with its costumes, banners, marching, war cries, and headlines, had been thrilling, but reruns might be dull. Gary Potter agreed. Brent had no interest in repetition, Potter believed. Focusing narrowly on June 6, he had never worked out a long-term protest strategy. Potter was discouraged by what struck him as the futility of a single rally and by what this lack of planning implied about Brent's motivation (did excitement trump effectiveness for Brent?). Joined by John Wisner, Potter left *Triumph* in 1970 to found a new conservative Catholic newsletter, *Rough Beast* (whose launch Brent graciously publicized in *Triumph*).[22]

Some conservative Catholics reviewed Brent's production unfavorably. For example, Paul Weyrich, commenting in *The Wanderer*, criticized the *Triumph* group for using "the worst possible method in view of the public attitude toward demonstrators these days." He added, "The number of people who will now equate abortion opposition with Black power and college lunacy [is], in my view, significant." Equally disapproving was the secular *National Review*. Labeling the rally a "Happening," *NR* condemned it as a self-indulgent romp, and one "politically worse than ineffective." The magazine observed that "Spanish Carlism, whatever its virtues in its native habitat, is surely exotic in the District of Columbia," and that the actions of the Sons of Thunder might well have turned the undecided in favor of abortion.

But Brent's supporters may have been more numerous than his critics. The many letters *The Wanderer* received on Weyrich's article ran two to one in Brent's favor. "Put simply," wrote one Weyrich opponent, "Brent Bozell has guts."[23]

The Sons of Thunder, June 6's public face, suffered harm from the rally. Angered by the bad publicity the violence had produced, the University of Dallas intended to expel the students who had gone to Washington to protest. But in the end, urged to show mercy by Buckley and seven cardinals, the school administration relented. (Not so lucky, Brad Evans got fired as an aide to a Kentucky congressman.) By the end of the year, the Sons had gone into decline. When members of a chapter formed by Georgetown students lobbied at a bishops' conference for a stepped-up antiabortion campaign, they were shown the door. The Sons staged only one more newsworthy demonstration, a protest rally in Manhattan during their 1971 Christmas holiday. The rally ended in arrests, and several protesters were jailed.

Meanwhile, the University of Dallas remained hostile, and students who might otherwise have joined the Sons now steered clear of the group, unwilling to risk clubbing, arrest, and jail. Among the Sons themselves, cohesion began to fray. Quarreling broke out over the issue of America's legitimacy, and by 1973, with the graduation of such key members as Chris Bozell and Joe Baker, nothing remained of the thunder but fading echoes.[24]

After his trial, Brent returned to everyday business. But a few months later, Bozell activism again made news, this time with Trish under the glare of the spotlight.

Triumph paid little attention to the women's movement, and its few articles on the subject were unstintingly hostile. It pictured feminism as an effort not to better women's lot but to destroy society's "central unit—the family" in order to advance the total revamping of the social order. "Hearth and Home," the editors contended, "are a creation of the woman. With her removed, they can be counted on to disappear." This claim held good especially for a Christian social order, another editorial asserted.[25] Feminists preached the opposite of Christian truth.

Trish was not a traditional stay-at-home housewife, and as the managing editor of a sharp-tongued opinion journal she in certain respects embodied a feminist ideal. But she detested feminism, which she accused of promoting "an unnatural view of existence." Although she wrote articles for *Triumph* only rarely, she contributed some scathing attacks on the women's movement. She particularly loathed feminists who pandered to anti-Catholic irreverence, and in 1971 she made this strikingly clear.[26]

The occasion arose when radical feminist Ti-Grace Atkinson was invited to speak at Catholic University. Grace Atkinson ("Ti-Grace" means "Little Grace" in the Cajun dialect of her native Louisiana) was raised as an Episcopalian. But as a child living in Rome (where her father, a Standard Oil executive, was stationed), she attended a Catholic, English-language school, which selected her to give flowers to the pope when he came to visit. Marrying at the age of seventeen, she was divorced five years later. In her twenties she worked for a time as a high fashion model but then gave up the runway for the feminist lecture circuit. At the podium she stood out as an advocate of legal abortion—in the 1960s, few feminists went this far in public—and for aiming blasphemous jibes at the Catholic Church.[27]

Atkinson's Church razing made her popular at Catholic colleges, where inviting her to speak became a student fad. When students at Catholic University invited her to their campus, the university's president canceled the invitation. But student leaders obtained a court order overturning his veto, and on March 10, 1971, Atkinson appeared at the university to put on her show. Word of her coming led Washington Catholics to protest. Some fifteen hundred attended a "reparation service" at the city's National Shrine of the Immaculate Conception. About twenty *Triumph* people—Brent, Kathy, some students, and a few Sons of Thunder—also took action, going to the university itself, where they knelt outside Atkinson's lecture hall saying the rosary. Trish went too, but carrying press credentials, and sat inside the hall as a member of the audience.

Accounts of exactly what happened that evening differ, but all agree that while speaking of the Virgin Mary's pregnancy, Atkinson uttered the phrase "knocked up." That exceeded what Trish was able to bear. Leaping to her feet, she cried, "I can't let her say that," then stormed down the aisle and up onto the stage, where she aimed a slap at the startled speaker's face. But the microphone stood in the way, Atkinson ducked back and raised an arm to ward off the blow, her bodyguards closed in, and the slap never landed. Whirling around, Trish raced down off the stage, back up the aisle, and out of the hall.

Once outside, she shouted, "To hell with Catholic University," took out a rosary, and knelt down beside Brent to pray. A short time later, the police appeared and arrested her, but she was soon released.[28]

Asked by reporters what she thought of her daughter's behavior, Trish's mother seemed unfazed by it. "Patricia always had a quick, redheaded temper," Mrs. Buckley replied. McCaffrey wouldn't criticize Trish either. "It wasn't something I would ever be tempted to do," he told Buckley, "but praise the saints that someone did it." Trish herself was blithely unrepentant. "I think I did what God would have wanted me to do," she told a *New York Post* reporter. Her one regret, she added, was that "I missed." And then, wrote the reporter, she laughed—"a gay, elegant, rippling laugh." But soon her buoyant mood began to fade. Flooded with requests for television appearances and interviews (including one from the day's top TV interviewer, David Frost), she began to feel as if she couldn't breathe and finally fled to Spain to escape the pressure. Did she ever accept a TV invitation, a visitor once asked her. "Oh, no," she said. "I was much too shy for that."[29]

With a photo of Trish in midswing as its April 1971 cover, *Triumph* reaped a windfall from the slap. Staggering under a burden of rising debt, Brent had decided to shut the magazine down. He would cease publication in the spring of 1971, he had confided to Trish the preceding winter, and focus his energy entirely on building his apostolate. But then came the Atkinson incident, and the short-term jump in subscriptions it produced enabled the dying *Triumph* to return to life.[30]

Although in theory Brent envisioned his apostolate as a mission to the world, in practice he gave his attention almost wholly to Americans. A notable exception arose toward the end of the 1960s when he developed an obsession with Ulster, the sole remaining British-ruled region of Ireland, where political conflict was escalating into revolt. In 1967 activists from Ulster's indigenous Catholic minority began to hold "civil rights" marches modeled on those of the American black civil rights movement. The violent response of the province's Protestant majority, determined to maintain its centuries-old union with Britain and the traditional Protestant "ascendancy" over the Catholics, led to the stationing of British troops in Ulster in 1969, at first to protect Catholic areas from Protestant attack and then to suppress "republican" (that is, Irish nationalist) rebellion by Catholics. The clashes also reenergized the outlawed Irish Republican Army (IRA), whose aim was to terminate British sovereignty in Ulster and join the province to the neighboring Irish Republic. Within the IRA, the Provisional faction (or "Provos") came to the fore, ready to resort to terror to attain these goals.

Understanding the word *Catholic* in its usual religious sense rather than as the political label (meaning "native") it was in this context, Brent reflexively sided with his coreligionists against the "Protestants" (also a primarily political label here, meaning "unionists" or "settlers," the descendants of Ulster's foreign occupiers). *Triumph* argued that to treat the Ulster upheaval as simply a civil rights conflict—to regard Ulster as "merely a British expression of Martin Luther King's Alabama"—was to misunderstand it; the situation must be seen as the national religious resurgence it really was. That IRA doctrine identified the enemy as "unionist," not "Protestant," and that the Catholic Church had condemned the IRA failed to make an impression on Brent. Mistaking IRA nationalism for a strand in a religious tradition, he thought the "Catholics" were fighting for the faith of St. Padraig and St. Brigid. "A revolt against the force that denies Ireland the unified expression of its national religion—that would be a truly Holy Cause," *Triumph* rhapsodized in an editorial titled "Criost Ri Abu" (Gaelic for "Viva Cristo Rey").[31]

In the 1970s the violence in Ulster worsened. Terror and counterterror became the order of the day. At times the struggle seemed *Triumph*'s principal subject—so much so that readers complained about the magazine's "disproportionate" attention to Ulster. Dismissing these complaints, the editors replied in a huffy tone, "We can answer only that when the gulf between truth and lie is so great—and when a Catholic people is being pushed into that gulf—we cannot be silent." Meanwhile, Brent's Gaelomania continued to grow. Ireland alone among Christian nations stood on a par with Spain as a nation that had "no other destiny than the permanent defense, and advancement, of the Incarnate Faith," *Triumph* proclaimed.[32] Brent could bestow no higher praise than that.

Writing in "Freedom or Virtue?" on political action, Brent had stressed the importance of prudence as a guide. But his regard for the IRA (in his eyes, a Celtic counterpart of the Carlist militia) made him rash. When the IRA denied responsibility for a series of bombings and American newspapers didn't publish the disclaimer, *Triumph* protested that the media were imposing an anti-Catholic "blackout"; Brent's magazine ran the denial to show Americans that "the IRA is innocent of terrorism." At the same time, *Triumph* called Britain "a Third Reich without a Hitler," accusing the British of viewing "Irish Catholics as *Untermenschen*." *Triumph* also wrote sympathetically of Noraid, an American "relief" organization for Ulster Catholics that was widely suspected of serving as a cover for Provo fund-raising and gun running. In 1975 Brent set up an SCC-based Irish Relief Fund to help American Catholics meet their "responsibilities" to Ulster Catholics families whose "men have been packed off to British concentration camps." "No, child," read a *Triumph* ad for the Irish Relief Fund, "Daddy won't be home for Christmas this year."[33]

But Brent began to agonize over his Celtic Requetés. Strict in his view of what God allowed Christians in warfare, he refused to exempt incidents that were clearly terrorist acts. Hence his moral cautions to the IRA. "The foundation of justice supporting the Irish cause may be eroding," *Triumph* warned in 1971. If the IRA employed "un-Christian" tactics, God would withdraw his protection from the rebel cause.

A year later Brent's misgivings about his heroes had grown stronger. In October 1972 he published a long article by a critic of the Provos, John P. McCarthy, who heaped scorn on the romantic myth of the IRA. The Ulster struggle stemmed not from the dream of a Catholic Ireland, McCarthy insisted, but from "that particularly heinous modern doctrine, secular nationalism." The IRA had no interest at all in a Catholic Ireland.

By now, Brent partly agreed. *Triumph* condemned the IRA's "anti-civilian excesses" and acknowledged the lack of "an integrally Catholic orientation in the IRA's war." The Provos didn't give a hoot about Catholicism, the magazine conceded in an editorial probably written by Brent. But *Triumph* blamed IRA terror on only "some" of the rebels, implying that most gave no cause for moral complaint. And it continued its general tolerance of rebel violence.[34]

If Brent developed mixed feelings about the IRA, there was no such ambivalence in his view of the Irish government. Dublin seemed ready to scrap the Catholic Church's special status in the Irish Republic, *Triumph* complained. It would happily "cut the Catholic heart out of the national constitution" (which contained a provision paying homage to the Catholic Church) if that would weaken Protestant resistance to reunification. But such a policy would be grotesque, the magazine went on, reverting to its romantic-religious interpretation of the conflict. For the point of the war was "an Irish Nation reunified in public confession of the Catholic Faith."[35] Hypnotized by Irish nationalist myths and dreams, Brent found it hard to accept unpleasant realities fully.

THIRTEEN

Time to Die

In the 1960s *Triumph* was an attack dog of a magazine, snarling, baring its fangs, and charging the liberal masters of Church and state. In the 1970s the magazine stayed on the offensive. But now immersed in building his apostolate, Brent paid more attention to the positive side of his work: mobilizing Catholics to press for a "Christian social order."

Global trends favored this objective, he believed. In a 1970 article called "The Confessional Tribe," he argued that around the world the dominant form of mass organization, the national state, which rested on "convenience" or "force," was giving way to the "tribe," a form based on "affinity," the tie of race or religion, for example.[1] Alongside the other tribes, a "worldwide Christian tribe" was emerging, its birth signaled by a new consciousness, by people asking themselves, "Am I an American? a Spaniard? an Englishman? Or am I a Christian?" To exist, he continued, a tribe must have a "presence." Christians, therefore, had to be "visible . . . in their apostolic role as teachers sent to the ends of the earth." And where could people find this Christian tribe? Wherever men hailed the cross before the flag.

In this time of transition, the article went on, *Triumph* was launching a movement on behalf of the cross. The aim of this movement—Brent's apostolate—was neither to reform "the American system" nor to destroy it but rather "to be the Christian system" in a country where the state encouraged conduct "antithetical to Christianity."

Despite America's much vaunted (but in fact fraudulent) pluralism, Christians were no longer permitted a "presence" in the country. Christ the King had been pushed outside the walls, and it was there with him that his subjects must now gather.

William A. Rusher, whom Brent asked to comment on the article, found its contentions extreme. The logic of Brent's position seemed to require "a revolutionary program," he noted. If America were making war on Christ, didn't it follow that Christians in turn would someday make war on America? Our true obligation, he advised, was to work for a better political order without letting devotion to an ideal drive us into "mortal enmity" toward our country, which perhaps more than any other offered "the practical opportunity" to attain our goal. Brent agreed that the article implied revolutionary action. But he rejected revolution, he said, because it would be "tactically infelicitous" and because "direct confrontation" between state and dissidents had become "obsolete." Rusher erred in doubting a tribal future, Brent added. The better order Rusher spoke of would surely be tribal, and it would come soon.[2]

"Brent is not so wrong in his diagnosis as in his cure," McCaffrey commented in a note on the article to Buckley. In a letter to Brent he said that although the country had indeed gone far in abandoning Christianity, the answer lay not in "proclaiming ourselves outcasts or playing at being martyrs" but in recovering the old morale in a time of demoralization. Brent's position seemed as much a response to personal problems as to those of the country, he observed: "I think you and your band are sublimating a private alienation." Buckley, to whom McCaffrey sent a copy of this letter, found it "absolutely brilliant—the best conceivable analysis."[3] Brent published the letter in *Triumph* but made no response.

After the publication of "The Confessional Tribe," *Triumph* began referring to American Catholics in a new way. Catholics, the editors declared, were neither a mass of lone individuals nor a collection of ethnic groups but rather "a People" (the word, as Brent here used it, synonymous with "tribe")—a body within, but separate from, the

American populace. This people had a historical mission to perform: in the short run, Catholics must "break the secular confinement of their politics on every front where they are presently barred from acting politically—publicly and explicitly—as Catholics"; in the long run, they must "wash the American public order in grace, cleanse it, make of it an offering to the Father, a place wherein His will might be done as it is in heaven."[4]

American Catholics, *Triumph* never stopped telling its readers, lived in a country philosophically, historically, culturally, and politically hostile to them. They must therefore stress their common identity and act as a pressure group, since the people who got what they wanted in America's democracy were those who formed lobbies to fight for their common goals. One group from whom Catholics could learn was America's Jewish population. An admiring *Triumph* reported that "Jews being and acting as a *people*" were able to blocking the passage of a U.S.-Soviet trade treaty President Nixon wanted until it included permission for Jewish emigration from the USSR. In contrast to diffident Catholics, so eager to prove themselves "good Americans," Jews had "the guts to create ... pressure"—and to use it.[5]

In 1973, to foster a similar pressure-group mentality among Catholics, *Triumph* launched a column called "The Catholic Interest," whose author, "Pertinax," wrote on issues he judged of special concern to Catholics. The idea of a "Catholic people" aggressively pursuing its collective interests inside "the American system" seemed to contradict Brent's depiction (in "The Confessional Tribe") of Catholics as a people outside the system, living beyond its walls with their exiled king. But it strongly appealed to the instinctively combative Brent.

Triumph found Catholic docility the more exasperating in that Catholics had potentially enormous political power. Not only did they form America's biggest voting bloc, the editors calculated. They were also more likely to vote than the average American, and most lived in states with more than average political weight. But because they failed to act as a political bloc, they were losing a chance to shape the country's "moral climate."⁶ Still, afire with his vision of Red Beret activists bringing Christ to America, Brent wasn't discouraged. Indeed, so compelling did he find the vision that he projected it beyond America to the entire world. In an article called "Toward a Catholic Realpolitik,"⁷ he conducted a global religiopolitical survey and concluded that if all the world's Catholics joined together in one huge pressure group, they could "eclipse all of the pretensions of the great powers."

In 1970, when Governor Nelson Rockefeller vetoed a bill before the New York State legislature to repeal the state's liberal abortion law, Brent seized the occasion to show how Catholics could operate as a pressure group. Imagining counteractions New York's archbishop might have urged on his flock, *Triumph* listed: repeated, grand-scale protest marches; nonstop picketing at the governor's office and mansion and at all clinics and hospitals that performed abortions; refusal to pay state income taxes; and sit-down strikes or resignations by state employees, with Catholic Charities and the archdiocese at the ready with financial help for state workers who lost their jobs.

Triumph denounced the archbishop's actual reply to the veto, a simple statement of regret. It was the kind of response that prompted Brent to remark after the Action for Life rally that what was once the "Church Militant" had turned into the "Church Complacent."⁸ But Brent himself held back from picketing and demonstrating. With his probationary status still hanging over his head, he instead mounted an attempt at "Catholic politics"—political horse trading on behalf of Catholic interests. Failure to exert political pressure, "or at least to try," he wrote in July 1972, "is a failure to be faithfully Catholic."⁹

The event that lured him into the stews of the Philistines was the Watergate crisis. Thinking that Catholics could profit from helping Nixon, in September 1973 he arranged a meeting with a friend from his Buckley period, Nixon aide Fred Buzhardt, to whom he suggested ways to strengthen the president's hand. Tell Attorney General Elliot Richardson to fire Watergate special prosecutor Archibald Cox, he proposed, and if Richardson balks, then fire him too and replace him with someone who will fire Cox. (Nixon did exactly this a few weeks later, but he doesn't seem to have taken his cue from Brent.) Nixon should also refuse to cooperate with the courts and should charge them with "usurpation of jurisdiction," he added. In exchange for this advice, Brent suggested, Buzhardt could urge Nixon to endorse a strong pro-life constitutional amendment or at least call for congressional hearings on proposed pro-life amendments. The president would be smart to heed "the Catholic interest," he told Buzhardt, because Catholics in return would heed the Nixon interest.

Buzhardt reacted with a polite show of interest but nothing more. Still hopeful, Brent turned to his brother-in-law Senator James L. Buckley of New York in hopes of a meeting with Nixon or Vice President Spiro Agnew. When no meeting was scheduled, he moved on to Nixon's secretary, Rose Mary Woods, another old friend from his *NR* conservative days. But Woods's office directed him to David Parker, Nixon's appointments secretary. A call to Parker's office brought a reply not from the appointments secretary but from Buzhardt, who told him that the president's schedule was too full to permit a meeting.

Nor was Brent able to set up a meeting with Barry Goldwater, whom he hoped to persuade to go after the vice presidency (soon to be vacated by Agnew, who had been indicted on a charge of taking bribes). Weary of getting the runaround, he finally gave up.[10] His *quid* had proved much too meager to call forth a *quo*.

Jarred by his failure, Brent decided to review his thinking in hopes of discovering what was "really in the Catholic interest." He concluded that his ideas and actions had sometimes been wrong. His pursuit of a deal with Nixon, for example, had risked diverting the SCC from its primary purpose of helping people "live their lives in a Christian way" and might also have harmed the souls of those who joined in the effort. Why he feared the latter he found hard to explain, he confessed, but he had "a feeling" it might have done harm, and lately he had grown more willing to trust his feelings. Moreover, these ventures could suggest the presence of sinful pride, for those pursuing such plans faced the problem "of presuming to know the key to the good of the civil order, and God's plan for turning it." Beyond that, he worried that he had been "reckless" in ending "The Confessional Tribe" with the words ("pompously rendered in probably bad Latin") "*Fiat hunc totiusque orbis Tribus Regis Christi*." It was God's prerogative, not the SCC's, to command that the whole world be the tribe of Christ the King. The SCC shouldn't let the "enticements of Catholic Politics" divert it from "the heart of [its] apostolate," the forming of Catholics.[11]

Brent didn't stop there. Regretting his 1968 article "The Autumn of the Church," he called what he was now writing "a message of contrition." His thinking then had been "correct," he said, but his attacks on the bishops had "probably" been "unfair and certainly contrary to the best interests of the Church," for they had only further inflamed its internal conflicts. Nor did he view "The Autumn of the Country" as he had then. Its diagnosis and prognosis had been right, though perhaps premature. America was sick and had gone a long way toward collapse. But convinced at the time that nothing could be worse than the present, *Triumph*'s editors wouldn't have minded America's fall—and would even have given the country "a small, last shove." Now, though, he thought they had gone too far toward "nihilism."[12] And although his central beliefs survived his review unaltered, he began to treat the bishops with a gentler hand.

Roe v. Wade caused no surprise at *Triumph*. Brent had predicted that if an abortion case reached the Supreme Court, the court would overturn laws banning the procedure. After the verdict, *Triumph* appeared with a black cover and a dedication reading "For the Children." The issue also ran an editorial called "The Catholic Obligation,"[13] in which Brent counseled Catholics on how to respond to the ruling.

In essence, he returned to the separatism of "The Confessional Tribe." Catholics should withdraw from "the civil order," he wrote.

America had forfeited its right to claim their allegiance. But Catholics must also campaign for a pro-life constitutional amendment—despite the near certainty that such a campaign would fail—because in the unlikely event that it succeeded, countless unborn children would be saved. (As it happened, Senator Buckley would put forward a pro-life amendment.) The bishops could underline the Catholic choice of separatism by stressing that Catholics, in their pro-life amendment campaign, were acting only as defenders of the unborn, not as citizen-participants in the political order. Catholics should realize, however, that an amendment campaign held dangers. They might forget that their struggle had more than one "battlefront," that many issues besides abortion had to be dealt with. Or they might fall under the illusion that they still belonged to the American civil order, that it was still possible to be loyal both to country and to faith, or worse, that the Constitution was "somehow the adjudicator of Catholic rights and duties," the adjudicator even of truth itself.

As enemies of the American civil order, Catholics should make their hostility plain to see. For example, they—and especially the bishops—should boycott patriotic and civic celebrations, such as Fourth of July festivities and presidential inaugurations. They should also refuse (as Brent himself did) to salute the flag. And they should engage in acts of civil disobedience, in "harassment and defiance of the existing constitutional order." Before Catholics could resume their loyalty to America, major changes would need to be made—and made in the American position, not the Catholic. In the near future, such changes looked anything but likely. Still, if *Roe v. Wade* were to rouse Catholics to action, it might one day be remembered not only as the horror it was but also as the spur that had moved Catholics on to their ordained mission: to serve as "Christ's apostles" to the world.

Roe's aftermath amply justified Brent's pessimism. Many Catholics showed no interest in the abortion issue, and among those who did, few were willing to adopt his separatist stance. Thus, one dismayed *Triumph* reader reported, at a meeting of about three hundred right-to-life Catholics, all but he had recited the Pledge of Allegiance.

The right-to-life movement was avoiding ties with religion, *Triumph* complained, and Senator Buckley's pro-life amendment needed tighter drafting to achieve its goal. In the end, the editors argued, there was only one way to stop the abortion holocaust: Americans as a nation would have to be won for the Church.[14]

In the war that broke out in the 1960s between the culture and the counterculture, Brent opposed both sides. No friend of a mainstream culture corrupted by liberalism, he could not smile on a counterculture defined by New Left radicalism and hippy hedonism. The culture he favored, he said, was "Christian culture."

Yet in some ways, starting with his rejection of the mainstream culture, he revealed an ambiguous kinship with the counterculture. In his writing, for example, he adopted (as did the counterculture) the word *tribe* to designate what were thoroughly nontribal human groupings, while in his views on living settings, he scorned suburbs, which he labeled "sterile." When President Nixon imposed wage and price controls in 1971, *Triumph* called the move "a step toward dictatorship" and urged its readers to protect themselves from "the servile state" by "dropping out."

Here, as in the magazine's advocacy of civic separatism, secession was the keynote—withdrawal from mainstream America into a life as independent of America as possible. Catholics could "learn to get along with less," the editors suggested. They could move to the country, "raise a garden and chickens or goats and bees if they prefer . . . learn how to bake bread and make their own clothes and repair things," and "share skills and products with fellow Christian dropouts."[15] Indeed, a "Catholic" economy consisting of quasi-communes might develop beyond the boundaries of the conventional American economy.

Other countercultural leanings also appealed to *Triumph*. For example, a 1972 article called "Baptizing Organiculture" sang the praises of purely organic farming, while a piece by Wilhelmsen (an enthusiastic technophile, ironically enough) charged that nature was "being raped by mechanization." Air and water pollution had causes less "physical" than "moral," *Triumph* charged. The best remedy would be "a human life-style that harmonizes with nature and nature's God." Nor did Brent see anything to admire in "industrial and technological" advances. When he wrote of progress now, he enclosed the word in irony-laden quotation marks. But he noticed a problem at the heart of the ecology craze. "In its current expression," he warned in a 1970 speech, environmentalism was "a kind of paganism which puts the earth above man instead of the other way around."[16]

Triumph had never found a "Catholic" economic philosophy. But in place of its earlier position, which, in tune with Leo XIII's *Rerum Novarum*, had called for a "third way" between "unfettered capitalism" and "materialistic socialism," the magazine now focused on personal economic behavior rather than on comprehensive economic systems and favored a monastic blend of communalism and austerity. "Accustom yourself to sacrifice," the editors instructed readers, "that you may know how to live."[17]

Papal prescriptions still shaped Brent's economic views. He had earlier rejected *Populorum Progressio*, Paul VI's 1967 encyclical advocating a global redistribution of wealth, as naive and unwittingly friendly to totalitarianism. In his 1967 article "Paul with Leo," he had used Leo XIII's economic teachings to criticize Paul's. But he came to defend *Populorum Progressio*. He had originally rejected the encyclical, he explained, because of its statism. Now he exhorted American Catholics to help meet the pope's goals, albeit through private conduits rather than corrupt and power-hungry government bureaucracies. The Church, *Triumph* insisted, must impress upon Catholics their duty to practice charity and upon governments their duty to ensure justice for the poor.

"Capitalism," a villainous conspiracy of the greedy in the eyes of the Left, also suffered *Triumph*'s lash. High on Brent's list of targets stood multinational corporations, which, the editors warned, posed "a special threat to Christian social values." The magazine criticized free markets as well. Writing of "Christian opposition to Communism and Capitalism," one editor declared, "Socialism with its slave-labor camps is hardly a worse system than one that allows the free exchange of money for goods and services which include [smut] and vacuum curettage machines."[18]

Simultaneously, *Triumph* moved left on Vietnam. In years past it had traced the root of America's Vietnam involvement to the theoretically anticommunist policy of containment. But in 1971 it embraced a leftist view of American motives. The containment explanation had been false from the start, it argued. Even then, "Great Power politics" had determined American policy, inspiring what was really "an effort . . . to thwart the spread of Chinese (and to an extent Russian) influence in Southeast Asia"—which is to say that the claim of a communist threat was only a smokescreen to conceal U.S. imperialism's maneuvers against rival imperialisms. Along with its Left-sounding identification of "U.S. imperialism" as the leitmotif of American policy, *Triumph* also came up with a Left-sounding plan for an Indochina peace settlement. The first three points of this seven-point proposal called for the United States to declare defeat, unilaterally withdraw its troops from Indochina, and end all bombing in the region.

By this time, Brent even accepted the New Left fashion of spelling *America* with a *k* instead of a *c*.[19] His anger was causing him to resemble the people he loathed.

Triumph's jump in subscriptions after the Ti-Grace incident proved short-lived, but the cost of publishing the magazine kept rising. In the autumn of 1971, in hopes of cutting expenses, Brent moved *Triumph*'s office from Washington to Warrenton, Virginia, a town less than an hour's drive from Huntly. Soon, however, the wolf returned to the door. In January 1973 Brent informed subscribers that the SCC "suddenly and unexpectedly" found itself "in imminent danger of having to suspend its activities"—activities that included publishing *Triumph*. To keep going, it would have to raise $35,000 by February 15. The target wasn't quite met, but enough money came in for the magazine to stay in business, and by summer the appeal had netted more than $40,000.[20] But 1974 turned out to be bleak. Brent described it as "perhaps the worst we have experienced." "Crippling" SCC staff cuts had to be made; *Catholic Currents* shrank to a single page placed in *Triumph*; and *Triumph* itself survived only because "two most generous friends" came to its rescue and members of the SCC's board of governors dug deep into their pockets to help pay the bills.[21]

By the beginning of 1975 the situation had again become "perilous," as Brent announced in a January fund-raising appeal. The SCC was now running an annual deficit of $150,000, most of which came from the cost of bringing out *Triumph* (whose paid circulation had fallen to about five thousand). To weather the storm, $37,000 had to be raised "*now.*" If *Triumph* got through the spring, it would find the means to go on. The primary reason for his confidence, Brent explained, was "spiritual," the bet he had made on "grace" when he founded the magazine. The Church had named 1975 a Holy Year, which made it a time when God would pour forth "special graces"—some of which, presumably, would flow to the aid of *Triumph*. "So we do not ask you to risk your generosity on the strength of our human projections, but on the promised extravagance of Him who is the common bond of us all." The appeal fell short of its goal by $4,000, but *Triumph* managed to survive by cutting its page count. The expected special graces failed to arrive, however, and with the SCC $50,000 in debt, the July issue announced that publication was being suspended.[22]

Triumph managed to come back in September—but this time as a four-page letter featuring only editorials. A notice in the first issue informed readers that this letter was a "temporary substitute" for *Triumph* magazine, which would resume publication when it found the money to do so. But after a second issue, in October, the substitute also shut down. The *Triumph* team revived the old format in January 1976 for a special publication called *The Spirit of Triumph*, a collection of some of the magazine's major pieces. Still dreaming of a full-scale resurrection, Brent introduced the collection with a "Dedication" that told the tale of *Triumph*'s money woes and then bade "the world" a hopeful "*hasta pronto*" ("See you soon").[23]

The Spirit of Triumph would have served as a fitting finale, but it turned out to be something less than final. In May, June, and July 1976 an eight-page *Triumph* newsletter appeared, edited by Gary Potter, who had returned to *Triumph* in 1974. It was only after no fourth issue came out that *Triumph* could at last be said to have finished its run.

But even then, not completely. Eight years later, some of the old *Triumph* crew—Brent, Trish, Mike Lawrence, and Warren Carroll among them—published a thick anthology called *The Best of "Triumph,"* a selection of numerous key editorials, articles, and reviews. Then, in 1986, Brent, Trish, and their children Maureen and Brent brought out a collection of Brent's own writings over the preceding twenty-five years. Called *Mustard Seeds: A Conservative Becomes a Catholic*, the volume consisted mainly of pieces from *Triumph*. It was only after *Mustard Seeds* that *Triumph*'s clarion voice fell quiet for good.

Why did *Triumph* have to close its doors? Lack of money is the obvious answer. But the magazine had always managed to get by while operating on a shoestring for almost its whole nine-year run (a point Brent himself would later make). Seen in retrospect, the 1975 crisis looks no worse than some earlier ones. Lawrence later wondered whether money had been the real problem. If Brent had truly wanted to keep *Triumph* going, Lawrence told an inquirer, he could probably have scraped together the needed funding.[24]

Trish blamed *Triumph*'s fall not only on money troubles but also on editorial conflicts. She recalled that Brent's anti-Americanism, as well as such claims as that birth control was worse than abortion, had led to friction with readers and, more destructively, between some editors and Brent. Lee Edwards, going further, thought that some of Brent's views had caused his isolation at *Triumph*.[25]

But above all else, *Triumph* fell prey to a hidden foe. Exactly when Brent became a victim of bipolar disorder (once more commonly known as manic depression) is impossible to pinpoint.[26] Swings in mood between periods of restlessness, high energy, euphoria, irritability, and grandiosity and periods of apathy, inertia, melancholy, chronic grieving, and despair suggest the presence of the disease, but if the episodes are rare and brief they may not be spotted as symptoms. To make recognition more difficult, in the middle stretch of the swings, victims may behave normally for long periods. Years after Brent's diagnosis (in 1976) some people who knew him had no idea he was sick.

Brent's illness probably dated from the later 1960s but went undetected for years. There are several possible reasons why his condition passed unnoticed. Attacks of mania or depression—at that early date infrequent and relatively mild—may have been taken for exaggerated instances of his normal behavior. ("Life with Brent was never a quiet sea," Trish once remarked.) Thus when Kathy sensed something "a little bit different" about her father in Spain in 1969, she didn't see anything worrisome in his behavior. Neal Freeman, who ran into Brent at Frank Meyer's funeral in 1972, described him as looking tired but still endowed with his familiar winning ways. Thomas Barbarie, an assistant editor at *Triumph* in the 1970s, later remembered the pleasure of spending time with him: "days of lively discussion, bourbon and bluegrass at the Huntsman [a Warrenton tavern] . . . and trips to Manassas where we would put *Triumph* to bed."[27] (An abiding likability and charm alongside irritability and anger is common in manic-depressives.) Moreover, the disorder has a strong genetic root, and none of Brent's known forebears seems to have had it. Also, it usually appears in the victim's teens or early twenties, whereas Brent was probably around forty when he fell ill.

Nonetheless, disquieting signs long preceded the diagnosis. For example, his rages at Buckley. These episodes were seemingly triggered by disagreements over birth control and abortion, and on a deeper level by the gap that had opened up between the two and Buckley's apparent indifference to Brent's wish to close it. Still, these explosions, in their disproportion to their visible cause, suggest the possible presence of pathology. As do the grandiose fantasies he entertained—converting the America people en masse to Catholicism; turning America into a confessional state; and, as spiritual heir to His Most Catholic Majesty Philip II and sometimes resident at that monarch's very command post, El Escorial, bringing the world under the scepter of Christ the King.

Also grandiose was his claim that he was frightening those he believed to be his adversaries. "Our enemies have sensed the danger of our rising impact on Church and national affairs," he wrote in a 1969 fund-raising appeal, "and are moving, with their imposing resources, to blunt the threat. *Time, Newsweek,* the *New York Times,* and countless other publications, secular and religious, have recently directed their fire at *Triumph*." Years later he would claim, "During the nine years of its existence, *Triumph* magazine was the only serious opponent of the American state."[28]

During these years he also made sudden changes that raised eyebrows. In October 1972, explaining that he needed more time for the SCC, he made Lawrence *Triumph*'s editor in chief and moved down to the lesser post of senior editor. He had told Kathy some years earlier that he might take just this step one day, so on the surface the move seems innocuous. But after he took on a lower title, he continued to rule the magazine as before. At the same time, with no explanation to anyone, not even Trish, he began to appear on the masthead under his full name, Leo Brent Bozell. This he did until *Triumph* went out of business, at which time he reverted to the familiar L. Brent Bozell.[29] What caused him to alter his name is still unclear, as is the meaning of the decision. But in Trish's view the change was surely significant. It probably had something to do with his inner commotion.

Weakening his judgment and strengthening his impulsive streak, Brent's illness couldn't fail to endanger *Triumph*. Brent was the force behind the magazine's conception and duration, Lawrence once observed, but also the principal reason behind its folding. Manic depression not only made him irresponsible. It also eroded his knack for raising money. Since none of his lieutenants could match him at this chore, his growing illness dealt *Triumph* a heavy blow.[30]

A decade later Brent offered several explanations for *Triumph*'s fall. He virtually dismissed what he called the "official" cause, inadequate funding, pointing out that despite a never-ending financial emergency, *Triumph* had always come up with the sums it needed. More important, he thought, was discord among the editors, and for that, he said, he bore the brunt of the blame. To what extent his illness had led to *Triumph*'s closing he couldn't say, but in the early 1970s, he now knew, he had suffered brief onsets of bipolar disorder, whose real significance no one had grasped at the time. He supposed they had helped push *Triumph* over the edge.

But in his eyes the "spiritual" causes of *Triumph*'s demise outweighed the "material" causes. "The problem," he wrote, "was that I and some of the others did not fully trust. There was no 'turning over' of *Triumph* to Christ, so that the hard choices and gambles would be his, even the seeming recklessness would be his." Worse, he said, *Triumph* didn't come up with "new ways" to cure the nation's ills, and it finally gave up trying.

The fatigue and frustration that settled over the magazine could be traced to an even greater failing. "At bottom," he concluded, *Triumph* misread the meaning of the Incarnation. It hadn't realized that the "old evangelization" (bringing God to men to help men become "self-reliant"), which he had called for in his speech "To Magnify the West," was giving way to a "new evangelization" (bringing men to God to enable them with love and mercy to help one another). So for *Triumph*, which had missed the change, "it was time to die."[31]

FOURTEEN

Manacled to a Roller Coaster

In the summer of 1975, right after deciding to shut *Triumph* down, Brent fell into a deep, four-month depression. His illness was now full-blown. The attack marked the start of the manic stage of his life, the years Mike Lawrence later referred to as his "lost decade." Swinging between depression, at whose low points he wished only to be dead, and mania, whose excitement and euphoria he loved, with sometimes long intervals of normality between the pendulum's extremes—this was the pattern that now took control of his life. Formally diagnosed as bipolar in mid-1976 during a second severe depression, he was prescribed lithium, the day's standard medication for bipolar disorder. Lithium could moderate the bipolar swinging that now ruled him, but he hated the feeling of mental suffocation it produced, and so for years he took the drug only sporadically. The result was a life never free of sharp changes in mood—a life lived, in a friend's words, as if "manacled to a roller coaster."[1]

As time passed, Brent's mental state grew worse. Not only did he continue to suffer from mood swings; he also began to fall victim to spells of delusion, and these too came and went for the rest of his life. But unlike the mood swings, the delusions tended to be brief. On one occasion, sensing that the Second Coming was about to take place, he phoned the news to David Schindler, a friend who taught at Catholic University. Schindler must come over immediately (the Bozells now lived in Washington) to await the event, he said in a voice filled with urgency. Recognizing that Brent was in a delusional state, and fearing he might come to harm if left alone, Schindler at once set out for the Bozells' apartment. But on opening the door, Brent was clearly surprised to find Schindler there. He had forgotten the phone call and even the Second Coming.

Another delusion made Brent—briefly—a major diplomat. Convinced that he had found a solution to the Arab-Israeli impasse, he telephoned Israel's prime minister, Menachem Begin, to describe the plan. Pretending to be a well-known American cabinet member, he disclosed his mission to the Begin aide who answered the phone, whereupon the aide summoned Begin from the Knesset to take the call. So authentic did Brent sound as he outlined his thinking to Begin that it took time for the latter to realize he was talking with a madman.

As his experience with Begin suggests, Brent had a knack for projecting credibility, doubtless strengthened by his firm belief in the claims he made. When he described to the archbishop of Boston, Humberto Medeiros, a plan he had worked out to bring peace to war-torn Ulster (Ireland remained a bee in his bonnet), Cardinal Medeiros, according to one account, gave him five thousand dollars to go to Ireland and promote the plan.

Sometimes, however, Brent's fantasies were filled with menace. He would sense that hostile powers were mustering their forces against him. Paranoia thus helped shape his delusional world, Trish recalled, and he couldn't be shaken free of his dark imaginings.[2]

Physical damage added to Brent's burden of woe. Injuries suffered during manic episodes, when his guard was down and his sensitivity to pain blunted, took a heavy toll. His indifference to physical discomfort could be perilous. One day during a winter visit to Connecticut, he took a walk in subzero weather wearing only sandals without socks on his feet. That he escaped frostbite could be considered a minor miracle. But luck didn't always protect him. Falling from the top of a high wall he had climbed while on a manic episode in Spain, he hit his head hard enough to do lasting harm to his memory. A walk he took in Manassas one day almost proved fatal. Ignoring traffic, he was knocked down in the street by a truck, an accident for which the truck's driver seems to have been blameless. This time, too, he recovered only partly, for never again could he stand fully upright.[3]

A heavy drinker in the past, as his mood swings grew more pronounced he crossed the line into alcoholism. This new compulsion made his troubles worse. His son Chris once speculated that drinking might have launched him on his manic flights. Whether or not this is so, alcohol could alter his personality, sometimes turning this most amiable of men into a boor. One night, for example, he appeared without warning at the door of his old ACU ally Robert Bauman and Bauman's wife, the former Carol Dawson, who had worked on his 1958 campaign for the Maryland legislature. The Baumans were busy hosting a dinner party but invited their surprise visitor in, even though he was shabbily dressed, scruffily bearded, and fairly drunk. Brent spent the evening putting away an impressive amount of vodka and delivering lengthy monologues on various topics. Carol remembers his leaving when the party ended, but Robert remembers that by that time he was too drunk to drive and had to spend the night at the Baumans'. It turned out that Brent had taken no medication that day, an omission that could easily derail him.

Since drinking cost money, he found himself forced to borrow. This meant more stress. He had never felt comfortable raising money to publish a magazine, and now he was trying to do so to cover his bar bills. Moreover, lenders began to grow scarce as he failed to repay them. As his need increased, Trish became more and more worried, fearing that he would try to pawn the family silver. He turned on people who refused to lend him money or to contribute to the various schemes he would dream up when in a manic state. But even when furious, he never threatened Trish.[4]

Much of the old Brent survived, however. For one thing, he never turned his back on his religious concerns. For another, his obsession with Ireland and Spain remained in force (while Latin America—a sort of junior Spain full of Catholics in need of help—soared in importance to him). Also, he could still draw others to his side, at least for a time, for his manic energy, buoyant spirits, and exciting talk could make him good and even inspiring company. But then people would drift away as he sank into a period of depression, or as the exciting talk failed to produce any action, or as it became unmistakably clear that he was sick.[5]

Brent's first grand manic struck in early 1976, a counterswing from his major depression of the previous summer. The adventure it triggered was an "SCC project" in Guatemala, a "Catholic mission" that almost cost him his life.

Since the early 1970s his interest in Latin America had been growing. From that Catholic world to the south, he had come to believe, could flow the vitality that would save the languishing North American Church. When an earthquake hit Guatemala in February 1976, he saw an opportunity to foster solidarity between spiritually needy North American Catholics and spiritually thriving Latin American Catholics—an *alianza para la Cristiandad*. The SCC (which now existed mainly in Brent's head) would spearhead a relief and reconstruction effort involving both materially thriving North American Catholics and materially needy Guatemalan villagers. In Gary Potter's words, Brent wanted to "act against indifference, against hostility, *against things as they have been*," to undertake revolutionary action not through violence but "organized around Christ." He also saw a chance to practice "the politics of mercy," the aim that would become the overriding purpose of his life.[6]

Two weeks after the earthquake, borne on the fiery wings of a manic swing, he flew to Guatemala to pursue an "exploratory mission." After spending a few days poking around the country, he wound up stranded in Guatemala City with a grand total of sixty-five cents in his pocket. Rescued by Chris, who rushed to his aid with money, he went home to do some fund-raising for his project. In late March he returned to Guatemala to begin his work. He found partners in Brad Evans (who had held open a side door for the Sons of Thunder at the George Washington University Hospital clinic during the 1970 demonstration) and later two more SCC workers along with his nephew Rob Bozell.

He chose as their work site the village of Vista Hermosa, a small settlement outside the town of Antigua, and there they worked on rebuilding damaged houses. The SCC flew its flag from the top of a fifty-foot flagpole Brent's crew had removed from an abandoned Red Cross compound. A second item also identified SCC workers: the red, beaked caps crew members took to wearing. For living quarters they rented a small apartment in Antigua, one of whose rooms they turned into the SCC's local "center." Their furnishings consisted of a table, a few chairs, some beds, a picture of the Holy Family, and a Pittsburgh Pirates pennant. The last item was a tribute to baseball Hall of Famer Roberto Clemente, who had played for the Pirates; Clemente had been killed in a plane crash on New Year's Eve 1972 while en route to deliver supplies to earthquake victims in Nicaragua.

Despite Brent's stress on the importance of Catholic solidarity, the SCC crew had almost no contact with the Guatemalan clergy. In a piece he wrote about the project, Brent explained that the Church had virtually no presence in the area. It was his hope that the SCC's coming would help fill that void by stimulating an increase in priestly vocations.

Despite Brent's dedication, the project soon came to grief. Little rebuilding got done. A dispute with a local bigwig brought Brent a short stay in jail. And a neglected cut on his elbow became badly infected ("providing a feast for a cluster of tiny insects," he said), raising his temperature to 105, sending him into delirium, and forcing his return home after only a few weeks' work.

But if Brent had little impact on Vista Hermosa, Vista Hermosa had a lasting impact on him. Having submerged him day after day in Third World poverty, life there sharpened his empathy with the Latin

American poor and deepened his sense of the meaning of *Populorum Progressio*. The experience, Rob Bozell wrote to Trish three decades later, "tempered much of his philosophy [for] the rest of his life."[7]

Once back home, Brent sank into a second severe depression. It was then that he was hospitalized, formally diagnosed as bipolar, and prescribed the lithium that he would so often fail to take.

Only sporadically treated, his condition failed to improve. Restlessness, one of his oldest traits (and one included in the standard description of the manic syndrome), burned in him more fiercely than ever. As in the past, he found relief in travel, a passion he could indulge all the more easily now that he had shed the duties imposed by *Triumph*. He journeyed all over America paying visits. The Southwest, with its rugged, open terrain and large Catholic, Spanish-speaking population held a special appeal for him.

His departures from home were often impromptu. Years later Juli Loesch, a fellow pro-life Catholic, recalled an encounter with Brent. Loesch had helped found the Pax Center, a Catholic peace and justice community in Erie, Pennsylvania, and by 1980 she had become active in the pro-life movement. One evening, she recalled, she received "an odd and disturbing phone call" at the Pax Center.

> The voice on the other end of the phone was ancient, masculine, raspy, and urgent. This man was calling to grill me about my stand on the various Life Issues, construed in the broadest possible way. What did I think of assassination? Euthanasia? Hiroshima? Purity? The Papacy? Poverty? Did I love Our Lady of Guadalupe? Had I ever considered suicide? Did I perchance speak Spanish?
>
> After 15 minutes of intense questioning, the sandpaper-voiced man said he'd just have to drive over to talk more about

these matters. "I could meet you for coffee sometime," I offered, thinking: Here's one hurtin' buckaroo. "Where are you calling from?" I asked. "Washington, D.C." Oh.

After midnight Loesch heard a knock at the door. She went to find a "scrawny gent, badly dressed, sockless, and somewhat slurry of speech." She brought him inside, prepared to refer him to the Pax Center's men's shelter. "But there wasn't any alcohol on his breath," Loesch said. "And he was talking about Aquinas and the Just War Theory." That is when she realized: "It's the same guy. He just hopped in his car and drove all the way up from D.C. to Erie through a blizzard because he has this urgent, driving need to discuss a Catholic vision of life and death."

Only then did she learn the man's name—though the name "didn't mean anything to me," recalled Loesch, who had come from the Catholic Left. She let Brent sleep on a sofa, and the next morning they discussed their pro-life activism, their mutual belief in the immorality of nuclear weapons, and much more. Brent, she said, "loved *Humanae Vitae*, loved his wife and 10 children with a reverence that made him shake, and he hated the loveless world of politics."

Loesch observed both the old and the new Brent in this encounter. "His body and voice seemed to be failing even then," she wrote. "He was a magnificent wreck: brilliant, ardent, relentless, and well-read, and yet a wreck, like a Mercedes in a ditch with a busted axle and broken glass on the seats." Qualities that had always drawn people to him were still alive in Brent. "He was unnervingly humble. He was here sitting at my feet almost, quizzing me and noting seriously everything I said, as if I were a font of wisdom, when his poorest, least coherent thoughts were more interesting than anything I had in my repertoire of small borrowed ideas."[8]

Brent also took many trips abroad, frequently believing he was traveling on "Catholic missions," with his favorite stops being Ireland, Spain, and Mexico (his halting Spanish improved markedly when he was manic, his son Brent noticed). His journeys were minimally planned, often with no itinerary drawn up for his family and no letters or postcards sent home from wherever he had landed. Traveling abroad in this almost clandestine fashion, he sometimes disappeared so completely that no one, not even Trish, was sure where to find him—until the State Department sent word that he had gotten sick or had an accident or been imprisoned. His wanderlust filled Trish with dread, for she knew that when seized by mania he grew reckless.[9]

Sometimes his roaming had its light moments. The younger Brent once tracked him down in Mexico City, where he found him registered at three different hotels at once—one for breakfast, one for lunch, and one for dinner, the father explained, as if such behavior were the most natural thing in the world. And Brent was about to register at a fourth; after all, he told his son, he needed an afternoon snack.[10]

Quite different, however, was what he called his "last Irish manic" flight. In Ulster, Catholics knew him simply as a pro-Catholic American magazine editor; no one seems to have realized he was mentally ill. So in the spring of 1983 he was invited to address a Catholic gathering in Belfast. Emerging from a pub to go to the meeting place, he could not find an unoccupied taxi. Then he spotted an empty bus in an adjacent British army compound and decided to take that "available" vehicle instead. Brent clambered over the fence, got the bus started, and rammed it through the compound's closed front gate. Given the wartime conditions prevailing in Belfast, any one of these stunts might easily have gotten him killed. But as things turned out, he was only halted and jailed. In custody, he kept insisting to his British captors that he was an Irish revolutionary, a claim not designed to hasten his release.

In jail he came to believe that he was the pope and simultaneously the commandant in chief of the IRA. He passed the time working on a volume he later self-mockingly referred to as a "'book,'" a production his jailers eventually threw out with the trash. Upon release, he found refuge in a shelter for homeless men, where his first significant action was to call a press conference. A number of serious journalists seem to have attended. Notified by the State Department that Brent was back in trouble, Trish followed his mayhem-filled course with bated breath, unable to do much more than watch and pray.[11]

Brent's illness plunged his family into turmoil. "A long nightmare," "unbelievable upheaval," "pain," "chaos"—those were among the words Kathy used to describe the situation. The depressions cast a pall over the household, while the manic periods triggered a state of alarm.

Although his individual mood swings couldn't be precisely foretold, young Brent and his sister Maureen developed a knack for sighting nascent manics. Even when their father appeared to be fully normal, small signs would reveal that a fire had started within him. For example, he might begin to carry a red handkerchief in his back pocket. He might also declare a sudden, urgent need for money to deal with some desperate emergency or to finance an utterly necessary trip (a "Catholic mission"), or announce some grandiose venture he planned to pursue. But catching an early warning usually did no good, for by the time mania had become even minimally detectable, it had already progressed beyond the point of stopping.

For years Brent fought hospitalization during periods of mania. Neither reasoning nor trickery could overcome this resistance. Only after a long bout of fit throwing—but never violence—might he finally give in. In the early 1980s, however, his attitude began to soften: he told family members to hospitalize him at the first hint of mania. But now as earlier, when the first outward signs appeared, the fire inside him had already started to blaze, and he might explode at the thought of hospital care.

The Bozells also tried a deterrence strategy against mania. Thinking the victim himself, if given enough incentive, might be able to quench the blaze through an exercise of will, family members began to "shun" him when the fire rose. But ostracism only made him angry (and had the added drawback of further demoralizing Trish). In any case, the tactic was doomed to fail: will power lacks the strength to quell the flames, which yield only to professional medical treatment or die down on their own.[12]

One day in the fall of 1976—after the depression that followed the Guatemala episode—Brent launched off on another manic flight. He took his two youngest sons from home and his younger daughters from school and simply drove away with them. Apprehended later that day, he couldn't explain where he was going, or for what purpose. Trish speculated that he might have been trying to get back at her for her efforts "to thwart him in some of his unbelievable reaches."

This new misadventure landed him back in the hospital, where he spent the next few months receiving treatment. It wasn't clear where he would go when discharged from the hospital. The thought of his living at home terrified Trish, who feared that he would pose a danger to the children. Deciding that she had no option but to "flee," she gathered up her brood and her Spanish servant, Mercedes, and rushed them up to the Buckley place in Sharon, Connecticut. After a brief stay in Trish's childhood home, they settled in rented quarters in nearby Lime Rock. When Brent's treatment was completed and his stability seemed assured, he joined them there. Lime Rock would "not be a permanent settling down place," he wrote to his sister, Patty, "but a place to be until Montejurra is sold and I figure out a new career as a successor to Triumph."[13]

Montejurra had gone on the market a few months earlier. With Brent not working, the Bozells were strapped for cash, and the farm was their only asset of significant value. It was Brent who had bitten the bullet and proposed selling. Yet the prospect of losing Montejurra filled him with grief. He was "DEEP in manics by this time," Trish later wrote, and after he had put the farm up for sale, he changed his mind, seduced by the illusion that selling wasn't necessary. But then, pushed by reality, he put Montejurra back on the market. He would repeat this on-again-off-again pattern more than once. Several prospective buyers came to look at the property but disappeared when it became clear that Brent hadn't made up his mind. At one point he actually did sell the farm, though he did so without saying a word to Trish. She was stunned one day when a stranger appeared at the door and identified himself as the owner of Montejurra.[14] This sale was canceled, but eventually another took place, and Montejurra passed into other hands.

The Bozells next rented a house in McLean, Virginia, a suburb of Washington. As Brent had said when writing to his sister about Lime Rock, they didn't intend to live in McLean for long—only "until we got our lives sorted out," as Trish told Buckley. But with Brent again seesawing between mania and depression, very little sorting out got done, and their stay in McLean lasted for five years. This was a trial for Brent, for although he had chosen the McLean location, his long-standing animus against suburbia hadn't abated. He simply had no hope of acquiring a new Montejurra, since the Bozells were now chronically short of money.

Money was in fact so scarce that Brent went looking for work. In 1981, hoping for a job, he visited Neal Freeman, whom the incoming Reagan administration had named to oversee a cluster of small federal agencies during the transition. He entered Freeman's outer office sporting a cyclist's helmet and spandex racing shorts—a bicycle racer in search of the Tour de France. A Freeman aide was astonished when he heard the visitor give his name to the receptionist. "Is that *the* L. Brent Bozell?" the aide asked his boss. Freeman found a job for the man whose 1964 primary campaign he had managed and whose 1966 book on the Supreme Court he had helped to edit. But the job involved little more than messenger's work, and Brent's stint as a federal employee didn't last long.[15]

In 1982 the Bozells left McLean for Washington. The apartment they had found would be their home for the rest of their lives. When they died, neither had lived anywhere else longer.

Brent's bipolar swings put a crushing burden on Trish. In effect, she now had another child to care for—a big, often deranged, and occasionally destructive and self-destructive child, whose legal status as an adult (he could rent a car, buy a plane ticket, etc.) compounded the other challenges he posed. Moreover, since he had lost his emotional balance, money management now fell entirely to her. Further complicating her new situation, she wrote to Buckley, Brent's illness made life "in its financial . . . aspects" less predictable. (Maureen and young Brent, students at the University of Dallas in the mid-1970s, offered to help, writing to their father that they would give up their allowance and get part-time jobs. But he wrote back with a different idea in mind. "Dear Maureen and Brent: Can I have an allowance?")

Buckley provided Trish with financial help, sending her money regularly for years. But she eventually furnished much of the Bozells' income herself. Unwilling to leave Brent alone all day, she needed work she was able do at home. Judging her decade as *Triumph*'s managing editor and her ties with conservative publishers to be her biggest assets, she decided to try her hand at freelance editing. Her choice was a wise one. She succeeded in coming up with editing jobs and over the years amassed a steady clientele. An old connection of Brent's, Regnery Publishing, proved to be especially important. According to Henry Regnery's son Alfred, she came to be viewed as the best editor the firm ever had.[16] With her career a success, she found it hard to retire and continued to wield her red pencil into her seventies.

But if Trish proved able to meet the challenges she faced—keeping her family financially afloat, assuring her children a greater measure of stability than might have seemed possible, dealing with the manifold tensions occasioned by Brent—her success was hard-won, for it required a struggle against not only Brent's demons but also her own. In the later 1970s, ceaselessly battered by the endless pressures surrounding her, she too slid into alcoholism. Fearing surrender would mean the collapse of her family, she dug in her heels and fought. "Tish is going to make another mighty effort to stop drinking, through AA, so please pray for her hard," Brent wrote to his sister in 1977.

Trish enlisted additional allies in her struggle. One of these was religion. She adopted the practice of going to Mass every morning, a routine that, whatever other benefits it afforded, furnished daily psychological reinforcement against drinking. Another was music. She had given up the piano in the early 1960s, convinced that interpretive playing lay beyond her reach, but during Brent's lost years she found her way back to the keyboard. She remained self-conscious about her supposed lack of talent. "I'm working on the most beautiful Largo movement of Beethoven," she confided to Buckley, but when he asked which largo, she was too shy to say. She also tried her hand at composition. Citing the annunciation, crucifixion, and resurrection of Christ as history's three most significant events, she wanted to compose a piano piece that would convey them musically. It is unclear whether she followed through on this wish, but she did compose several pieces that Buckley called "marvelous."[17] Whether religion or music or sheer grit enabled her to win, in the end she overcame alcohol once and for all.

Trish's mettle was brutally tested by Brent's illness. But she never faltered, unprepared though she was for the troubles confronting her. Shouldering the cross that fate had thrust upon her, she doggedly accompanied Brent down his fiery road, unaware that she was making her life a moral triumph.

Brent first commented publicly on his illness in the short spiritual biography with which he prefaced his 1986 collection, *Mustard Seeds*. Some family members and friends opposed his doing so, thinking he should keep his bipolar problem private. But he waved away their objections, convinced that important matters were at stake. He wanted to speak "forthrightly," he said. But more than that, he suspected the disease was meant to serve a purpose. The medical diagnosis of manic depression (a "bio-chemical imbalance") struck him as superficial, as failing (in his case, at least) to understand its most basic cause. In reality, he ventured, his illness was probably "God-given," visited upon him in pursuit of a double aim. On one hand, God was punishing him for his sins. On the other—and this, he believed, was God's fundamental purpose—by making him suffer, God was working to teach him "about mercy. In a hundred ways."[18] The path to grasping mercy was paved with pain.

FIFTEEN

Mercy

"Brent is doing magnificently, quiet, showing his recent years' illness, coping," Trish wrote to Buckley on Christmas Day 1983. It was a fine Christmas, she went on. Most of the children were at home, and she was very happy. It had been a long time since a letter of hers had voiced such a mood. "I think joy is returning," Buckley answered. Time passed, and the news continued to be hopeful. "Brent [is] better than in years," Trish reported several weeks later. "His increasing mental abilities simply give the lie to the scientific prognosis." March saw a downturn in Brent's condition, but not a severe one. "All is well here, though Brent [is] into a depression," Trish told Buckley. But she still wrote in her recent cheerful tone, noting that the current depression was "not nearly as devastating as prior ones, thank God."

About this depression, or maybe a later one, or possibly a manic, Buckley wrote six months later to his nephew Michael Bozell, a monk living at a Benedictine house in France, "The good news is that [Brent] went voluntarily to the hospital and received intense treatment." There was "not-so-good" news too, but it concerned new aspects of Brent's current treatment, not a further decline in his mental health. From now on, he would have to take daily medication "in highly recorded doses," and Trish would have to report to his doctor "on a very regular basis any change in his mood."

By the end of the year Brent's improvement began to look permanent.

Brent himself later identified this period as his turning point, calling 1984 the time when "my new life" began.[1]

Since manic depression is incurable, "new" was perhaps too strong. Nonetheless, the disease can be held in check, and this is what Brent finally succeeded in doing. Oddly, mania proved to be its own best antidote. While psychologically as capable as ever of catching fire, after a decade of physical pummeling he was exhausted. Battered and broken, stooped and lame, lacking the energy and stamina manics require, he could no longer answer the manic summons on anything like the scale of times gone by. So it was that he began taking lithium regularly, accepted the need for occasional hospital stays, and gave up drinking. The toll of mania had ruled out further sprees.[2]

Although Brent had been made stable by medication and physical breakdown, his brilliance at oratory was gone for good. Able to address an audience only briefly, he was forced to give up the art at which he had excelled.

He did résumé writing, however. During his lost decade he had found what he called "serious" writing beyond him. When depressed, he had lacked the energy such writing demanded. What he had written when manic later struck him as "wild and false." One of his few pieces of competent prose during this dismal time was a letter in 1981 to *National Review* criticizing the social critic George Gilder's bestseller *Wealth and Poverty*, a celebration of free-market economies on "spiritual" grounds. Gilder was trying to "sacramentalize self-interest, even greed," Brent complained. *Wealth and Poverty* discouraged concern for "the common good," the basic principle of Christian economics.[3] Brent had once rejected the liberal Catholic accusation that market economics contradicted Catholic social morality, but now he fully espoused that view.

As he came out of his lost decade, Brent began devoting a good deal of time to writing. His efforts were daunting. He could spend a day working on a single paragraph. He had never been a fast writer, and now his physical and mental condition kept his output low. To aid his concentration, he rented a room for writing from a religious order, the Oblates of St. Francis de Sales.

In 1984 he published a full-length article in *NR*, his first since his *Triumph* days.[4] Called "Poland's Cross—and America's," the piece contrasted the American public's feeble protest against the Supreme Court's ban on prayer in public schools with the Polish public's resistance to its Marxist government's attempt to take crucifixes out of classrooms.

It was no accident that Poland was the subject of his return to writing. Brent had discovered a new magic kingdom, with Poland joining Spain and Ireland in his charmed circle. Poland had splendid credentials to present. Historically a defender of Christendom against the Eastern hordes, it had now resumed this mission, giving birth to the anticommunist, largely Catholic Solidarity movement, which was locked in struggle with Poland's communist rulers. Solidarity exercised a heavy influence on Brent, not only because he admired grassroots Catholic resistance to communism but also because he learned much about "Catholic economics" from Solidarity writers. These writers grew in importance for him as the question of the Christian duty toward the poor became his special concern.

Equally important to Brent's thinking was the Polish pope, the tough-minded traditionalist John Paul II. If any one piece of writing of the 1980s could be called definitive for Brent's thought at this stage of his life, it would have to be John Paul's 1980 encyclical *Dives in Misericordia* (Rich in Mercy).[5]

Unlike his *Triumph* jeremiads, Brent's later pieces never thundered. His critical writing no longer aimed at the secular liberal state (though he still opposed it). Instead he took on "capitalism" because it was "self-seeking" and "socialism" because it was based on state "coercion." Only "Self-denying Christianity," he insisted, could serve as the basis for a morally worthy economy. Poland's Solidarity movement, which taught that *"every man is expected to help carry the burden of the other man,"* exemplified the Christian economic outlook. Whereas capitalism told you, "Make as many bucks for yourself as you can," Christianity told you, "Make as many bucks as you and your family need, then start looking after the brother."

Translated into institutional form, this ethic would require "collectivization"—that is, a centralized welfare state. Although Brent rejected state "coercion," in a 1986 essay in the *New Oxford Review* he wrote that collectivization should be achieved

> by the adoption of government policies that, in effect, impose "compulsory self-denial" on the rest of us in order to help the poor. Paying taxes for social welfare, because individual charities fall short, may not seem like an exercise in self-denial, but it *is* a denial of self, is it not? And it can become an authentic spiritual act of self-denial if by an act of will you take as your primary sanction, not the IRS's gun, but love for the poor. In this way, the governing standard of the American economy could become mercy.[6]

Mercy, which Brent defined as "an attempt to alleviate the suffering of another, motivated by love," now formed the cornerstone of his economic philosophy. It became the primary subject of his writing. His 1985 article "The Politics of Mercy" illustrates the way he typically handled the subject.[7]

Inspired by John Paul's *Dives in Misericordia*, Brent began by delving into the Pauline epistles 2 Corinthians and Colossians to illuminate the message on mercy he thought they contained. He pronounced the duty of mercy binding on all Christians, identifying, in particular, a North American obligation to aid poverty-stricken Central America (especially given the Cold War struggle with communism, which was working hard to take power in Central America). He next argued for the pope's contention that mercy transcended justice and could even give justice "a new content"—namely, the bestowal of mercy, "the supreme goal and standard of Christian politics." It was because God so made the world, Brent wrote, that John Paul could call mercy "an obligation—the *dominant* obligation—of every country's foreign policy." He concluded that once North American mercy had saved Central America from poverty and communism, then (here he succumbed to his weakness for grandiose schemes) it could "truly embark on a world politics of mercy."[8]

Whether the needy suffered from material or spiritual want, in Brent's view the bestowal of mercy took a single course. The bestower gave up something (money, comfort, time, possibly his life) to help the burdened one, and in this act of self-denial he also became a sufferer, one who gave the merit earned by his suffering to someone else. This pattern underlay all acts of mercy, including the Crucifixion, the supreme act of mercy that opened salvation to mankind. In bestowing mercy, in suffering to help another, the bestower becomes a "surrogate" Christ, "another Christ," who thereby helps lessen the torment borne by the Savior. Brent concluded, "It seems sure—in some way, to some extent—that Christ depends on *us* to do the work given by the Father of mercies."[9]

So crucial did such thinking become to Brent that this later period of his life could be called the "mercy stage." He was influenced by another Pole, Sister Faustina Kowalska (1905–1938), a nun to whom Christ had appeared on several occasions and who had labored to spread his worship as "King of mercy." She believed that, as Brent put it, "the worst sinners" enjoyed "a right of priority" for Christ's mercy, as long as they repented of their sins. Brent admired Sister Faustina immensely, singing her praises as a leading missionary of mercy.[10]

Even more influential were the teachings of an eighteenth-century French Jesuit, Jean Pierre de Caussade, author of the treatise *Abandonment to Divine Providence*. Brent took up Caussade's work in a 1988 piece called "The Politics of Abandonment."[11] Caussade, he wrote, urged a spiritual life based on "abandonment" of self to God, so that rather than our doing God's will, God does his will through us. The "abandoned" man, Brent noted, thus becomes "a wholly dependent and docile instrument of God's power" and in effect "wields" that power. But such men may not cut noteworthy figures in the world. As Caussade had written:

> [They] are often flung into a corner like a useless bit of broken pottery. There they lie, forsaken by everyone. . . . The world thinks them useless, and it seems as if they are. Yet it is quite certain that by various means and through hidden channels they pour out spiritual help on people who are often quite unaware of it. . . . But note that there is nothing pathetic about the abandoned man. By preferring God to himself, by choosing God's will over his own, the exercise of God's power has been placed in his hands.[12]

The most vivid impression left of Brent's writings on mercy is of his wonder over God's eagerness to forgive sinners. That God suffered—still suffers—to help sinners left Brent dazzled, and the excitement he felt gripped him for the rest of his life. One day not long before his death, he received a visit from his son Brent, who, finding him smiling blissfully at a picture of the Sacred Heart, asked what was making him smile. He answered that he was marveling "at Christ's mercy." "Learning more about mercy . . . is the name of my new life," he wrote in 1986. That animating purpose never faded.[13]

Brent never explained his excitement about the mystery of mercy. But the feelings it stirred in him sprang from his emotional core.

Guilt-ridden over his manic days, especially over the troubles he had inflicted on his family (but perhaps also over a whole life he may have regarded as misspent), he surely felt a desperate need for mercy. But something besides guilt may have been at work. He had suffered a striking reversal of fortune in the past quarter century, falling from the status of a conservative star to that of a burned-out has-been, someone people liked but now mostly felt sorry for. Yet with his discovery of mercy and "abandonment," he saw things differently. "Note that there is nothing pathetic about the abandoned man," Caussade wrote. "The exercise of God's power has been placed in his hands."

Brent had again discovered a life he wanted to lead. Thanks to the power to bestow mercy his suffering gave him, he could see his troubles not as meaningless misfortune or himself as a pitiful victim of rotten luck. Instead, he became a man whose woes exalted him, since they gave him a formidable power to bestow mercy. He was the last person on earth people should feel sorry for.

"Blessed are the merciful, for they shall obtain mercy." Brent quoted Christ's words to readers of "The Politics of Mercy." And those who pray for mercy, he noted in another article, "God Is Mercy," must join works of mercy to their prayers. God withholds mercy from those who withhold it from others.[14] He took these words with the utmost seriousness, systematically performing what the Church called the "corporal works of mercy": he fed the hungry, gave drink to the thirsty, clothed the naked, welcomed strangers, brought care and comfort to the sick, and visited prisoners. He omitted only the seventh work, burying the dead, since the times no longer provided occasions for doing so. Bestowing mercy became his defining trait, as editing *Triumph* had once been.

Usually he acted by volunteering for Catholic charitable work. He all but ignored political life, now caring only about bringing mercy to the poor. His friend Kevin Lynch, a former *NR* editor, identified him not with politics but with kindness. Julia Poppelier, a fellow volunteer at the hospice Mother Teresa founded in Washington, considered sheer goodness to be his most visible trait. Raymond T. Gawronski, a Jesuit friend, called him a "great intellectual-become-holy-fool" and marveled at the love he showed for the helpless and needy.[15]

Brent's work took him far and wide across the Washington area. A few of the organizations he regularly served included a home for indigent old people, a soup kitchen operating in a poor Hispanic enclave, a visitors' association serving Lorton prison in northern Virginia, a shelter for the poor established by the Sisters of Charity, and Mother Teresa's hospice for AIDS patients, where he washed, dressed, and helped feed the dying. Gaunt, stooped, his hair now suggesting rust more than fire, he looked barely capable of maintaining his strenuous pace. Indeed, it could be hard to tell him from the people he aided. (Three things had wrecked him, he explained to fellow volunteers: coffee, whiskey, and cigarettes.)[16] Yet year after year, he managed to keep limping along, held up by the will to bestow and receive mercy.

Brent's favorite agency of mercy was his own creation. In 1985, under the influence of *Dives in Misericordia* and the social philosophy of Solidarity, he was trying to come up with new "projects of mercy" when he had a brainstorm. He would launch an apostolate to Hispanics in the United States and focus mainly on poor Hispanic immigrants. (The question of "illegal" immigration left him indifferent. All that mattered in his eyes was bestowing mercy.) He called his projected enterprise Misión Guadalupe, named for Mexico's patroness, Our Lady of Guadalupe.

At first he envisaged his immigrants not only as receivers of mercy but also as restorers of North American Catholicism. But on a trip to New York's Spanish Harlem to reconnoiter the immigrant scene, he discovered that many Hispanics had shed Catholicism either for no religion at all or for evangelical Protestantism, whose pastors were busy recruiting for their storefront churches. This situation led him to alter his plans. Now his revivalist target would be the Hispanics, and only later would North American Catholics come into play, with reenergized Hispanics evangelizing their Anglo coreligionists. After this would begin—and here appeared Brent's inveterate preference for the grand scale—"a new Spanish mission to the world." This apostolate, he wrote, would be his work for the rest of his life.[17]

At first he wavered over how to implement his plan, sure only that it should enlist "the poor to help the poor." But talks he had at monasteries in the West, capped by a trip to Mexico City's shrine of

Our Lady of Guadalupe, seem to have yielded answers. Organization would be loose and simple. Misión Guadalupe would grow as members found friends and neighbors who wanted to join. All the Misión's activities would be works of mercy, intended to lessen the burdens the immigrants faced—for example, helping in the hunt for food, shelter, clothing, jobs, and medical care. Members would also help through visits to the sick, teaching English, driving people to church, or simply spending time with the old and lonely. As Misión's headquarters, Brent rented a house in tumbledown northeast Washington, where he put up a sign reading THIS IS MISIÓN GUADALUPE and set out an array of pamphlets and instructional literature.[18]

Beset by illness, mishap, and failure, Brent went on performing the corporal works of mercy to the fullest extent his worsening health allowed. Even on the verge of death, he was still at it.

Despite his frequent traveling and his high regard for Poland, Brent had never set foot on Polish soil. Then, in the mid-1980s, he met the perfect guide, Raymond Gawronski, a young Jesuit of Polish background who had recently been assigned to serve at a church in Washington. Before he knew Brent, Father Gawronski had read and admired "Poland's Cross—and America's." Brent, for his part, knew Father Gawronski only from the Jesuit's 1985 article "Pilgrimage to Poland and Byelorussia," a "meditation" on Slavic spirituality based on a trip he had taken through Poland and western Byelorussia. Brent found the priest's observations on Poland fascinating, and his eagerness to visit the country mounted.

Eventually introduced by a mutual acquaintance, the Bozells and Father Gawronski hit it off, and in 1987 Brent, Trish, and their new friend set off together on a ten-day trip through Poland. Starting in Warsaw, they drove to Gdansk, where their hotel overlooked the Lenin Shipyard, Solidarity's birthplace. Then on to Kraków, the country's ancient capital; Auschwitz, where they visited the cell of Father Maximilian Kolbe, Catholic priest and also ethnic Jew; and the shrine of the Black Virgin of Częstochowa, Poland's national protectress, whose intervention in battle in 1655 enabled the Poles to smash a Swedish siege.

The trip was a great success. Despite his trouble walking, Brent seemed enraptured much of the time, and his eagerness never waned. One Polish region reminded him of America's Great Lakes country, where in his childhood he had spent some of his summers. Poland's ubiquitous Catholicism enchanted him. Coming out of his hotel in the morning, he would look around, turn on his sunbeam smile, and announce to the world in tones of utter delight, "Ah! No Protestants!"[19]

Trish, too, fell in love with Poland and Solidarity. In 1988, moved by the previous year's trip, she published an article ("The Polish Church, the Workers Movement") hailing the Church-Solidarity battle against communism. The following year Poland's faltering communist bosses threw in the towel, and the Bozells rejoiced. Brent, overjoyed but astounded by Solidarity's victory, thought that nothing less than supernatural intervention could explain it. The key, he insisted, was the involvement of Our Lady of Częstochowa.[20]

So well had the 1987 trip turned out that in 1988 the same trio set off on a new one. This time they decided to visit the Balkans, another terra incognita for the Bozells. From Rome they flew to the Dalmatian town of Split, then drove north to Dubrovnik. They turned inland to look at Sarajevo and then pushed east into the heartland of Balkans Orthodox Christianity. First they visited Serbia, then Bulgaria, then Macedonian Greek Thessalonica and Lake Ohrid, and finally Montenegro.

The Balkans tour took place without a hitch. Throughout the trip Brent showed an otherwise-seldom-glimpsed ecumenical spirit, neither hesitating to frequent Orthodox churches and monasteries nor declaring his delight at the absence of Protestants. Still, Father Gawronksi noticed that Brent was having more trouble walking than he had had in Poland.[21] His ability to travel seemed to be running out.

Although Brent's health was poor, his interior fire kept burning. But now, in his new life, it lost its connection with religious and political warfare. Where once Brent had displayed anger and a readiness for confrontation, he came to convey serenity, the contentment of the hearthside, and a desire to help others. Brent's son Brent once said that the subtitle of *Mustard Seeds: A Conservative Becomes a Catholic*, might more aptly have read *A Conservative Becomes a Contemplative Catholic*. David Schindler of Catholic University counted among Brent's traits at this stage of his life not only "a fierce courage" but also "a profound gentleness." Elsa Thompson, a friend of Trish's, spoke of the graciousness Brent could express simply by smiling his "extraordinarily angelic smile."[22]

Brent's serenity appeared in his bearing toward the saints to whom he prayed. He began to address them by nicknames he assigned. St. Anthony of Padua, for example, became "Tony" and St. Thérèse of Lisieux "Tessie." Jesus himself received this informal treatment: for reasons unknown, Brent took to calling him "Spike." And although he also continued to pray in conventional fashion, his praying often turned into informal chats.[23]

As Brent grew older, his aptitude for leisure increased. With his friend the former *NR* hand Kevin Lynch at the wheel, he went for drives in the Virginia countryside, where he liked to walk and meditate. He also enjoyed visiting a friend with a cottage in Virginia, an elderly man named Mac, at whose tranquil retreat he would relax and pass the time. And in rural Virginia he found a Russian Orthodox monastery, which—the ecumenical outlook he had shown in the Balkans still with him—became a favorite place of his to pray.[24]

Despite his age (sixty-five in January 1991) and his many ailments, he still made his regular rounds on behalf of mercy. His routine was grinding. He rose in darkness to attend a daily 5:30 a.m. prayer service at St. Anselm's Abbey, a Benedictine monastery not far from the desolate streets of northeast Washington. When the service ended, he would race to Mass at a nearby Franciscan monastery, always entering the chapel a few minutes late. It was possible to set a clock by the moment the chronically tardy redheaded stranger, sometimes bearded or dressed in the garb of a street person, limped through the chapel door. After Mass, he would drive to a diner where homeless people congregated, and there, drinking coffee and smoking cigarettes with the drifting and the desperate, he would joke, gossip, and speak of Christ's ever flowing mercy. He became a familiar figure in the neighborhood. "Yo, Red! How you doin', man?" friendly voices would greet him as he hobbled over broken sidewalks to the diner. After a while he would leave for work at Mother Teresa's, or report for duty serving food at a convent soup kitchen, or drive to Virginia to visit the inmates at Lorton.[25]

Friends worried about Brent. For one thing, he drove his car with what one called "abandon"; for another, he spent much time with Washington's "dangerous classes." But Trish backed his pursuit of mercy to the hilt. Lynch believed the two made a model couple. They epitomized what marriage was supposed to be, he said.[26]

Others thought Brent was drawn to a different vocation. Schindler suspected he was strongly attracted to the monastic life. Young Brent shared Schindler's hunch. By the 1990s, he once remarked, his father wanted (though not necessarily consciously) to become a monk. In 1992 the senior Brent found a way—by becoming not a full-fledged monk but an associate of a monastic order. He had long admired the Carmelites, who, as one writer put it, embraced "solitude, silence, abandonment, recollection, and . . . contemplation" to forge "a mystical oneness with Christ" and in hopes of "saving souls through redemptive prayer." In April 1992 Brent became a Third Order Discalced ("unshod") Carmelite. Accepted as an associate of the order, he continued to live in the secular world and didn't take all the Carmelite monastic vows. He called the step a birthday present for Trish. The monastic name he chose was "Brother Anthony of Padua."[27]

However great Brent's happiness over his Carmelite membership may have been, even greater was his happiness when his Benedictine son, Michael, decided to enter the priesthood. The ordination—or "coronation," as the Bozells jokingly called it—took place in 1994 at Michael's medieval monastery in France. Many guests attended, including Michael's uncle Bill Buckley, who flew several guests to the ceremony at his own expense.

In the 1980s, as Brent committed himself to mercy, his hostility toward Buckley began to ebb. "Dear Will," he wrote in 1984 in reply to a letter Buckley had sent him, "I am most grateful for your note, which is but another testimony to your good heart." Neal Freeman, pleased by the growing reconciliation, encouraged Buckley to show an equal warmth. But if the rift appeared finally to have ended, a faint mutual wariness still lingered. It was only in the emotion-filled atmosphere of Michael's ordination, Chris Bozell believed, that surviving hesitations dissolved.[28]

The evening preceding the ordination ceremony, the guests gathered for a banquet in the monastery's hall. Antique tapestries covering the walls and a large stone fireplace created a lofty ambience. After Michael himself, Trish and Brent were the center of attention. Trish's sister Carol described the couple: "Patricia, small and thin, with sculpted features and rose-soft coloring; Brent, stooped now, walking with a cane, humbled before the occasion of his son's ordination, a frail and good man."[29]

Buckley, one of the banquet speakers, succumbed in midspeech to feelings too strong to contain. Bursting into tears and unable to stop weeping, he had to abandon his speech and return to his seat. Perhaps he was thinking not only of the present moment (among all his nephews, he had the closest relationship with Michael, with whom he had long corresponded about religious concerns) but also of the twists and turns of his decades-long friendship with Brent, and of the sadness that settles like ashes on human life.

Brent spoke too, reading a short "letter to Michael" he had worked on for weeks. Pushing himself out of a wheelchair, he succeeded in delivering his message on his feet. The letter put the theme of mercy in the forefront (and sometimes seemed to be about himself as much as about Michael). Brent informed his guests that Michael was "a fool for suffering, of which he has had much, and which he has managed to transform into joy. For himself, Michael has never acknowledged that the joy of helping Christ is his way of dealing with suffering. But I know it is." He closed by saying of Michael, the only Bozell child to enter the clergy, "You are the largest public glory of my life."[30]

How Brent managed to keep going is hard to fathom. He was suffering from so many ailments by the mid-1990s that his condition amounted to a Homeric catalogue of infirmities. His manic depression, though well managed, was still active. Moreover, symptoms of Alzheimer's had begun to appear, a stomach operation brought on intestinal problems, and a heart condition contributed its own special woes. His back pain, often severe, made a wheelchair part of his everyday equipment. The loss of peripheral vision ended his driving, and apnea, asthma, and osteoporosis joined the list. "You name it, he had it," his son Brent recalled.[31]

Despite all this, in January 1996 Trish threw what turned out to be a genuinely festive seventieth birthday party for him. One guest presented him with a University of Nebraska football warm-up jacket, which seemed to delight him. Buckley gave him an airplane ticket good for any destination in the world (which his awful health prevented him from using).

But a moment of merriment couldn't stem the fatal tide. His condition worsened till he could no longer be cared for at home, and in late 1996 he moved to the assisted-living section of a nursing home. Hating his new surroundings, he grew sullen and withdrawn, and soon left for another nursing home more to his liking. Since his physical state made his old routine impossible, he had to give up most corporal works of mercy. Yet he continued the little he could still handle. In the last weeks of his life, he would limp through the wards of a nursing home near his own, trying to console patients (thus following the injunction to care for and comfort the sick). For all his good works, he showed nervousness as death closed in, as if worried that somehow he had failed to become a Catholic.[32]

In April 1997, now seventy-one, he came down with pneumonia, and on April 15 he died of it while sleeping. Family members were keeping him company at the end. Buckley had asked to be notified as soon as Brent died. When the phone brought the news, he let out a sob and, unable to speak, hung up.

Among Brent's last acts was the completion of his Carmelite vows, and he lay in Carmelite robes in his coffin at the funeral home. The onetime admirer of Carlist Requetés thus wound up a Carmelite semimonk, a gauge of the unorthodox course his life had taken (though Carlists and Carmelites harbored a characteristic in common, one the French writer Stendhal called "*espagnolisme*," a kind of unrestrained, go-for-broke ardor).

Brent's funeral, held at Washington's Our Lady of Mount Carmel, was a grand affair. Michael flew in from France to say the funeral Mass, at which he was assisted by eight concelebrants. One of these was Father Lucius Cervantes, the priest who had been Brent's mentor at Creighton Prep and officiated at his marriage to Trish. Many conservative notables—libertarian, anticommunist, traditionalist, eclectic—attended; they had never ceased to regard him as one of their own. He was buried in St. Mary's Cemetery in northeast Washington, where as "Red" he had tried to help the poor and needy. His tombstone reads, "A just and honest man."[33]

"Red"

EPILOGUE

Viewing Brent Bozell's life from a conventional secular vantage point, many people would probably judge it a failure. The man who had started out with so much promise—and gained so much prominence—wound up helping nuns serve soup to Washington derelicts.

But if judged by the standards he himself came to embrace, his life would surely prompt a different verdict. For whatever people might think of its total trajectory, its ultimate stage would have to be called a triumph.

NOTES

One: The Bozells of Omaha

1 Scott Moore, current president of Bozell & Jacobs, to author, January 27, 2007.
2 Patricia Bozell Prom to author, January 4, 2007.
3 Maureen Bozell to author, February 27, 2007.
4 Patricia Buckley Bozell (hereafter, PBB) to author, July 11, 2006.
5 Copies of the speeches, along with newspaper clippings and photographs relating to the contest, provided by PBB.
6 Leo Bozell's letter provided by PBB.
7 Patricia Bozell Prom to author, January 4, 2007; L. Brent Bozell (hereafter, LBB) to Patricia Bozell Prom, October 3, 1947, letter provided by PBB.
8 LBB, *Mustard Seeds: A Conservative Becomes a Catholic* (Front Royal, VA: Christendom Press, 2001), 2; Lucius Cervantes, SJ, to author, February 7, 2007; LBB to Patricia Bozell Prom, April 3, 1950, provided by PBB; LBB, "The New Catholic: Quo Vadis?" *New Oxford Review* 55 (March 1988): 20.
9 PBB to author, July 11, 2007.
10 PBB to author, July 11, 2007.

Two: Bulldog

1 LBB to Patricia Bozell Prom, February 20, 1949, letter provided by PBB.
2 Ibid., November 22, 1948, and February 20, 1949, letters provided by PBB.
3 Garry Wills, *Confessions of a Conservative* (Garden City, NY: Doubleday, 1979), 14–15.
4 John Judis, *William F. Buckley Jr.: Patron Saint of the Conservatives* (New York: Simon and Schuster, 1988), 56–57; William F. Buckley Jr., *Nearer, My God: An Autobiography of Faith* (Garden City, NY: Doubleday, 1997), 258.
5 Judis, *Buckley*, 74; Charles Lam Markmann, *The Buckleys: A Family Examined*

(New York: William Morrow, 1973), 59–60; PBB to author, November 20, 2007.
6   Buckley, *Nearer, My God*, 258–59; Judis, *Buckley*, 64; *Yale Daily News*, January 16, 1948, January 22, 1948, February 26, 1948.
7   Dwight Macdonald, *Memoirs of a Revolutionist: Essays in Political Criticism* (New York: Meridian Books, 1957), 333.
8   George H. Nash, *The Conservative Intellectual Movement in America since 1945* (New York: Basic Books, 1976), 427n72.
9   LBB to Patricia Bozell Prom, November 22, 1948, letter provided by PBB.
10 Ibid., October 3, 1948, and November 22, 1948, letters provided by PBB.
11 Ibid., October 7, 1948, letter provided by PBB.
12 Official Campaign Biography of L. Brent Bozell, 1964 Republican primary in Maryland's Sixth Congressional District, provided by Neal B. Freeman; LBB, "Mustard Seeds," *Mustard Seeds*, 2.
13 William F. Buckley Jr., *Cruising Speed: A Documentary* (New York: Putnam, 1971), 219; William F. Buckley Jr. to PBB, January 28, 2007, e-mail provided by PBB.
14 PBB to author, October 31, 2006.
15 Buckley, *Nearer, My God*, 260.
16 PBB to her parents, late 1938, William F. Buckley Jr. Papers, Sterling Memorial Library, Yale University.
17 William F. Buckley Jr., *Miles Gone By: A Literary Autobiography* (Washington, DC: Regnery Publishing, 2004), 5–6.
18 Ibid., 27.
19 *New York Post*, March 20, 1971; Osterweis quoted by Markmann, *The Buckleys*, 87; Carol Buckley, *At the Still Point* (New York: Simon and Schuster, 1996), 44.
20 PBB to author, October 31, 2006.
21 Ibid.; Judis, *Buckley*, 57.
22 LBB to Patricia Bozell Prom, January 12, 1949; PBB to author, November 20, 2007; LBB to Patricia Bozell Prom, February 20, 1949. Letters provided by PBB.
23 LBB to Patricia Bozell Prom, February 20, 1949, letter provided by PBB.
24 LBB to Patricia Bozell Prom, April 3, 1950, letter provided by PBB.

Three: McCarthy and His Friends

1   PBB to author, October 31, 2006.
2   Judis, *Buckley*, 87.
3   WFB to author, November 30, 2007.
4   William F. Buckley Jr. and L. Brent Bozell Jr., *McCarthy and His Enemies: The Record and Its Meaning* (Chicago: Henry Regnery, 1954), 59–60.
5   Ibid., 277, 281, 301, 302, 335, 340. Italics in the original.
6   WFB, ed., *Odyssey of a Friend: Whittaker Chambers's Letters to William F. Buck-

ley Jr., 1954–1961 (New York: Putnam, 1969), 47; McCarthy quoted by Judis, *Buckley*, 108–9; Buckley, *Nearer, My God*, 261.
7   Arthur M. Schlesinger Jr., "The Pendulum of Dogma," *Saturday Review* 37 (April 3, 1954): 61.
8   Henry Regnery to LBB, February 22, 1954; LBB to Henry Regnery, June 21, 1954, Henry Regnery Papers, Hoover Institution.
9   Maureen Bozell to author, February 27, 2007.
10 LBB to Henry Regnery, June 2, 1954; Henry Regnery to LBB, June 25, 1954, Henry Regnery Papers.
11 Henry Regnery to LBB, June 25, 1954; LBB to Henry Regnery, June 21, 1954; Henry Regnery to LBB, September 2, 1954; Henry Regnery to LBB, April 30, 1962, Henry Regnery Papers.
12 Henry Regnery to LBB, June 25, 1954; LBB to Henry Regnery, June 21, 1954; Henry Regnery to LBB, July 26, 1954; Henry Regnery to LBB, September 2, 1964, Henry Regnery Papers.
13 *New York Times*, November 10, 1954.
14 PBB to author, April 13, 2006; July 11, 2006; October 29, 2006.
15 PBB to author, July 11, 2006.
16 Joseph R. McCarthy, "Acheson Looks at Acheson," a review of Dean Acheson's *A Democrat Looks at His Party*, *National Review* (hereafter, *NR*) 1 (December 28, 1955): 26–28; Gary Potter to author, July 27, 2009.
17 LBB to WFB, July 5, 1962, William F. Buckley Jr. Papers.
18 LBB, "This Was a Man," *NR* 3 (May 18, 1957): 26–28.
19 LBB, "National Trends," *NR* 1 (November 19, 1955): 12.

Four: Standing athwart History

1   WFB to LBB, April 13, 1955, and August 8, 1955, William F. Buckley Jr. Papers.
2   Priscilla L. Buckley, *NR* 9 (November 19, 1960): 308.
3   LBB, National Trends: "Wait Till Next Year: Some Notes on the 85th Congress," *NR* 4 (September 14, 1957): 224; LBB, "Should We Impeach Earl Warren?" *NR* 11 (September 9, 1961): 153ff.
4   Henry Regnery to LBB, May 7, 1957; LBB to Henry Regnery, n.d., but probably mid-1957; Henry Regnery to LBB, June 22, 1960; LBB to Henry Regnery, September 24, 1960; Henry Regnery to LBB, October 4, 1960, Henry Regnery Papers.
5   LBB, National Trends: "The Great American Slumber," *NR* 2 (October 6, 1956): 9.
6   LBB, "Nuclear Tests: Hedge against Disaster," *NR* 6 (March 14, 1959): 581; LBB, "The Great American Slumber."
7   LBB, National Trends: "Eisenhower's Premises, Stevenson's Conclusions," *NR* 2 (October 27, 1956): 8; LBB, National Trends: "Operation Tenderizing," *NR* 7 (August 1, 1959): 235; LBB, National Trends: "World Approval or National Security?" *NR* 6 (January 16, 1960): 35; LBB, National Trends: "Congress

Speaks," *NR* 6 (August 16, 1958): 128; LBB, "The Strange Drift of Liberal Catholicism," *NR* 11 (August 12, 1961): 84; LBB, National Trends: "Retreat in Lebanon. Mr. Hammarskjold Pulls a Fast One," *NR* 6 (July 19, 1958): 80.

8   William A. Rusher, *The Rise of the Right* (New York: William Morrow, 1984): 76–77.
9   PBB to author, December 14, 2007, and April 29, 2008.
10 Whittaker Chambers to WFB, October 14, 1959, in WFB, ed., *Odyssey of a Friend*, 264.
11 LBB, National Trends: "Wait Till Next Year," 224; LBB, National Trends: "Why Mr. Rovere Likes Ike," *NR* 2 (July 4, 1956): 7ff.; McCarthy [LBB], "Acheson Looks at Acheson," 26–28; LBB, National Trends: "Public Lobby Got Public Spending," *NR* 7 (August 15, 1959): 267; LBB, National Trends: "The Road Ahead," *NR* 2 (November 24, 1956): 10ff.; LBB, National Trends: "Senator Wiley Repudiated," *NR* 2 (June 13, 1966): 10; LBB, National Trends: "Death Throes of a Proud Party," *NR* 6 (January 31, 1959): 487; LBB, National Trends: "More 'Interlocking Subversion'?" *NR* 3 (March 23, 1957): 276.
12 LBB, "Nuclear Tests: Hedge against Disaster," 579; Kevin J. Smant, *Principles and Heresies: Frank S. Meyer and the Shaping of the American Conservative Movement* (Wilmington, DE: ISI Books, 2002): 46.
13 LBB, "The Open Question," *NR* 4 (September 7, 1957): 209.
14 "The Week," *NR* 11 (July 29, 1961): 38; "For the Record," *NR* 11 (August 12, 1961): 77; Judis, *Buckley*, 318.
15 WFB, ed., *Odyssey of a Friend*, 161, 260.
16 David Franke to author, November 27, 2006; Carol Dawson Smith to author, November 28, 2006.
17 LBB letter to Alfred Kohlberg, November 22, 1958, Alfred Kohlberg Papers, Hoover Institution.

Five: Ghostwriter

1   LBB, "The 1958 Election: Coroner's Report," *NR* 6 (November 22, 1958): 333–35. Italics in the original.
2   Stephen Shadegg, *What Happened to Goldwater? The Inside Story of the 1964 Republican Campaign* (New York: Holt, Rhinehart, and Winston, 1965), 18.
3   Ibid., 7, 8, 24–26; Gregory L. Schneider, *Cadres for Conservatives: Young Americans for Freedom and the Rise of the Contemporary Right* (New York: New York University Press, 1999), 24–25.
4   Clarence Manion to J. Bracken Lee, March 25, 1959, Clarence Manion Papers, Chicago Historical Society.
5   See Manion's numerous letters of May 1959 promoting a Draft Goldwater committee, Clarence Manion Papers; Lee Edwards, *Goldwater: The Man Who Made a Revolution* (Washington, DC: Regnery Publishing, 1995), 105–7.

6 Clarence Manion to Hubbard Russell, December 4, 1959, Clarence Manion Papers.
7 WFB, *Nearer, My God*, 261; WFB to author, November 30, 2008; PBB to author, November 6, 2006.
8 Edwards, *Goldwater*, 114–15.
9 Barry Goldwater, *Why Not Victory? A Fresh Look at American Foreign Policy* (New York: McGraw-Hill, 1962), 18; Barry Goldwater, *With No Apologies* (New York: William Morrow, 1979), 99; Barry Goldwater with Jack Cassidy, *Goldwater* (New York: Doubleday, 1988), 120; Neal B. Freeman to author, June 8, 2006, and November 11, 2006.
10 PBB to author, February 16, 2008.
11 F. Clifton White, *Suite 3505: The Story of the Draft Goldwater Movement* (New Rochelle, NY: Arlington House, 1967), 204–5.
12 Barry Goldwater, *The Conscience of a Conservative* (Shepherdsville, KY: Victor Publishing, 1960), foreword, n.p.
13 Ibid., 23, 66.
14 Ibid., 87–88.
15 Gerald W. Johnson, "Mutterings from Tombstone Territory," a review of *The Conscience of a Conservative* by Barry Goldwater, *New Republic* 142 (May 23, 1960): 20; Frank S. Meyer, "A Man of Principle," a review of *The Conscience of a Conservative* by Senator Barry Goldwater, *NR* 8 (April 23, 1960): 269–70.
16 Goldwater to Clarence Manion, May 5, 1963, Clarence Manion Papers; Nash, *The Conservative Intellectual Movement*, 291.
17 WFB to author, November 30, 2007; Edwards, *Goldwater*, 112; Goldwater to Clarence Manion, November 4, 1960; Clarence Manion to LBB, November 9, 1960; Clarence Manion to LBB, October 18, 1960; Clarence Manion to Barry Goldwater (n.d., but probably April 1963); LBB to Clarence Manion, November 4, 1960; Clarence Manion to LBB, November 9, 1960, Clarence Manion Papers; Christopher Manion to author, December 2, 2006.
18 LBB, National Trends: "Goldwater on the First Ballot," *NR* 8 (June 18, 1960): 388. Italics in the original.
19 Rusher, *Rise of the Right*, 86–89; Edwards, *Goldwater*, 134.
20 Clarence Manion to Hubbard Russell, July 27, 1960, Clarence Manion Papers; LBB quoted by Marvin Liebman, *Coming Out Conservative: An Autobiography* (San Francisco: Chronicle Books, 1992), 149.
21 LBB, National Trends: "Goldwater's Leadership: An Assessment," *NR* 9 (August 13, 1960): 74; LBB, National Trends: "Putting Power to Use," *NR* 9 (December 17, 1960): 373.
22 Priscilla L. Buckley, *NR* 9 (November 19, 1960): 308; LBB, National Trends: "The Intimidation of Richard Nixon," *NR* 9 (November 19, 1960): 304.
23 LBB, National Trends: "The Challenge to Conservatives, I," *NR* 9 (December 3, 1960): 343; LBB, National Trends: "The Challenge to Conservatives, II," *NR* 10 (January 14, 1961): 12. Italics in the original.

24 "Senator Goldwater Speaks His Mind: An Interview with L. Brent Bozell," *NR* 10 (January 14, 1961): 13–14.
25 Barry Goldwater, "A Foreign Policy for America," *NR* 10 (March 25, 1961): 177–81.
26 LBB to Stephen Shadegg, telephone transcript, September 19 or 20, 1963, Stephen Shadegg/Barry Goldwater Collection, 1945–65, Center for American History, University of Texas at Austin.

Six: Magic Kingdom

1 Patrick Allitt, *Catholic Intellectuals and Conservative Politics in America, 1950–1985* (Ithaca, NY: Cornell University Press, 1993), 144.
2 PBB to author, July 11, 2006.
3 Frederick D. Wilhelmsen quoted by Russell Kirk, *Confessions of a Bohemian Tory: Episodes and Reflections of a Vagrant Career* (New York: Fleet Publishing, 1963), 143.
4 PBB to author, June 5, 2006; Fr. Joseph M. Baker, "The End of an Era," eulogy for Frederick D. Wilhelmsen and L. Brent Bozell, University of Dallas Tribute, 62–65; WFB to author, November 30, 2007; Nash, *The Conservative Intellectual Movement in America*, 427.
5 PBB to Allitt, *Catholic Intellectuals and Conservative Politics*, 144–45.
6 LBB to WFB, December 31, 1962, William F. Buckley Jr. Papers.
7 L. Brent Bozell III to author, October 30, 2006.
8 PBB to WFB, February 25, 1964, William F. Buckley Jr. Papers; PBB to author, July 11, 2006.
9 PBB to WFB, December 10, 1962, William F. Buckley Jr. Papers.
10 PBB to WFB, n.d. 1962, William F. Buckley Jr. Papers.
11 Ibid.; PBB to author, May 26, 2006.
12 LBB, "Capitalist Self-Seeking or Christian Self-Denial?," *New Oxford Review* 53 (October 1986): 18; Nash, *The Conservative Intellectual Movement in America*, 427; PBB to author, October 29, 2006; PBB to author, April 5, 2006.
13 George H. Dunne, SJ, and C. J. McNaspy, SJ, "How We Look to Others," *America* 105 (May 13, 1961): 272–74.
14 LBB, "The Strange Drift of Liberal Catholicism," *NR* 6 (August 12, 1961): 81–85.
15 LBB, "To Magnify the West," *Mustard Seeds*, 7–14.
16 Carol Dawson Smith to author, November 28, 2006; Linda Bridges and John R. Coyne, *Strictly Right: William F. Buckley Jr. and the American Conservative Movement* (Hoboken, NJ: John F. Wiley & Sons, 2007), 77; Rusher, *Rise of the Right*, 130; Schneider, *Cadres for Conservatism*, 52; Lee and Anne Edwards to author, November 2, 2006.
17 Priscilla L. Buckley, *NR* 11 (November 18, 1960): 308.
18 Frank S. Meyer, "The Twisted Tree of Liberty," *NR* 12 (January 16, 1962): 25–26.
19 LBB, "Mary's Bread," *Mustard Seeds*, 338.

20 LBB, "Freedom or Virtue?," *NR* 13 (September 11, 1962): 181–87ff.
21 Frank S. Meyer, "Why Freedom?," *NR* 13 (September 25, 1962): 223–25.
22 PBB to author, April 5, 2008; Allitt, *Catholic Intellectuals and Conservative Politics*, 144–45.
23 LBB to WFB, December 31, 1962, William F. Buckley Jr. Papers.
24 Maureen Bozell to author, September 8, 2008; Christopher Bozell to author, March 31, 2008.

Seven: Pulling Up Stakes

1 LBB to Dr. Paul O'Halloran, June 27, 1964; Frederick D. Wilhelmsen to WFB, December 28, 1964, William F. Buckley Jr. Papers.
2 PBB to WFB, February 25, 1964, William F. Buckley Jr. Papers; PBB to author, October 31, 2006.
3 PBB to WFB, February 25, 1964, William F. Buckley Jr. Papers.
4 PBB to WFB, (probably December) 1968, William F. Buckley Jr. Papers.
5 LBB to WFB, December 31, 1962, William F. Buckley Jr. Papers.
6 *NR* 14 (April 23, 1963): 310.
7 LBB-Hutchins debate in Steve Allen et al., ed., *Dialogues in Americanism* (Chicago: Henry Regnery, 1964), 74–92; PBB to WFB, February 6, 1964, William F. Buckley Jr. Papers.
8 Shadegg, *What Happened to Goldwater?*, 46.
9 LBB to Neil McCaffrey, January 9, 1961, Neil McCaffrey Papers, in the possession of Mrs. Neil McCaffrey (my thanks to Mrs. McCaffrey for providing me with copies of these papers).
10 Shadegg, *What Happened to Goldwater?*, 54, 57–58; Edwards, *Goldwater*, 166–67; Shadegg to LBB, September 19 or 20, 1963, Stephen Shadegg/Barry Goldwater Collection.
11 LBB to Stephen Shadegg, September 19 or 20, 1963, Stephen Shadegg/Barry Goldwater Collection.
12 Ibid.
13 *New York Times*, September 16, 1963.
14 White, *Suite 3505*, 205–7; LBB to Stephen Shadegg, September 19 or 20, 1963; Shadegg, *What Happened to Goldwater?*, 69–70; Edwards, *Goldwater*, 183–84; Goldwater, *Goldwater*, 147–48, 188–90.
15 Edwards, *Goldwater*, 196–99.
16 LBB to WFB, May 31, 1964, William F. Buckley Jr. Papers; PBB to author, October 31, 2006; Judis, *Buckley*, 319.
17 PBB to WFB, February 25, 1964, William F. Buckley Jr. Papers; Neal B. Freeman to author, August 29, 2008.
18 Freeman to author, June 8, 2006; WFB to author, November 30, 2007; PBB to author, April 3, 2006.

19 Freeman to author, June 8, 2006.
20 LBB to WFB, May 31, 1964, William F. Buckley Jr. Papers.
21 E. Michael Lawrence, introduction to *Mustard Seeds*, xii.
22 Bozell campaign literature, Neal B. Freeman Papers (my thanks to Mr. Freeman for allowing me to examine these papers); L. Brent Bozell III to author, October 22, 2008.
23 Clipping from the *Washington Post*, n.d., William F. Buckley Jr. Papers.
24 Bozell campaign literature, Neal B. Freeman Papers; Freeman to author, June 8, 2006; E. Michael Lawrence to author, November 1, 2006; Freeman to author, May 15, 2006.
25 LBB to Freeman, May 28, 1964, Neal B. Freeman Papers; LBB to WFB, May 31, 1964, William F. Buckley Jr. Papers; Freeman to author, April 5, 2007.
26 Smant, *Principles and Heresies*, 154.
27 American Conservative Union, *Confidential Preliminary Report* (n.d., but probably January 1965), Marvin Liebman Papers, Hoover Institution.
28 Robert E. Bauman to author, December 5, 2006; Jameson Campaigne Jr. to author, September 21, 2006; Carol Dawson Smith to author, November 28, 2006.
29 Marvin Liebman to John Ashbrook, February 2, 1966, Marvin Liebman Papers.
30 Bauman to author, December 5, 2006; minutes of the ACU board of directors meetings, Marvin Liebman Papers.
31 LBB to John Ashbrook, March 10, 1966, William F. Buckley Jr. Papers; Bauman to author, December 5, 2006; David R. Jones proposal of February 8, 1966, Marvin Liebman Papers.
32 Minutes of the ACU board of directors special meeting, March 2, 1966, Marvin Liebman Papers.
33 LBB to John Ashbrook, March 10, 1966; LBB to Ashbrook, March 15, 1966, William F. Buckley Jr. Papers.
34 Bridges and Coyne, *Strictly Right*, 102; William Campbell to author, October 31, 2008; Guy Davenport, "The Need to Maintain a Civilization," *NR* 17 (April 6, 1965): 283–84.
35 LBB to WFB, May 23, 1963, William F. Buckley Jr. Papers.
36 LBB to WFB, October 28, 1965; WFB to LBB, November 1, 1965; LBB to WFB, November 1, 1965; WFB to LBB, November 4, 1965. All in William F. Buckley Jr. Papers.
37 WFB, On the Right: "The Catholic Church and Abortion," *NR* 18 (April 5, 1966): 308; LBB to WFB, April 5, 1966, and in *NR* 18 (May 3, 1966): 390; WFB to LBB, not sent; WFB to LBB, "To the Editor," *NR* 18 (May 3, 1966): 390; LBB to WFB, April 6, 1966, William F. Buckley Jr. Papers.

Eight: Defender of the Constitution

1. LBB to Alex Hillman, November 26, 1963; PBB to WFB, February 25, 1964, William F. Buckley Jr. Papers.
2. PBB to author, July 11, 2006; Henry Regnery to LBB, November 20, 1963, Henry Regnery Papers; Bozell campaign literature, Neal B. Freeman Papers.
3. Neal B. Freeman to author, April 5, 2008.
4. Ibid.; PBB to author, October 9, 2006; David Franke to author, November 27, 2006.
5. L. Brent Bozell, *The Warren Revolution: Reflections on the Consensus Society* (New Rochelle, NY: Arlington House, 1966).
6. Ibid., 30. Italics in the original.
7. Ibid., 34, 232–33 et passim; LBB, "Should We Impeach Earl Warren?" *NR* 11 (September 9, 1961): 153ff.
8. LBB, *The Warren Revolution*, 112, 116–18.
9. Ibid., 338–39.
10. Ibid., 336.
11. Ibid., 15, 219.
12. Neal B. Freeman to author, November 6, 2008.
13. E. Michael Lawrence, introduction to *Mustard Seeds*, x; William F. Buckley Jr., ed., *Did You Ever See a Dream Walking?: American Conservative Thought in the Twentieth Century* (Indianapolis: Bobbs Merrill, 1970), 5; WFB to LBB, December 13, 1966, William F. Buckley Jr. Papers.
14. Martin Diamond, "Challenge to the Court," a review of *The Warren Revolution* by L. Brent Bozell, *NR* 19 (June 13, 1967): 642–44; James McClellan, "On Judicial Subversion," a review of *The Warren Revolution* by L. Brent Bozell, *Modern Age* 11 (Spring 1967): 207–10; George Carey, "The Constitution v. Warren et al.," a review of *The Warren Revolution* by L. Brent Bozell, *Triumph* 2 (January 1967): 27–29.
15. Author to PBB, n.d.; Joseph Sobran to PBB, February 2, 2008.
16. PBB to author, October 9, 2006.
17. LBB, "The Death of the Constitution," *Triumph* 3 (February 1968): 383–90.

Nine: Defender of the Faith

1. LBB quoted by Gary Potter to author, July 27, 2009.
2. LBB, "The Strange Drift of Liberal Catholicism," *NR* 11 (August 12, 1961): 85; LBB, Notes and Asides, *NR* 13 (August 14, 1962): 93.
3. *Washington Daily News*, June 8, 1970.
4. Kathryn Bozell Brewster to author, December 4, 2006; Robert E. Bauman to author, December 5, 2008.
5. E. Michael Lawrence, Introduction, *The Best of "Triumph"* (Front Royal, VA:

Christendom Press, 2001), xviii; E. Michael Lawrence to author, November 1, 2006.
6   LBB, "Who Is Accommodating to What?," *NR* 17 (May 5, 1965): 374ff.
7   PBB to author, April 3, 2006.
8   LBB, "Mustard Seeds," *Mustard Seeds*, 2.
9   Allitt, *Catholic Intellectuals and Conservative Politics*, 140–41.
10 WFB, On the Right: "The Birth Rate," *NR* 17 (March 23, 1965): 231; Garry Wills, "Catholics and Population," *NR* 17 (July 27, 1965): 643–48.
11 LBB, "*Humanae Vitae*, Part Two: Thou Shalt Live Love," *Best of "Triumph,"* 225–30.
12 LBB, "The Open Question: Mater si, Magistra si!," *NR* 17 (September 17, 1965): 772.
13 Garry Wills, "On the Present Position of Catholics," *NR* 17 (March 4, 1965): 375–77.
14 Allitt, *Catholic Intellectuals and Conservative Politics*, 142.
15 Farley Clinton to author, March 20, 2008; Christopher Bozell to author, March 31, 2008; Wills, *Confessions of a Conservative*, 12.
16 Neal B. Freeman to author, June 8, 2006.
17 Rusher, *Rise of the Right*, 133; Kendall quoted by Wills, *Confessions of a Conservative*, 22; Willmoore Kendall to LBB, n.d., but probably 1966, William F. Buckley Jr. Papers.
18 PBB to WFB, n.d., Wednesday, 1968, William F. Buckley Jr. Papers.
19 Russell Kirk to LBB, September 24, 1965, Russell Kirk Papers, Clarke Historical Library, Central Michigan University.
20 Committee for a Conservative Catholic Magazine fund-raising letter, September 8, 1965, Russell Kirk Papers. Emphasis in the original.
21 Committee for a Conservative Catholic Magazine fund-raising letter, September 21, 1965, William F. Buckley Jr. Papers; "A Preliminary Report from the Committee for a Conservative Catholic Magazine," William F. Buckley Jr. Papers.
22 Committee for a Conservative Catholic Magazine brochure, William F. Buckley Jr. Papers.
23 E. Michael Lawrence to author, November 1, 2006.
24 LBB, statement included in a letter to Russell Kirk, August 26, 1966; Lawrence, Introduction, *Best of "Triumph,"* xix.
25 LBB, "A Declaration," *Mustard Seeds*, 283.
26 LBB to WFB, March 1, 1966; PBB to WFB, March 6, 1968; PBB to WFB, September n.d., 1969, William F. Buckley Jr. Papers; L. Brent Bozell III to author, October 30, 2006; PBB to author, December 26, 2006; Kathryn Bozell Brewster to author, December 4, 2006.
27 LBB to Nicholas von Hoffman, *Washington Post*, May 22, 1966.
28 LBB to Russell Kirk, December 28, 1965, Russell Kirk Papers.
29 E. Michael Lawrence to WFB, July 20, 1966; WFB to E. Michael Lawrence, July 28, 1966, William F. Buckley Jr. Papers.

Notes

30 Anne Edwards to author, November 2, 1966.
31 LBB to WFB, July 8, 1966; Carl D. Hall to WFB, July 26, 1966; WFB to Jaycee official, July 20, 1966; WFB to J. A. Friedrich, August 10, 1966, William F. Buckley Jr. Papers.
32 LBB to Russell Kirk, August 26, 1966, Russell Kirk Papers.
33 Ibid.
34 Lee Edwards to Henry Regnery, November 3, 1966, Henry Regnery Papers.

Ten: The Cutting Edge

1   Farley Clinton to author, March 31, 2008; Farley Clinton to author, April 2, 2008.
2   Willmoore Kendall to LBB, late 1966, William F. Buckley Jr. Papers.
3   Russell Kirk to LBB, November 29, 1966, Russell Kirk Papers.
4   LBB to Russell Kirk, June 12, 1967, Russell Kirk Papers; LBB, "Paul and Leo," *Mustard Seeds*, 48.
5   The editors, "The War," *Triumph* 3 (March 1968): 7; LBB, "Mustard Seeds," *Mustard Seeds*, 2; Lawrence, introduction to *Mustard Seeds*, xiii; Anne Edwards to author, November 2, 2006; Gary Potter to author, July 27, 2009.
6   *New York Times*, September 18, 1966; LBB to Henry Regnery, January 13, 1970, Henry Regnery Papers; LBB to WFB, July 20, 1966, William F. Buckley Jr. Papers.
7   Anne Edwards to author, November 2, 2006.
8   Russell Kirk quoted by Judis, *Buckley*, 319.
9   LBB, "The Coming American Schism," *Mustard Seeds*, 67–70; LBB to Nicholas von Hoffman, *Washington Post*, May 22, 1966; Gary Potter, "The Liturgy Club," *Best of "Triumph,"* 77–90.
10 LBB, "The New Missal II," *Triumph* 4 (July 1969): 42.
11 Lee and Anne Edwards to author, November 2, 2006.
12 PBB to WFB, March 8, 1966; PBB to John J. Russell, Bishop of Richmond, March 10, 1969; WFB to PBB, March 12, 1969, William F. Buckley Jr. Papers.
13 The Editors, "Mater No, Magistra No," *Triumph* 2 (October 1967): 42; The Editors, "The End of Catholic Education," *Triumph* 3 (July 1968): 37; The Editors, "A Model for the Bishops," *Triumph* 4 (June 1969): 10; The Editors, "The Seminaries," *Triumph* 5 (May 1970): 42.
14 Kathryn Bozell Brewster to author, December 4, 2006.
15 Speech quoted in Neil McCaffrey to LBB, August 22, 1970, Neil McCaffrey Papers.
16 The Editors, "Eucharistic Euphemy," *Triumph* 7 (February 1972): 8; The Editors, "Cost Analysis Saves?" *Triumph* 7 (October 1972): 10; The Editors, "Ecumenicism or Catholicism: Two Politics," *Triumph* 8 (January 1973): 46.
17 LBB, Fund Appeal Letter of January 15, 1970, Neil McCaffrey Papers.
18 The Editors, "The Merciful Penalty," *Triumph* 3 (June 1968): 9–10;

Thomas J. Higgins, SJ, "Why the Death Penalty," *Triumph* 8 (February 1973): 20–23; David Schindler to author, July 12, 2006.
19. The Editors, "The Silent Church," *Triumph* 5 (January 1970): 42; LBB, "Live Politics: Catholic," *Mustard Seeds,* 205.
20. The Editors, "Alone, If Necessary," *Triumph* 2 (April 1967): 38; The Editors, "The Herodians," *Triumph* 5 (March 1970): 7; The Editors, "Democratic Murder," *Triumph* 3 (February 1968): 9; The Editors, "Birthright," *Triumph* 6 (March 1971): 9.
21. LBB, "Stop the Death Merchants," *Mustard Seeds*, 211; The Editors, "Machismo," *Triumph* 4 (May 1969): 10; The Editors, "The Final Solution," *Best of "Triumph,"* 236.
22. The Editors, "Great Day in the Morning," *Best of "Triumph,"* 212–14; LBB, "*Humanae Vitae*, Part One: Thou Shalt Love Life," *Best of "Triumph,"* 215–25; LBB, "*Humanae Vitae*, Part Two," 226–30; PBB to author, October 31, 2006.
23. Neil McCaffrey to LBB, September 18, 1968, Neil McCaffrey Papers; The Editors, "The Encyclical," *NR* 20 (August 18, 1968): 786.
24. LBB, "The Coming American Schism," 71; Ralph McInerny, *What Went Wrong with Vatican II: The Catholic Crisis Explained* (Manchester, NH: Sophia Institute Press, 1998): 79–80; PBB to author, July 11, 2006, and March 1, 2008.
25. LBB, "The Coming American Schism," 57–72.
26. LBB, "Whither Anti-Communism?" *Mustard Seeds*, 53–54; LBB, "The Church and the Republic," *Mustard Seeds*, 239; LBB, "Dialogue in Vermont," *NR* 17 (December 14, 1965): 1153–56.
27. The Editors, "Democracy's Revenge," *Triumph* 2 (October 1967): 41; The Editors, "Viet Riddles," *Triumph* 3 (February 1968): 7–8; The Editors, "The Second Vietnam War," *Triumph* 3 (June 1968): 8; The Editors, "Nixon's Redemption," *Triumph* 4 (July 1969): 41.
28. The Editors, "War: Left, Right, Christian," *Triumph* 5 (January 1970): 41; The Editors, "McNamara's Valedictory," *Triumph* 5 (March 1968): 38; The Editors, "Our Toothless Terror," *Triumph* 4 (April 1969): 42; LBB, "Defending America: Impractical?" *Triumph* 6 (November 1971): 31 (italics in the original); The Editors, "Stop CBW," *Triumph* 4 (March 1969): 7.
29. The Editors, "The Negro Revolution," *Triumph* 2 (August 1967): 38; The Editors, "Black Power," *Triumph* 2 (January 1967): 8.
30. The Editors, "Soul, Brother," *Best of "Triumph,"* 338–56; E. Michael Lawrence, "Our First Three Years," *Triumph* 4 (September 1967): 12.
31. LBB, "Mary's Bread," *Mustard Seeds*, 338–39; LBB, "The Servile State Revisited," *Mustard Seeds*, 161–69.
32. The Editors, "At Last: A Conservative Catholic Magazine," *NR* 18 (September 6, 1966): 870–72; LBB to Neal B. Freeman, November 2, 1966, Neal B. Freeman Papers; Neal B. Freeman to LBB, November 9, 1966, Neal B. Freeman Papers; Maria Augusta Trapp to the editors, *Triumph* 1 (September 1966): 2.
33. *Commonwealth* 85 (November 1966): 124.

Eleven: Autumn in America

1. The Editors in the introduction to an article called "Radical Christianity" by Erik von Kuehnelt-Leddihn, *Triumph* 2 (February 1967): 19.
2. The Editors, "Quo," *Best of "Triumph,"* 253.
3. Thomas Molnar to author, June 6, 2006; WFB, *Nearer, My God*, 261; WFB, "L. Brent Bozell, RIP," *NR* 49 (May 19, 1997): 22–23; Kirk quoted by Markmann, *The Buckleys*, 318; E. Michael Lawrence, Introduction, *Best of "Triumph,"* xxii–xxiii; Neal Freeman to author, June 8, 2006; Stuart Gudowitz, "Moving Toward Jesus," a review of *Mustard Seeds* by L. Brent Bozell, *Fidelity* 7 (February 1987): 47.
4. LBB to Russell Kirk, February 2, 1968, Russell Kirk Papers; LBB, "The Death of the Constitution," *Best of "Triumph,"* 381–91.
5. LBB, "The Autumn of the Church," *Mustard Seeds*, 97–104. Italics in the original.
6. The Editors, "The New Missal II," *Triumph* 4 (July 1969): 42; John Courtney Murray, SJ, *We Hold These Truths: Catholic Reflections on the American Proposition* (New York: Sheed and Ward, 1960).
7. The Editors, "The Silent Church," *Triumph* 5 (January 1970): 42.
8. LBB, "The Autumn of the Country," *Mustard Seeds*, 89–96.
9. The Editors, *Triumph* 1(September 1966): 37.
10. Anne W. Carroll, "The American School," *Best of "Triumph,"* 552; LBB, "The Tapes and the Truth," *Mustard Seeds*, 254; The Editors, "The Unsinkable R.C.," *Triumph* 7 (July 1972): 45.
11. Molnar to author, June 6, 2006; Gary Potter to author, July 27, 2009; PBB to author, October 31, 2006; Farley Clinton to author, April 2, 2008; Lawrence, Introduction, *Best of "Triumph,"* xvii, xxv; E. Michael Lawrence to author, September 8, 2009.
12. Lee Edwards to author, November 2, 2006; Neil McCaffrey to LBB, November 28, 1967, Neil McCaffrey Papers; LBB to McCaffrey, December 14, 1967, William F. Buckley Jr. Papers; LBB to McCaffrey, February 2, 1968, William F. Buckley Jr. Papers; Neil McCaffrey, *Triumph* 3 (February 1968), Neil McCaffrey Papers; Neil McCaffrey to LBB, June 8, 1968, William F. Buckley Jr. Papers.
13. LBB, "True Sin, True Myth," *Triumph* 7 (January 1972): 15–16.
14. Sister Isabel to LBB, July 9, 1969, William F. Buckley Jr. Papers.
15. WFB, *Nearer, My God*, 260; WFB, *Cruising Speed*, 215–16; WFB to LBB, August 30, 1967, William F. Buckley Jr. Papers; WFB, *Triumph* 3 (April 1968): 3–4.
16. Bozell file, Correspondence, Box 48, William F. Buckley Jr. Papers.
17. LBB to WFB, October 11, 1968, William F. Buckley Jr. Papers; LBB to Neal Freeman, May 24, 1965, Neal B. Freeman Papers.
18. PBB to WFB, n.d., but probably October 1968, William F. Buckley Jr. Papers.
19. WFB to LBB, January 29, 1969; LBB, "The Truth-Seeker," *NR* 24 (April 1972): 473; Judis, *Buckley*, 320.

20 LBB, "Letter to Yourselves," *Triumph* 4 (March 1969): 11–14.
21 E. Michael Lawrence, Introduction, *Best of "Triumph,"* xxvi; Farley Clinton to author, March 3, 2008; LBB, "Letter to Yourselves," 11.
22 LBB, "Politics of the Poor," *Triumph* 4 (April 1969): 11–13. Italics in the original.
23 LBB, "Near to the Escorial: 1563," *Triumph* 5 (December 1970): 26.
24 "Letters from Yourselves," *Triumph* 4 (June 1969): 17–19ff.
25 LBB to William A. Rusher, February 24, 1969, William A. Rusher Papers; William A. Rusher to LBB, March 6, 1969, William A. Rusher Papers; PBB to WFB, March 1969, William F. Buckley Jr. Papers.
26 *Triumph* Reader Survey, 1969, William F. Buckley Jr. Papers.
27 LBB, fund-raising letter, October 11, 1967, William F. Buckley Jr. Papers; Gary Potter to author, July 27, 2009; Kevin Lynch, "Mission of Mercy," a review of *Mustard Seeds* by L. Brent Bozell, *NR* 39 (June 5, 1987): 45–46; Judis, *Buckley*, 320–21; Allitt, *Catholic Intellectuals and Conservative Politics*, 158; Warren H. Carroll, Foreword, *Best of "Triumph,"* xiv.
28 LBB, report to subscribers, October 11, 1967, Neil McCaffrey Papers; The Editors, fund-raising letter, November 8, 1967, Neil McCaffrey Papers.
29 Freeman to author, June 8, 2006; PBB to author, October 31, 2006; Molnar to author, June 6, 2006.
30 Christopher Bozell to author, March 31, 2008; LBB, fund-raising letter, January 17, 1969, William F. Buckley Jr. Papers; LBB to Neil McCaffrey, January 15, 1970, Neil McCaffrey Papers; LBB to Gen. Albert C. Wedemeyer, August 7, 1969, Albert C. Wedemeyer Papers; Donald G. McClane to *Triumph*'s special friends, April 1969, Neil McCaffrey Papers.

Twelve: Phantom Empire

1 PBB to author, October 29, 2007; LBB, "A Preliminary Report from the Committee for a Conservative Catholic Magazine," William F. Buckley Jr. Papers; Kathryn Bozell Brewster to author, December 4, 2006; *Triumph* fund-raising letter, January 17, 1969, William F. Buckley Jr. Papers.
2 LBB, "Life—Money? Diaspora?" *Triumph* 8 (February 1973): 8.
3 Advertisement, *Triumph* 5 (January 1970): n.p.
4 Advertisement, *Triumph* 6 (January 1971): 24.
5 LBB to Neil McCaffrey, August 8, 1972, Neil McCaffrey Papers; LBB, "Life—Money? Diaspora?," 8.
6 LBB, "Life—Money? Diaspora?"; The Editors, "The SCC Guild Program," *Triumph* 7 (March 1972): 15; LBB, "The JBS and the SCC," *Triumph* 6 (October 1971): 31.
7 Kathryn Bozell Brewster to author, December 4, 2006.
8 Advertisement, *Triumph* 9 (January 1974): n.p.

9 Cyrus Brewster to author, November 29, 2006; Fr. Joseph Baker to author, July 31, 2006; Buckley, *Cruising Speed*, 215–16.
10 Allitt, *Catholic Intellectuals and Conservative Politics*, 149; Markmann, *The Buckleys*, 185.
11 LBB, "The Church and the Republic," *Mustard Seeds*, 242–43; Warren H. Carroll, *Memories* (a privately printed collection of reminiscences of L. Brent Bozell), 21.
12 LBB, "The Confessional Tribe," *Best of "Triumph,"* 33–37.
13 The Editors, "The Reign in Spain," *Triumph* 4 (February 1969): 8–9; The Editors, "The Magazine's for Burning," *Triumph* 4 (July 1969): 7.
14 E. Michael Lawrence to author, November 1, 2006; The Editors, "Action for Life," *Best of "Triumph,"* 19–20; LBB, "Mustard Seeds," *Mustard Seeds*, 3–4.
15 The Editors, "Action for Life," 21.
16 Baker to author, July 31, 2006; Baker, "The End of an Era," 62–65; M[ichael] L[awrence], "June 6," *Triumph* 5 (July 1970): 9–10.
17 The Editors, "The Sons of Thunder," *Triumph* 5 (March 1970): 8; Baker, "The End of an Era," 63.
18 M[ichael] L[awrence], "June 6," 8–10ff.; *Washington Post*, June 7, 1970; *Washington Star*, June 6, 1970.
19 *Washington Daily News*, June 8, 1970; M[ichael] L[awrence], "June 6," 42.
20 LBB, "Encouraging Murder," *New York Times*, October 13, 1970; The Editors, *Triumph* 5 (November 1970): 14; The Editors, *Triumph* 6 (April 1971): 7; LBB to Neil McCaffrey, March 12, 1971, Neil McCaffrey Papers.
21 Kathryn Bozell Brewster to author, December 4, 2006; LBB, "On Going to Jail," *Mustard Seeds*, 197.
22 E. Michael Lawrence to author, November 1, 2006; Gary Potter to author, July 27, 2009; The Editors, "Rough Beast," *Triumph* 5 (June 1970): 10.
23 Paul Weyrich, "On Militancy and Responsibility (Some Reflections)," *The Wanderer*, June 18, 1970; The Editors, "Abortion," *NR* 22 (June 30, 1970): 359.
24 Baker, "The End of an Era," 64; Baker to author, July 31, 2006; The Editors, "Bishops and Sons," *Triumph* 5 (December 1970): 8.
25 The Editors, "The First Lady," *Best of "Triumph,"* 285; The Editors, "Men's Lib," *Triumph* 5 (October 1970): 42.
26 PBB, "The Sexual Dialectic," *Triumph* 6 (January 1971): 17.
27 *New York Post*, March 20, 1971; The Editors, "God and Woman at Catholic U.," *Best of "Triumph,"* 48.
28 The Editors, "God and Woman at Catholic U.," 48; *New York Post*, March 20, 1971; *New York Times*, March 12, 1971; *Time*, March 22, 1971; *Newsweek*, March 22, 1971.
29 Mrs. William F. Buckley Sr. quoted by the *New York Post*, March 20, 1971; Neil McCaffrey to WFB, March 18, 1971, Neil McCaffrey Papers; PBB's comments, an undated clipping from an unnamed newspaper, Neil McCaffrey Papers; PBB to author, October 31, 2006.

30 PBB to author, October 31, 2006.
31 The Editors, "Ireland for the Irish," *Triumph* 4 (October 1969): 7; The Editors, "Criost Ri Abu," *Triumph* 4 (February 1969): 10.
32 The Editors, "England v. Ireland," *Triumph* 9 (December 1974): 10; The Editors, "Ireland and Spain: Mirrors of Christendom," *Triumph* 6 (March 1971): 45.
33 The Editors, "IRA Denies Bombing Role," *Triumph* 8 (October 1973): 43; The Editors, "Bombs, Bias, and a Bishop's Blessing," *Triumph* 8 (October 1973): 45; Thomas J. Barbarie, "From the Bronx, with Love," *Triumph* 8 (June 1973): 16–17; The Editors, "Help for Ireland!," *Triumph* 8 (December 1973): 9; Irish Relief Fund advertisement, *Triumph* 8 (December 1973): 45.
34 John P. McCarthy, "Will the Catholic Nation Survive?," *Triumph* 7 (October 1972): 29; The Editors, "The Greening of Ulster," *Triumph* 6 (October 1971): 9; The Editors, "Erin Goes Blah," *Triumph* 8 (January 1973): 8; The Editors, "The IRA and Ireland's Future," *Triumph* 8 (April 1973): 46.
35 The Editors, "Nation Time," *Triumph* 7 (July 1972): 9.

Thirteen: Time to Die

1 LBB, "The Confessional Tribe," *Best of "Triumph,"* 32–42.
2 William A. Rusher to LBB, August 4, 1970, William A. Rusher Papers; LBB to William A. Rusher, August 19, 1970, William A. Rusher Papers.
3 Neil McCaffrey to WFB, June 27, 1970, Neil McCaffrey Papers; Neil McCaffrey to LBB, July 21, 1970, Neil McCaffrey Papers, and to *Triumph* 5 (October 1970): 22; WFB to Neil McCaffrey, August 8, 1970, Neil McCaffrey Papers.
4 The Editors, "1972: Acceptable Year of the Lord," *Triumph* 7 (November 1972): 45.
5 The Editors, "Catechism for a Catholic ADL," *Triumph* 8 (April 1973): 45; The Editors, "Balance of Power, U.S.A.," *Triumph* 8 (April 1973): 8–9; The Editors, "America and Israel," *Triumph* 9 (January 1974): 8; The Editors, "People Who Need Peoplehood," *Triumph* 8 (June 1973): 9.
6 The Editors, "The Catholic Vote," *Triumph* 9 (June 1974): 11; The Editors, "Life and the Facts of Life," *Triumph* 9 (July 1974): 46.
7 LBB, "Toward a Catholic Realpolitik," *Best of "Triumph,"* 630–43.
8 The Editors, "Catholics Act!" *Best of "Triumph,"* 31; LBB as reported by the *Washington Daily News*, June 8, 1970.
9 LBB, "Live Politics: Catholic," *Mustard Seeds*, 204.
10 LBB, "The Church and the Republic," *Mustard Seeds*, 236–42.
11 Ibid., 242–45.
12 Ibid., 232–35.
13 The Editors (LBB), "The Catholic Obligation," *Mustard Seeds*, 217–23.
14 William Devlin, "America: There's a Nigger in the Woodpile," *Triumph* 8 (May 1973): 27; John Short, "Wanted: A Pro-Life Movement," *Triumph* 8 (November

1973): 16; The Editors, "The Buckley Amendment," *Triumph* 8 (July 1973): 46; The Editors, "Life and the Facts of Life," *Triumph* 9 (July 1974): 46.
15 The Editors, "The Servile State," *Best of "Triumph,"* 441–42.
16 Mario de Solenni, "Baptizing Organiculture," *Triumph* 7 (February 1972): 28–29; Frederick D. Wilhelmsen, "Toward an Incarnational Politics," *Best of "Triumph,"* 563; The Editors, "Ecology: Whose Rebellion?" *Triumph* 5 (March 1870): 41; LBB, "Doing *Populorum Progressio*," *Mustard Seeds*, 275; LBB, "A Bridge to the Future," (April 1970), Neil McCaffrey Papers.
17 The Editors, "The Dry Look," *Triumph* 4 (February 1974): 7; The Editors, "A Lenten Meditation," *Triumph* 9 (March 1974): 46.
18 LBB, "Doing *Populorum Progressio*," 277–79; The Editors, "*Mater et Magistra*," *Triumph* 8 (April 1973): 9; The Editors, "The Debasers," *Triumph* 8 (April 1973): 7; Thomas J. Barbarie, "A Christian Manifesto," *Triumph* 9 (December 1874): 20.
19 The Editors, "An American Summer," *Triumph* 6 (October 1971): 45; The Editors, "Seven Points," *Triumph* 7 (March 1972): 7–8; Neil McCaffrey to E. Michael Lawrence, February 23, 1971, Neil McCaffrey Papers.
20 LBB, "Life—Money? Diaspora?," 8; LBB, "A Letter You May Have Missed," *Triumph* 10 (February 1975): 9.
21 LBB, "A Letter You May Have Missed," 9.
22 Ibid. (italics in the original); The Editors, "TRIUMPH Lives!" *Triumph* 10 (March 1975): 10; LBB, "A Dedication," *Mustard Seeds*, 281; E. Michael Lawrence to author, February 19, 2010.
23 The Editors, *Triumph* 10 (September 1975): 1; LBB, "A Dedication," 281.
24 Lawrence to author, November 1, 2006; LBB, "Mustard Seeds," *Mustard Seeds*, 4.
25 PBB to author, July 11, 2006; Lee Edwards to author, November 2, 2006; LBB, "Mustard Seeds," 4.
26 For a comprehensive discussion of bipolar disorder, see Kay Redfield Jamison, *Touched with Fire: Manic-Depressive Illness and the Artistic Temperament* (New York: Free Press, 1994).
27 Neal B. Freeman to author, June 8, 2006; Barbarie, *Memories*, 59.
28 LBB, fund-raising appeal, January 19, 1969, William F. Buckley Jr. Papers; LBB, "Mustard Seeds," 3.
29 Lawrence, to author, September 8, 2008; PBB to author, May 2008.
30 Lawrence to author, November 1, 2006.
31 LBB, "Mustard Seeds," 4; LBB, "Mary Falls," *Mustard Seeds*, 372–73.

Fourteen: Manacled to a Roller Coaster

1 LBB, "Mustard Seeds," *Mustard Seeds*, 4–5; Lawrence, introduction to *Mustard Seeds*, xiii; Carroll, *Memories*, 23; Christopher Bozell to author, March 31, 2008; Richard Wheeler to LBB, September 27, 1984, William F. Buckley Jr. Papers.

2   David Schindler to author, July 12, 2006; Lawrence to author, November 1, 2006; Potter to author, July 27, 2009; PBB to author, July 11, 2006.
3   Kathryn Bozell Brewster to author, December 4, 2006; L. Brent Bozell III to author, October 30. 2006.
4   L. Brent Bozell III to author, October 30, 2006; PBB to author, July 11, 2006; Robert E. Bauman to author, December 5, 2006; Carol Dawson Smith to author, November 28, 2006; Christopher Bozell to author, March 31, 2008.
5   L. Brent Bozell III to author, October 30, 2006.
6   The Editors, "Alianza para la Cristiandad," *Triumph* 8 (March 1973): 46; Gary Potter, "Triumph and the Future," *Triumph* (March 1976): 8 (italics in the original); LBB, "Pretty View—the SCC in Guatemala," *Triumph* (June 1976): 7; LBB, "The Politics of Mercy," *Mustard Seeds*, 296.
7   LBB, "Pretty View—the SCC in Guatemala," 4–8; LBB, "Pretty View—the SCC in Guatemala (Part II)," *Triumph* (July 1976): 6–8; Rob Bozell to PBB, June 5, 2008.
8   Juli Loesch Wiley, Letter: "Meeting Brent Bozell," *New Oxford Review* 64 (October 1997).
9   L. Brent Bozell III to author, October 30, 2006; PBB to author, October 31, 2006.
10 L. Brent Bozell III to author, October 30, 2006.
11 LBB, "Mustard Seeds," *Mustard Seeds*, 5; Lawrence to author, November 1, 2006; L. Brent Bozell III to author, October 30, 2006; Kevin Lynch to author, October 30, 2006; PBB to author, October 31, 2006.
12 Kathryn Bozell Brewster to author, December 4, 2006; L. Brent Bozell III to author, October 30, 2006; Lawrence to author, November 1, 2006.
13 PBB to author, January 15, 2007; Maureen Bozell to author, September 6, 2008; LBB to Patricia Bozell Prom, October 3, 1977.
14 PBB to author, January 11, 2007; Farley Clinton to author, March 20, 2008.
15 PBB to author, January 11, 2007; PBB to author, January 15, 2009; Neal B. Freeman to author, October 30, 2009.
16 L. Brent Bozell III to author, October 30, 2006; L. Brent Bozell III, *Memories*, 5; PBB to WFB, October 3, 1984, William F. Buckley Jr. Papers; Alfred Regnery to L. Brent Bozell III, May 18, 2010; L. Brent Bozell to author, May 24, 2010.
17 LBB to Patricia Bozell Prom, October 31, 1977; PBB to WFB, July 9, 1984, William F. Buckley Jr. Papers; PBB to WFB, February 20, 1984, William F. Buckley Jr. Papers; PBB to WFB, March 14, 1984, William F. Buckley Jr. Papers; PBB to WFB, August 6, 1984, William F. Buckley Jr. Papers; PBB to WFB, August 15, 1984, William F. Buckley Jr. Papers.
18 Kathryn Bozell Brewster to author, December 4, 2006; LBB, "Mustard Seeds," 4–6.

Fifteen: Mercy

1   PBB to WFB, December 25, 1983, William F. Buckley Jr. Papers; WFB to PBB, January 25, 1984, William F. Buckley Jr. Papers; PBB to WFB, February 10,

1984, William F. Buckley Jr. Papers; PBB to WFB, March 1, 1984, William F. Buckley Jr. Papers; WFB to Br. Michael Bozell, September 26, 1984, William F. Buckley Jr. Papers; LBB, "Mustard Seeds," *Mustard Seeds*, 1, 5–6.
2. PBB to author, April 18, 2005; L. Brent Bozell III to author, October 30, 2006; Gary K. Potter to author, July 27, 2009; LBB, "Mustard Seeds," 6.
3. LBB, "Mustard Seeds," 5; LBB, letter to *National Review* 35 (May 15, 1981): 516.
4. LBB, "Mustard Seeds," 5–6; LBB, "Poland's Cross—and America's," *Mustard Seeds*, 287–94.
5. L. Brent Bozell III to author, October 30, 2006; Lawrence to author, November 1, 2006; Carroll, *Memories*, 23; Kathryn Bozell Brewster to author, December 4, 2006; LBB to WFB, April 10, 1984, William F. Buckley Jr. Papers.
6. LBB, "Capitalist Self-Seeking, or Christian Self-Denial?," *New Oxford Review* (October 1986), reprinted as "Mary's Bread," *Mustard Seeds*, 341, 345. Italics in the original.
7. LBB, "The Politics of Mercy," *Mustard Seeds*, 295–314.
8. Ibid., 303, 305. The italics are in the original.
9. Ibid., 313.
10. LBB, "God Is Mercy," 325–26.
11. LBB, "The Politics of Abandonment," *New Oxford Review* 55 (January–February 1988), 18–22.
12. Ibid., 20–22.
13. L. Brent Bozell III to author, October 30, 2006; LBB, "Mustard Seeds," 6.
14. LBB, "The Politics of Mercy," 303; LBB, "God Is Mercy," *Mustard Seeds*, 328.
15. L. Brent Bozell III to author, October 30, 2006; Kevin Lynch to author, October 30, 2006; Julia Poppelier to author, November 27, 2006; Fr. Raymond T. Gawronski, SJ, *Memories*, 14.
16. Poppelier to author, November 27, 2006.
17. LBB, "Mary Falls," *Mustard Seeds*, 367–68; LBB, "Misión Guadalupe," *Mustard Seeds*, 360–81; LBB and Eduardo Miles-Campos, *Misión Guadalupe* (Front Royal, VA: Christendom Press, 1998), 90.
18. LBB, "Misión Guadalupe," 368; John Janaro, "Publisher's Headnote," *Misión Guadalupe*, ix, xi–xii; LBB and Miles-Campos, *Misión Guadalupe*, 4; Lynch to author, October 30, 2008; L. Brent Bozell III to author, October 30, 2006.
19. Raymond T. Gawronski, SJ, to author, October 1, 2007; PBB to author, September 1, 2007.
20. PBB, "The Polish Church, the Workers Movement," *Fidelity* 7 (September 1988): 12–16; LBB and Miles-Campos, *Misión Guadalupe*, 92.
21. PBB to author, September 3, 2007; Gawronski to author, October 1, 2007.
22. L. Brent Bozell III to author, October 30, 2006; David L. Schindler to author, July 12, 2006; Elsa Thompson quoted by PBB to author, February 2, 2008.
23. Eduardo Miles-Campos reported by PBB to author, December 17, 2006; Lawrence to author, November 1, 2006.
24. Lynch to author, October 30, 2006; Christopher Bozell to author, March 31, 2008.

25 Schindler to author, July 12, 2006; Miles-Campos reported by PBB to author, May 4, 2008.
26 Lynch to author, October 30, 2006.
27 Schindler to author, July 12, 2006; L. Brent Bozell III to author, October 30, 2006; *Memories*, insert on the Carmelites, n.p.
28 L. Brent Bozell III to author, October 30, 2006; Neal B. Freeman to author, June 17, 2010; LBB to WFB, April 10, 1984, William F. Buckley Jr. Papers; Christopher Bozell to author, March 31, 2008.
29 Carol Buckley, *At the Still Point*, 250.
30 L. Brent Bozell III to author, October 27, 2008; LBB quoted by WFB, *Nearer, My God*, 252–63.
31 L. Brent Bozell III, *Memories*, 7–8.
32 Lynch to author, October 30, 2006; Poppelier to author, November 26, 2006; L. Brent Bozell III to author, October 31, 2006.
33 Christopher Bozell to author, March 31, 2008; L. Brent Bozell III to author, October 30, 2006; WFB, "L. Brent Bozell, RIP," 22–23; *Memories*, 39, 80.

ACKNOWLEDGMENTS

Many people helped me in my labors. First and foremost comes Brent Bozell's wife, Patricia Buckley Bozell, whose many kindnesses to me and patience with my endless questioning made the book possible. I also profited from information, speculation, comment, criticism, and correction from Father Joseph Baker; Robert E. Bauman; Christopher Bozell; L. Brent Bozell III; Maureen Bozell; Cyrus Brewster; Kathryn Bozell Brewster; William F. Buckley Jr.; Jameson Campaigne Jr.; William Campbell; Lucius Cervantes, SJ; Farley Clinton; Anne Edwards; Lee Edwards; John Englund; David Franke; Neal B. Freeman; Raymond Gawronski, SJ; Jeffrey Hart; E. Michael Lawrence; Sidney Lovett; Kevin Lynch; Christopher Manion; Mrs. Neil McCaffrey; Thomas Molnar; Scott Moore; Julia Poppelier; Gary Potter; Patricia Bozell Prom; Thomas C. Reeves; Alfred S. Regnery; David L. Schindler; Carol Dawson Smith; Thomas N. Tripp; and Alexandra Wilhelmsen. The Bozell family was also kind enough to supply the photographs included in this book. My thanks to all.

Thanks are due also to the Association of Yale Alumni, the Boston Public Library, the Center for American History at the University of Texas at Austin, the Chicago Historical Society, the Clarke Historical Library at Central Michigan University, Creighton Prep, the Dimond Library at the University of New Hampshire, the Hoover Institution, the Library of Congress, the New York Public Library, the Thomas P. O'Neill Jr. Library at Boston College, and Yale University's St. Thomas More Chapel and Sterling Library.

And of course, as always, I benefited immeasurably from the encouragement, criticism, and forbearance of my wife, Wendy Anne Korbel Kelly.

INDEX

abandonment, 207–9
Abandonment to Divine Providence (Caussade), 207–9
abortion: antiabortion organizations, 156; antiabortion protests, 160–66; Bozell's Catholic politics and, 176; Bozell's opposition to, 125, 160–66, 178–80; conflict between Bozell and Buckley over, 91–92
Acheson, Dean, 33
Action for Life protest, 160–66
"Foreign Policy for America, A" (*Conscience of a Conservative*), 58–59
alcohol and alcoholism, 74, 77, 191–92
America magazine, 132
American Catholics: Bozell's notions of, 173–75. *See also* Catholic America
American Conservative Union, 87–89
American Enterprise Institute (AEI), 81
Americans for Goldwater, 56
Americans United for Life, 156
antiabortion organizations, 156
antiabortion protests, 160–66
anti-birth-control protests, 162

anticommunism: the Bozell-Buckley friendship and, 11; Bozell's conversion to conservatism and, 13; Bozell's view of the Vietnam War and, 128; Bozell's views in the *National Review*, 39–43; Bozell's views in *Triumph*, 127–28
antiliberalism: the *National Review* and, 35
apostolate: Action for Life protest, 160–66; Bozell's conception and planning of, 155–58; Bozell's views of Ireland and the violence in Ulster, 168–71; El Escorial summer school, 156–58; guild networks, 156; Misión Guadalupe, 210–11; notions of a Catholic America, 158–60; Patricia's antifeminism and the Atkinson incident, 166–68; Society for the Christian Commonwealth and, 158
Arlington House, 94
Ashbrook, John, 79, 87–88
Atkinson, Ti-Grace, 167–68
"Autumn of the Church, The" (*Triumph*, Bozell), 139–41

"Autumn of the Country, The" (*Triumph*, Bozell), 141

Baker, Joe, 157, 158
Balkans, 212
Barbarie, Thomas, 185
Baroody, William J., 81
Bauman, Robert, 87–88, 191
Begin, Menachem, 190
Belfast (Ireland), 196–97
Belloc, Hilaire, 130
Berlin wall, 69–70
Best of Triumph, The, 184
bipolar disorder: Bozell's episodes of depression and mania, 189–97; Bozell's public comments on, 201–2; Bozell's stabilization, 203–4; impact on Bozell and *Triumph* magazine, 185–87; impact on Patricia, 200–201; impact on the Bozell family, 197–99
birth control: anti-birth-control protests, 162; Bozell's opposition to, 107, 125–27; the *National Review* on, 106–7
Black Power, 129
black riots, 129
black vote, 43
"Boys' Town," 1–2
Boys' Town (film), 1–2
Bozell, Aloise, 62
Bozell, Brent, 213, 214
Bozell, Christopher, 23, 192–93
Bozell, James, 77
Bozell, John, 62
Bozell, Kathy, 28, 78, 123, 157, 185, 197
Bozell, L. Brent, Jr.: alcohol and alcoholism, 74, 191–92; American Conservative Union and, 87, 88, 89; anti-American views, 141–44; anticommunism and (*see* anticommunism); bipolar disorder and (*see* bipolar disorder); birth and childhood, 2; birth of children, 23, 28, 62, 73; campaigns for political office, 44–45, 82–86; Carmelites and, 214, 217; "the Catholic cause" and, 83, 104, 106; cigarette smoking and, 65; *Conscience of a Conservative* and, 49–55; on conservatism after the 1960 presidential election, 57–58; conversion to Catholicism, 6–7, 15–16; conversion to conservatism, 10, 13–15; corporal works of mercy, 209–11, 213–14; countercultural views of, 180–82; criticism of Catholic bishops, 137–38, 139–40, 160, 178; criticism of Catholic schools, 122–23, 124; criticism of ecumenicism, 124; criticism of "secular conservatism," 149–52; death and burial of, 218; defends and joins McCarthy, 29–33; defense of *Humanae Vitae*, 126–27; development of religion-based argumentation, 67–73; early political views of, 3–4; education of his children, 123; failing health and last years of, 213–17; "Freedom or Virtue?" article (*National Review*), 70–73; Goldwater and, 50–51, 54–55, 57, 58–59, 80–81; high school and oratory, 3–5; later writings of, 204–9; Michael Lawrence and, 84; lecturing and debating tours, 78–79; *McCarthy and His Enemies*, 25–29; meets and marries Patricia

Buckley, 18–20; in the Merchant Marine and Navy, 5; move to Huntly, VA, 92; move to Washington, D.C., 32; *National Review* and, 33, 36–44, 78, 90–92 (*see also* National Review); opposition to abortion, 125, 160–66, 178–80; opposition to birth control, 107, 125–27; opposition to Khrushchev's U.S. visit, 41–42; opposition to liturgical reform, 121–22; ordination of Michael Bozell, 214–16; physical appearance, 4–5; psychology of, 44; "A Purpose for Our Foreign Policy" speech, 89; radicalization of, 137–41; relationship with Buckley, 11, 13, 14, 15, 44, 75, 83, 90–92, 107–9, 119, 120, 144–49, 215; relationship with Meyer, 71, 142; on the Republican Party in the 1958 elections, 47; response to *God and Man at Yale*, 24; San Francisco and, 28, 31; in Spain (*see* Spain); "To Magnify the West" speech, 68–70; trips to Poland and the Balkans, 211–12; *Triumph* magazine (*see* Triumph magazine); views of Ireland and violence in Ulster, 168–71; views of nuclear weapons, 128–29; views on communism and the Cold War, 39–43; writings on mercy, 206–9; at Yale University, 9–15, 23

Bozell, Leo, 1–3, 6
Bozell, Lois, 2–3, 7, 16
Bozell, Maureen, 28
Bozell, Michael, 28, 214–16, 217
Bozell, Patricia: alcohol and, 74, 77; antifeminism and the Atkinson incident, 166–68; birth of children, 23, 28, 62, 73, 77; Brent's bipolar disorder and, 200–201, 203; on Brent's development of religion-based argumentation, 67; on the closing of *Triumph*, 184–86; on the contrasts between America and Spain, 77–78; effort to save the Brent-Buckley relationship, 147–48; life in Spain, 65–66; as managing editor of *Triumph*, 112–13; move to Spain, 62 (*see also* Spain); move to Washington, D.C., 32; opposition to Khrushchev's U.S. visit, 41–42; opposition to liturgical reform, 122; return to America from Spain, 73–75; San Francisco and, 28, 31; support for Brent's corporal works of mercy, 214; trips to Poland and the Balkans, 211–12. *See also* Buckley, Patricia
Bozell, Patricia (daughter), 9–10, 62
Bozell, Rob, 193, 194
Bozell, William, 73
Bozell and Jacobs agency, 1–2
Brewster, Cyrus, 157
Brown, Aaron, 95
Brown v. Board of Education, 79
Bruce, Donald C., 87–88
Buckley, Patricia: Catholicism and, 18; childhood and college, 16–19; meets and marries Bozell, 18–20. *See also* Bozell, Patricia
Buckley, Reid, 61
Buckley, William F., Jr.: American Conservative Union and, 87; anticommunism and, 11; on birth control, 106; on Bozell's bipolar disorder, 203; on Bozell's conversion to Catholicism, 15–16;

Buckley, William F., Jr. (cont'd)
  Bozell's death and, 217; Bozell's 1964 political campaign and, 83; on Bozell's radicalism, 138; childhood, 16, 17; debating in college, 11, 19; *God and Man at Yale*, 23–24; Goldwater's 1964 presidential campaign and, 80–81; marriage and children, 23; *McCarthy and His Enemies*, 25–27; at Michael Bozell's ordination, 215; *National Review* and, 33, 35 (*see also* National Review); opposition to Khrushchev's U.S. visit, 41; relationship with Bozell, 11, 13, 14, 15, 44, 75, 83, 90–92, 107–9, 119, 120, 144–49, 215; relationship with sister Patricia, 16; response to Patricia's criticism of liturgical reform, 122; support for Bozell's *The Warren Revolution*, 99–100; *Triumph* magazine and, 113, 119; at Yale with Bozell, 11, 13, 14, 15
Burnham, James, 36
Buzhardt, Fred, 176–77

capitalism, 130, 181–82
capital punishment, 124–25
Carey, George, 100–101
Carlists, 62–63, 66; American, 158
Carmelites, 214, 217
Carroll, Warren H., 153, 158
Casti Connubii, 106–7
Catholic America: Bozell's antiabortion position and response to *Roe v. Wade*, 178–80; Bozell's apostolate (*see* apostolate); Bozell's concept of, 159–60; Bozell's goal of creating, 158; Bozell's notions of American Catholics and Catholic politics, 173–78
Catholic bishops: Bozell's softens his criticism of, 178; criticized by Bozell and the editors of *Triumph*, 137–38, 139–40, 160
Catholic Currents newsletter, 155, 182
Catholicism: Leo Bozell and, 2–3, 6; Bozell's apostolate (*see* apostolate); Bozell's conversion to, 6–7, 15–16; Bozell's corporal works of mercy, 209–11, 213–14; Bozell's criticism of liberal Catholicism, 104–5, 120–27, 139–41; Bozell's defense of in the *National Review*, 90; Bozell's experience of Spain and, 61–62, 64, 73; Bozell's writings on mercy, 206–9; Patricia Buckley and, 18; Patricia's attack on Grace Atkinson and Church razing, 167–68; positions in the *National Review* on Catholic issues, 106–7. *See also* Catholic America; religion
"Catholic Obligation, The" (*Triumph*, Bozell), 178–79
Catholic politics, 175–78
Catholic schools: Bozell's criticism of, 122–23, 124; El Escorial summer school, 156–58
Catholic theocracy, 129–30
Catholic University, 167–68
Caussade, Jean Pierre de, 207–9
Cervantes, Rev. Lucius, 6, 20, 217
Chambers, Whittaker, 42, 44
Christendom College, 156–58
Christian Commonwealth Institute, 156–58
Christian economy, 205–6
Christian society, 151–52

"Christian tribe," 173–75
Clinton, Farley, 108, 142, 149
Cold War, 40–43, 58–59
Committee for a Conservative Catholic Magazine, 109–11, 124
Commonweal magazine, 132
community/commonwealth: Bozell's views of, 71–73
"Confessional Tribe, The" (*Triumph*, Bozell), 173–74, 178
Conscience of a Conservative (Goldwater): Bozell's authorship of, 50–51; Bozell's conservative views in, 51–54; impact on Bozell's status among conservatives, 55; Clarence Manion and the origin of, 49–50; public response to, 54; royalties to Bozell and Goldwater, 54–55
conservatism: American Conservative Union, 87–89; Bozell on conservatism after the 1960 presidential election, 57–58; Bozell's appeal to conservatives in the startup of *Triumph* magazine, 110–11; Bozell's conversion to, 10, 13–15; Bozell's criticism of "secular conservatism" in *Triumph*, 149–52; Bozell's lecturing and debating tours, 78–79; Bozell's 1964 political campaign, 82–86; development of Bozell's religion-based argumentation, 67–73; Goldwater, Bozell, and *Conscience of a Conservative*, 49–55; Goldwater's 1964 presidential campaign, 79–82, 87
Conservative Book Club, 94, 99
Conservative View (newspaper), 14
Creighton Prep high school, 3, 5, 6

Creighton University, 1, 3
Cruising Speed (Buckley), 15–16

Dallas anti-birth-control protest, 162
Daniélou, Jean, 151
Dawson, Carol, 191
Dawson, Christopher, 113
"Death of the Constitution, The" (*Triumph*, Bozell), 139, 143, 145
death penalty, 124–25
debating: Bozell and Buckley at Vassar, 19; Bozell at Yale, 10–13; Bozell's lecturing and debating tours, 78–79
Declaration on Religious Liberty, 91
de Toledano, Ralph, 89
Diamond, Martin, 100
Dives in Misericorida, 205, 206–7
Don Carlos and rise of Carlism, 62, 63
Dunne, George H., 67

East Berlin, 75
economics: Bozell on Christian economy, 205–6; Bozell's critique of Gilder's *Wealth and Poverty*, 204; views of Bozell and *Triumph* magazine, 130, 180, 181–82
ecumenicism, 124
Edwards, Anne, 113–14, 119
Edwards, Lee, 70, 81, 115, 185
Eisenhower, Dwight D., 39, 40–41, 42, 47
El Escorial (Spain), 65–67, 156–58
"Encouraging Murder" (*New York Times*, Bozell), 163–64
environmentalism, 181
Evans, Brad, 163, 165, 193

feminism: Patricia's opposition to, 166–68

Fitzpatrick, James K., 144
Flannagan, Edward J., 1–2
Fox, Robert, 124
freedom: in *Conscience of a Conservative*, 52–53; in "Freedom or Virtue?" (*National Review*), 73
"Freedom or Virtue?" (*National Review*, Bozell), 70–73
Freeman, Neal: on Bozell in 1972, 185; Bozell's bipolar disorder and, 199; Bozell's 1964 political campaign and, 83, 86; on Bozell's radicalization, 138; Bozell's *The Warren Revolution* and, 94, 95; opinion of *Triumph*, 131

Gawronski, Raymond T., 209, 211–12
George Washington University Hospital, 161–63
Gilder, George, 204
God and Man at Yale (Buckley), 23–24
Goldwater, Barry: Bozell's ghost writing for and disillusionment with, 49–55, 57, 58–59; *Conscience of a Conservative*, 49–55; 1958 elections and, 48; "How Do You Stand, Sir?" column, 48; 1960 presidential campaign, 48–49, 56–57; 1964 presidential campaign, 79–82, 87; visit to Bozell in Spain, 66; at the 1962 World Liberation from Communism rally, 68, 70
Goldwater for President committee, 80, 81
Guatemala relief project, 192–94
guild networks, 156

Hall, Jay, 81
Hispanics, 210–11

"How We Look to Others" (Dunne), 67
Hughes, Charles Evans, 97
Humanae Vitae, 126–27
Human Destiny (Lecomte du Noüy), 15
Hunt, E. Howard, 83, 84
Huntly (VA), 92
Hutchins, Robert Maynard, 79

Ireland, 168–71, 196–97
Irish Relief Fund, 170
Irish Republican Army, 169–71

Jacobs, Morris, 1–2
Jesuits, 140
Jews, 175
John Birch Society, 90–91, 156
John Paul II (pope), 205, 206–7
Johnson, Lyndon B., 82, 128
John XXIII (pope), 43–44
Jones, David R., 88–89
judicial review, 95–99
Junior Chamber of Commerce, 114

Kendall, Willmoore: on the Bozell-Buckley relationship, 109; Bozell's decision to move to Spain and, 61; Bozell's 1964 political campaign and, 83; contributions to *McCarthy and His Enemies*, 25; with the *National Review*, 36; political views of, 13–14; *Triumph* magazine and, 117–18
Kennedy, John F., 80, 94
Khrushchev, Nikita, 41–42
Kirk, Russell: on Bozell's radicalization, 138; with the *National Review*, 36; *Triumph* magazine and, 110, 117–18, 120
Kitchel, Denison, 81

Kohlberg, Alfred, 45
Kowalska, Sr. Faustina, 207

Lawrence, Michael: with Bozell in defending *Humanae Vitae*, 126–27; on Bozell's Action for Life protest, 164–65; on Bozell's anti-Americanism in *Triumph*, 142; on Bozell's "Letter to Yourselves," 149; Bozell's 1964 political campaign and, 84; on Bozell's radicalization, 138; call for a Catholic theocracy, 129–30; *Triumph* magazine and, 104, 110, 112, 113, 117, 129–30, 155
Lecomte du Noüy, Pierre, 15
Leo XIII (pope), 130, 181
"Letter to Yourselves" (*Triumph*, Bozell), 149–50, 151–52
liberal Catholicism: Bozell's criticism of, 104–5, 120–27, 139–41
liberalism: Bozell's criticism of, 39, 69, 141; in Bozell's early political views, 10; *Conscience of a Conservative* on, 53
libertarianism, 72
Liebman, Marvin, 87–88
Lindsay, John V., 88
lithium, 189, 194, 204
liturgical reform, 121–22
Loesch, Juli, 194–95
Lynch, Kevin, 209, 213, 214

Macdonald, Dwight, 13
Manion, Clarence, 48–50, 54, 55, 56, 57
Marbury v. Madison, 98
market economics, 130
Marshall, John, 98
Maryland: Bozell's campaigns for political office, 44–45, 82–86

Mater et Magistra, 43–44
Mathias, Charles, 82, 84–85, 86
McCaffrey, Neil: criticism of Bozell's views in *Triumph*, 143–44; criticism of *Humanae Vitae*, 126; on Patricia's attack on Grace Atkinson, 168; publication of the *Warren Revolution*, 94, 95; response to "The Confessional Tribe," 174
McCarthy, Jean, 26–27, 31, 41
McCarthy, John P., 170–71
McCarthy, Joseph: Army hearings, 29–30; Bozell defends and joins, 29–33; death of, 33; *McCarthy and His Enemies*, 25–29; McCarthyism and, 24–25; Senate censure of, 30–31
McCarthy and His Enemies (Buckley and Bozell), 25–29, 94
McCarthyism, 24–25
McClane, Donald G., 154
McClellan, James, 100
McFarland, Ernest, 48
Medeiros, Humberto, 190
Merchant Marine, 5
mercy: Bozell's corporal works of, 209–11, 213–14; Bozell's writings on, 206–9
Meyer, Frank: American Conservative Union and, 87, 88, 89; article with Bozell on nuclear strategy, 43; Bozell's "Freedom or Virtue?" article and, 70–73; with the *National Review*, 36; relationship with Bozell, 71, 142; response to *Conscience of a Conservative*, 54
Misión Guadalupe, 210–11
Molnar, Thomas, 110, 112, 132, 138, 153
"Montejurra" (Bozell home), 92, 198–99

Montejurra (Spain), 66
Murray, John Courtney, 140
Mustard Seeds (Bozell), 184, 201–2
mutual assured destruction (MAD), 128

National Committee against the Treaty of Moscow, 43
National Review: Bozell returns to from Spain, 78; on Bozell's Action for Life protest, 165; Bozell's contribution to the first issue, 33; Bozell's critique of George Gilder, 204; Bozell's critique of the Second Vatican Council, 104–5; Bozell's dissenting opinions within, 43–44; Bozell's "Freedom or Virtue?" article, 70–73; Bozell's withdrawal from, 90–92; Buckley's purpose with, 35; conflicts between Bozell and Buckley, 90–92; criticism of *Humanae Vitae*, 126; editors and columnists, 36; overall view propounded by the staff, 36; positions on Catholic issues, 106–7; response to *Conscience of a Conservative*, 54; subjects addressed by Bozell, 36–43, 90; support for Bozell's *The Warren Revolution*, 99–100; *Triumph* magazine and, 119–20, 131
New Deal, 4
New Science of Politics, The (Voegelin), 69
Nixon, Richard M., 46–47, 49, 128, 176–77, 180
Noraid, 170
nuclear weapons, 43, 128–29

Office of Policy Coordination, 23–24
"Operation 72," 89
oratory, 3–5. *See also* debating
Osterweis, Rollin G., 18

Paul VI (pope), 126, 130, 181
Pax Center, 194–95
Philadelphia Society, 89
Pius XI (pope), 106–7
Poland, 205–6, 211–12
"Politics of Abandonment, The" (*New Oxford Review*, Bozell), 207–8
"Politics of Mercy, The" (*Mustard Seeds*, Bozell), 206–7
"Politics of the Poor" (*Triumph*, Bozell), 150–51
Poppelier, Julia, 209
Populorum Progressio, 130, 181
Potter, Gary, 119, 121, 165, 192
Progressive Citizens of America, 12–13
pro-life amendment, 179, 180
Provos, 169, 170–71
"Purpose for Our Foreign Policy, A" (Bozell speech), 89

Reagan, Ronald, 70
Regnery, Henry: Bozell's Supreme Court book and, 38, 93, 94–95; publication of *God and Man at Yale*, 24; publication of *McCarthy and His Enemies*, 25, 27, 28, 29; urges Bozell to write another book on McCarthy, 29, 38–39
religion: Christendom theme in Bozell's lecturing, 79; development of Bozell's religion-based argumentation, 67–73; as a subject in Bozell's *National Review* columns, 90. *See also* apostolate; Catholic America; Catholicism

religious pluralism, 125
Republican Party: 1958 elections, 47–48; Goldwater's 1960 presidential campaign, 48–49, 56–57 (*see also* Goldwater, Barry); Goldwater's 1964 presidential campaign, 79–82, 87
Requetés, 62, 63
Rerum Novarum, 130, 181
Reuther, Walter, 38
Rockefeller, Nelson A., 46–47, 48, 49, 176
Roe v. Wade, 178–79
Roosevelt, Franklin Delano, 17–18
Rusher, William A.: on the Bozell-Buckley relationship, 109; on Bozell's "To Magnify the West" speech, 70; Goldwater's 1964 campaign and, 79; response to Bozell's anti-Americanism, 142–43; response to "Letter to Yourselves," 152; response to "The Confessional Tribe," 174

Schindler, David, 189–90, 213, 214
Schlesinger, Arthur, Jr., 27
Schwartz, Michael, 162
Second Vatican Council, 91, 104–5
"secular conservatism," 149–52
Servile State, The (Belloc), 130
Shadegg, Stephen, 48, 80, 81
Simms, Harry, 85
Sobran, Joseph, 101
social disorder, 129
socialism, 130, 182
Society for the Christian Commonwealth: Bozell's Catholic politics and, 178; Bozell's Guatemala relief project, 192–94; financial problems and the closing of *Triumph*, 182–83; founding of, 158; notions of a Catholic America, 158–60. *See also* apostolate
Solidarity, 205–6, 212
Sons of Thunder, 161–63, 165–66, 167
Spain: American Carlists, 158; Patricia Bozell on the contrasts between America and Spain, 77–78; Bozell's Catholicism and, 61–62, 64, 73; Bozell's decision to move to, 61–62; Bozell's decision to return to America, 73–75; Bozell's El Escorial summer school, 156–58; Bozell's first visit to, 14; Bozell's life in, 64–67; Carlists, 62–63; development of Bozell's religion-based argumentation in, 67–73
Spirit of Triumph, The, 184
"Strange Drift of Liberal Catholicism, The" (Bozell), 67–68

Tenth Amendment, 4
Thomas Aquinas College, 123
Thompson, Elsa, 213
"To Magnify the West" (*Mustard Seeds*, Bozell), 68–70
"Toward a Catholic Realpolitik" (*Triumph*, Bozell), 176
Trapp, Maria Augusta von, 131
"Treaty of Fifth Avenue," 56–57
"triumphalism," 114–15
Triumph magazine: antiabortion position and response to *Roe v. Wade*, 178–80; Bozell and the radicalization of, 137–41, 153–54; Bozell on the function and guiding notions of, 118–19; Bozell's anti-American views and reactions to them, 141–44;

Triumph magazine (cont'd)
Bozell's apostolate and, 155;
Bozell's bipolar disorder and, 185–87; Bozell's criticism of "secular conservatism," 149–52; Bozell's description of a Catholic America in, 159–60; Bozell's dominant role in, 118, 119, 120; Bozell's motivations in founding, 103–9; Bozell's notions of American Catholics and Catholic politics, 173–78; Buckley's criticism of, 145; the Catholic experience of the editors, 117; "The Catholic Interest" column, 175; closing of, 182–87; conservative contributors, 117–18; countercultural viewpoints in, 180–82; criticism of Catholic bishops, 137–38, 139–40, 160, 178; criticism of liberal Catholicism, 120–27; debut issue, 113–15; declining readership and financial problems, 152–54, 182–84; demographics of subscribers, 152; on economics, 130, 180, 181–82; fund-raising in the startup of, 109–11; imitative/adversarial relationship to *National Review*, 119–20; impact of Patricia's attack on Grace Atkinson, 168; naming of, 112, 114–15; opposition to feminism, 166; Patricia as managing editor, 112–13; popular reaction to, 131–32; secular subjects addressed in, 127–30; senior editors, 112; on the violence in Ulster, 169–71

Ulster (Ireland), 168–71
United Auto Workers, 38
United World Federalists. *See* World Federalism
University of Dallas, 123, 161, 165, 166
urban riots, 129
U.S. Constitution: Bozell's assault on, 139; Bozell's defense of in *The Warren Revolution*, 95–98
U.S. Navy, 5
U.S. Senate: censure of McCarthy, 30–31
U.S. Supreme Court: Bozell debates the *Brown v. Board of Education* decision, 79; Bozell's critique of the Warren Court and judicial review, 37–39, 95–99 (*see also Warren Revolution, The*)

Vassar College, 18–19
Vecchione, P. J., 12–13
Victor Publishing, 50, 55
Vietnam War, 128, 182
virtue, 71–73
Vista Hermosa (Guatemala), 193–94
Voegelin, Eric, 69

Wallace, Henry A., 12
Warren, Earl, 37–39
Warren Court, 37–39, 95–99
Warren Revolution, The (Bozell): Bozell's critique of judicial supremacy and judicial review in, 95–99; Bozell's writing of, 38, 93–94; popular reception and critical reviews of, 99–101; publication of, 94–95; Regnery and, 38, 93, 94–95
Watergate crisis, 176–77
Watkins, Arthur V., 30
Watkins committee, 30–31
Wealth and Poverty (Gilder), 204

Wedemeyer, Albert C., 45, 84, 154
We Hold These Truths (Murray), 140
Welch, Robert, 90–91, 156
White, F. Clifton, 51, 79, 80, 81
Why Not Victory? (Goldwater), 59
Wilhelmsen, Frederick D.: Bozell's decision to move to Spain and, 61, 62; Bozell's 1964 political campaign and, 83; countercultural viewpoints, 181; fascination with Spain, 62–64; relationship with Bozell in Spain, 64, 66; Sons of Thunder and the Action for Life protest, 161, 162–63; *Triumph* magazine and, 103, 104, 110, 112, 118; at the University of Dallas, 123
Wills, Garry, 106–7, 108
Wilson, Francis Graham, 110
Wisner, John, 112
women's movement: Patricia's antifeminism and the Atkinson incident, 166–68
World Federalism, 10, 11, 14–15
World Liberation from Communism rally, 68–70

Yale University, 9–15, 23
Young Americans for Freedom, 68, 88–89, 161

ISI Books is the publishing imprint of the Intercollegiate Studies Institute. Since its founding in 1953, ISI has been inspiring college students to discover, embrace, and advance the principles and virtues that make America free and prosperous.

ISI reaches thousands of college students across the country through an integrated program of campus speakers, conferences, seminars, publications, student groups, and fellowships and scholarships, along with a rich repository of online resources.

ISI is a nonprofit, nonpartisan, tax-exempt educational organization. The Institute relies on the financial support of the general public—individuals, foundations, and corporations—and receives no funding or any other aid from any level of the government.

To learn more about ISI,
visit www.isi.org or call (800) 526-7022